NAPOLEON
ON ST HELENA

NAPOLEON
ON ST HELENA

MABEL BROOKES

FONTHILL

Fonthill Media Limited
Fonthill Media LLC
www.fonthillmedia.com
office@fonthillmedia.com

This edition published in the United Kingdom 2012

British Library Cataloguing in Publication Data:
A catalogue record for this book is available from the British Library

ISBN 978-1-78155-171-4 (print)
ISBN 978-1-78155-190-5 (e-book)

Typeset in 10.5pt on 14pt Sabon
Printed and bound in England

Connect with us
 facebook.com/fonthillmedia twitter.com/fonthillmedia

Contents

Foreword

BY THE RT. HON. R. G. MENZIES, C.H., Q.C.
PRIME MINISTER OF AUSTRALIA

Dame Mabel Brookes is a very remarkable woman. She is also a very old friend of mine. These two facts have no logical connection but, between them, they will explain why I am delighted to have been asked by her to contribute a brief foreword to this book.

In her own right she has made a great contribution to the City of Melbourne and to the State of Victoria. A very great women's hospital owes more to her than may ever be fully recorded.

Inheriting from her father a lawyer-like capacity for analysis and possessing herself a remarkable executive faculty, she has, ever since I first knew her, commanded the minds and judgments of politicians and of businessmen so that in the result they found it easier to agree with her. If this gives you the impression that she has any domineering mannerism, I have not conveyed myself accurately. The truth is that she is one of those advocates who not only persuade you that they are right but leave you faintly ashamed to have thought temporarily that they might have been wrong.

This kind of advocacy is not simply professional. It arises from a powerful conviction in the mind of the advocate that something ought to be done and that you ought to help it to be done.

Looking back over my long experience of public affairs, I cannot readily remember anybody who had this persuasive power more richly than Mabel Brookes. It was not a power that arose from political experience, for I am bound to say about this dear friend of mine that politically she always seemed to me to do what her famous husband would never have dreamed of doing — play the ball off the wrong foot. But this doesn't matter. Her life's work has been conducted with immeasurable skill and to the great benefit of the community in which she has lived.

It is not given to everybody who is strong in persuasion or valiant in action to be a distinguished writer. Yet Mabel Brookes has, by some miracle which

I do not profess to understand, made herself a writer of immense versatility. She began by writing novels and, if I may confess it, very readable ones. She then gave up writing for quite a long time while she put her great hospital on the map.

She went around the world quite a bit with her husband, Sir Norman Brookes, whom I shall always think of as the one fantastic genius of the game of lawn tennis, of which he was one of the pioneers and became one of the most persistently brilliant exponents.

In recent years she has turned once more to her pen. Her book *Crowded Galleries* is, if you omit the over-kind passages about myself, one of the most delicious essays in social history that it has ever been my privilege to read. It is gay, perceptive, and illuminating. She has now turned her hand to a piece of history. She has not fallen into the error of setting out to be the professional historian. She has rather chosen to explore with great charm some of the by-ways of history. She has, so to speak, wandered along the somewhat forgotten lanes.

The very early association of her own family with the great Napoleon has led her, on the spot, and by reference to family records and documents, to give us a new light on Napoleon, and to introduce us to human relationships. Such a book improves upon the works of the professional historian by letting us see that man in his setting and the kind of intimate world in which he lived.

It has long been a theory of mine that history should not be left unaided to the professional student of the documents, the speeches and the despatches. It may well be that all of us who had contact with affairs should take whatever opportunity offers to set down a few pictures, a few tales, a few judgments which may some day help to set the record right.

If Mabel Brookes had lived in the very days of Napoleon and had later set down her memories, they would be invaluable. As it is, she has gone a long way back. She has pursued her family researches. And in the course of these researches she has produced a story which cannot fail to illuminate the events of far more than a century ago, and thus to add not only to the sum of human knowledge but to an understanding of the great truth that history is the story of human beings.

Canberra, 1958

ROBERT GORDON MENZIES

Introduction to the 2013 Edition

The capture and final incarceration of Napoleon on the island of St Helena has fascinated many historians, and few more so than Mabel Brookes. Her grandfather, as a little boy, was bounced upon Napoleon's knee. He remembered him as a 'nice man' with a stout frame and small hands, and he particularly recalled the frogs on his famous green coat and some star or other that scratched. The stories he told of Napoleon instilled within Mabel a lifelong fascination of the Emperor's final years on that remote tropical island.

Dame Mabel Balcombe Brookes (1890-1975) was born at Raveloe, South Yarra, Melbourne, the only child of Harry Emmerton, a solicitor from England, and Alice Mabel Maude, née Balcombe. Mabel was a grand-daughter of Alexander Balcombe, and great-grand-daughter of William Balcombe, who had initially hosted Napoleon on his arrival at St Helena at The Briars, the Balcombe family home.

In 1911, at the age of 21, Mabel married Norman Brookes, the first non-Briton to win Wimbledon. Norman also came from a wealthy family and the couple spent much of their time touring the fashionable tennis circuits of England, France and the USA. Norman's fame increased further in 1914 when he won his second singles and doubles titles at Wimbledon and helped to regain the Davis Cup. Upon the outbreak of war, Mabel and Norman returned to Australia.

Mabel became a society celebrity in Australia and was heavily involved in charitable works. Her greatest contribution was as president of the Queen Victoria Hospital (1923-70), staffed by women for women. Under her leadership three new wings—one named after her—were added in ten years. Mabel Brookes twice stood for parliament: in 1943 for the Federal seat of Flinders as a 'Women for Canberra' candidate; and in 1952 for the State seat of Toorak for the Electoral Reform League. A vigorous campaigner, she attracted few votes but much public attention. She described herself as a liberal conservative. Her main goals were free education, a health service to reduce infant mortality, reform of mental hospitals, and housing for the poor.

After the Second World War, Mabel's leadership in Melbourne society was undisputed. She was appointed CBE in 1933 and DBE in 1955 for services to hospitals and charities. Her name and photograph—usually wearing a bold floral dress under a plain coat, big-bosomed and commanding—were constantly before the public. She entertained an extraordinary range of visitors to Melbourne, frequently at the request of State or Federal Governments. She had special pleasure in welcoming US President, Lyndon B. Johnson to her home; an occasion marked by a political demonstration.

Dame Mabel Brookes wrote several works of fiction and several on history. *Napoleon on St Helena*, originally published in 1960 as *St Helena Story*, was the culmination of much research, aided by her great-aunt's diaries and notebooks. Her great-aunt was Betsy Balcombe (later known in married life as Lucia Elizabeth Abell); she was Napoleon's favourite, and her memoirs, *Napoleon and Betsy: Recollections of Napoleon and St Helena*, have also been published by Fonthill.

Perhaps unsurprisingly, *Napoleon on St Helena* has inherited a degree of family bias. The extent to which the book centres on Mabel Brookes' family might leave the reader with the impression that Napoleon's stay at The Briars was of some duration. In fact it was little more than two months, although it was a very eventful two months. Mabel is also overzealous in her treatment of Sir Hudson Lowe, whom she portrays as a villain without any thought of his instructions from Lord Bathurst. Betsy's age is also amended; she was only 13 years old when she first met Napoleon, but Mabel prefers to add a few years. These are, however, trifling matters in what is a landmark account of this fascinating period of Napoleon's life.

Additional notes have been added to this edition, together with a much larger plate section. Dame Mabel Brookes' text has been left as it is, and when, in the last chapter, she mentions the island as it is 'today', the reader should bear in mind that she was writing in 1958 and 1959.

CHAPTER I

An Emperor's Island-Prison

Time, enemy to memory, spreads a dust-film over incidents that were once stark and dramatic, changes stormy backgrounds into shadows and dims high-lighted desires, tragedies and triumphs. No narrative of past lives can hope to throb with the energy of present happenings. Trends of thought and speech all help to vitalise the written story and when the word-fashions and undercurrents of a past century become buried under the hurrying years, something of history dies. Incidents of this drama are brought as near today as possible by voices that have passed on family gossip from the lips of the actors themselves, and as nearly as can be are related in the actual words remembered.

The story of our family's association with Napoleon was homely stuff, and not unduly emphasised, for there was heartbreak in it and the domestic circle found it more interesting to dwell on their later adventures on coming to Australia, five years after their departure from St Helena. My grandfather Balcombe (Alexander Beatson, aged four when Napoleon came to the island) knew the Emperor as 'a nice man' on whose knee he clambered and whose fobs and seals he fingered and played with. He remembered the soft lap, the stout figure, the small hands and the frogs on the famous green jacket, and some star or other that scratched. He soon overcame the fear of 'Boney' implanted in him, as in most English children, and bore with the Emperor's habit of tweaking his ears and nose. To him the Emperor was just another person in the regulated orbit of a child's existence. Perhaps, in the four-year-old Alexander, Napoleon re-created the image of his own son, and his questions to Mrs Balcombe as to the child's upbringing emerged from an effort to follow vicariously his own boy's progress in the simpler and more intimate functions of his life. So Alexander, unhindered, clambered on the Emperor's lap, clung to his collar and played with the green jacket that had been worn at Waterloo. This story is a breath blown on the dying embers of the conflagration that swept Europe one hundred and forty years ago, and on the spark that lit it — Napoleon.

A connoisseur of such things once gave me a Chinese painting on rice-paper of St Helena, and the capital, Jamestown. It was executed with the exquisite precision of the oriental artist. The expert, apologising for its tattered condition, said it was "an interesting eighteenth-century example" and that he vaguely remembered the Balcombes once had some connection with the island. The picture shows stark peaks, a gulf between and a cluster of buildings like residue fallen from the barren hills. In the foreground, full-rigged ships ride a formalised, sea that fringes a natural fortress. A magnifying glass will pick up the finer detail: the paraphernalia of a sailing vessel of the eighteenth century, the British flag, the spars and ropes and strange-shaped canvas, and in the background the carefully limed roofs and windows of the little town, while a further perspective gives a glimpse of yet more buildings around the turn of the valley. In the sky, vapour-trailing clouds are dissipated before the sunrise. The Rock, the Fortress, the Island — St Helena has answered to all three names. An important anchorage for ships of the East India Company, and a port of call of the British Fleet, it was the chief re-victualling stop for vessels on the trade route to the Orient, to India and the vast half-comprehended bulk of China, with Australia a vague outline beyond. Although deserted as a forgotten fragment of history, St Helena was fiercely spotlighted in the Napoleonic era and shared in the last phase of the Napoleonic legend. Whereas it is strategically and commercially negligible today, history holds a permanent niche for this forbidding upsurge of rock, which rates honourable mention in national annals other than Napoleonic. English commentators affirm that, but for St Helena, none of the great British possessions in the Far East could have been secured. Once the Suez Canal wrote finis to her usefulness in 1868, however, few vessels anchored in James Roads, where once barquentines displayed their trim lines and the British Fleet came in with a flurry of spreading sail and precise manoeuvring. But on the political map of the time it was important and strategic and convenient, one of the assets of the potent 'John Company' of the past.

The East India Company had offices in the little town, in the building which, still intact, now functions as the Jamestown Post Office. Traders and merchants found business good and a number of English families lived in comfortable, sub-tropical surroundings behind the outer mountain barrier. Its disadvantages were few, but occasionally troublesome. Fever was endemic, regular food supplies unpredictable — meat particularly — and the island was always open to the possibility of epidemic, some legacy from a passing ship. (A bundle of washing sent ashore from a measles-infected slave-ship resulted in more than one-hundred-and-sixty deaths among the islanders, their burial presenting a serious problem.) The English expatriates lived in a world of slave-carriers and unlimited slave households, tropical fruits and English flowers, crinolines and canned provisions, both newly come into vogue, Chinese porcelain, Indian carpets, home-made amusements, balls and dinners (these often necessitating carrying a gown in a tin box), horses and farm-carts for transport, bridle-paths for roads, wide hats and, for the adolescent, pantaloons to the ankles. Children of the East India Company's employees were sent to England for schooling, and the journey back, as in the case of the *Northumberland* with Napoleon on board, took more than two months.

To Betsy Balcombe and her sister Jane, returning from school in 1813, the island appeared probably much as it does today — the sharp peaks, the trade wind carrying land scents across the ultramarine-blue water to their anchored ship, the whitewashed houses, the sheltered landing-steps for passengers. All this still remains; only the vessels in James Roads differ. There are no longer barques and brigantines, sloops-of-war and pot-bellied merchantmen. A mauve-hulled Union Castle liner, a rusty tramp, a Government launch, now superimpose their utilitarian shapes on the fading picture of sail, and, to bring the scene right up to date, an oil-slick marks the site of a tanker sunk in the last war.

In 1810, the Napoleonic battles and depredations that were frightening the world became somewhat academic when viewed from the distance of St Helena. Bonaparte was accepted in the mind's eye as a tyrant astride Europe, a disrupter, destroyer of world peace, a dictator, in some manner a logical outcome of the French Revolution — yet physically so far off as to be no menace. Children rated him an Ogre. "Be good or Boney will get you" and "Go to sleep or Boney will come" had been woven into the consciousness of their youthful lives by mothers and nurses.

Thackeray, writing in *The Roundabout Papers*, tells of a later impression when at six years of age he visited the island. "My black servant took me for a long walk over rocks and hills until we reached a garden where we saw a man talking. 'That is he,' said the black man. 'That's Bonaparte. He eats three sheep every day and all the little children he can lay hands on.'"

In 1814, to England — within striking distance of France — he had become a figure of terror and death, the slayer of thousands. The martello towers built along the shores against his invasion now appear slightly ridiculous in their impotence. Once, driven by desire, expediency and ambition, he had stood on the French coast with troops massed behind him, and gazed at the cliffs and intervening sea, seeing England as a tremendous threat and the stumbling-block to his domination of Europe — indeed of the civilised world.

The two Balcombe girls, scarcely emerged from childhood, watched the peaks of St Helena, the morning haze already rolled away and the sun deepening the shadows on their sides. At their age (fourteen and sixteen), newly released from an English school and about to rejoin their family, the forbidding mountains held no threat, only the promise of fun and enjoyment with a regiment stationed there, ensigns for beaux, and race-meetings and dances for rendezvous. The future looked rosy. William Balcombe, appointed to the East India Company a few years before, and Naval Agent for the British Fleet, had created a comfortable home for his wife and two boys younger than Betsy and Jane — another, an older boy, remaining at school in England. They lived at the Briars, believed, until recently, to be an East India Company house, built a mile and a half behind the town. (I have since discovered that he actually owned the Briars, the surrounding land and the waterfall behind, about one hundred acres, which are now the property of the Cable and Wireless Company.)

A certain mystery had been woven around William Balcombe, and the townsfolk made the most of it. Today one knows only hearsay; then there was speculation as to his antecedents and gossip played with the possibility of a royal father. It made an item of interest in the little community, which became rather proud of it. Born in England, he and his brother were educated by the King's Bounty — their father, captain of a frigate, having reputedly been lost at sea with his ship. Rumour circulated at the time that these two boys were natural sons of one of the Georges. They spent much time at Carlton House during their young life, and probably the speculation arose from this and the circumstances of their education, which, however, was usual procedure in those days: the sons of officers lost at sea while in the service of their country were often assisted in their schooling by such means.

William's elder brother, a soldier, remained equerry to the Regent for many years and eventually retired as Inspector-General of Yeomanry about 1847. William's lot as a sailor held more in it of drama. Hot-tempered and impulsive, he fell foul of a superior officer by refusing to transmit his order for a flogging which he considered unjust, and, but for the Regent's intervention, he would have been summarily cashiered. He was allowed to resign his commission, however, and in due course a post was found for him abroad as Naval Agent and Purveyor for the East India Company in St Helena. Although it made him a virtual exile, the post held promise for anyone who knew and understood sailors and ships. William had fought in the Battle of the Nile and was content to live away from England. His wife sailed for the island with no misgiving, but, to judge from their recorded comments, her family considered she had been little better than transported to Botany Bay. One letter, a folded document, written before the days of envelopes and criss-crossed in careful lines of script, bewails the fact that she was lost to her own people for ever.

It is not easy to recapture her quality. She had been widowed once, probably by war, and was appraised as puritanical by her contemporaries, but by Napoleon was considered almost the living image of Josephine. The family hold memories of her good looks and good housekeeping, when she finally reached Sydney and settled in the Colonial Treasurer's house, while William Balcombe was beginning to arrange the new office to which he had been appointed.

Betsy seldom wrote of her. She must have had a certain fortitude, for although frequently ill over the years, from chronic hepatitis, she remained on the island until 1818, and in due course, without apparent comment or objection, took ship to the almost unknown continent, there to remake a home and finally to die.

Great-grandmother's was a life of un-favoured incident, and, herself a background to activities manifestly foreign to her precise Anglo-Saxon upbringing, she met it all with high courage.

Napoleon respected her and, albeit reluctantly, submitted on occasions to her household remedies.

In my possession remains a picture of the Briars; a pale water-colour painted in 1813, which Betsy once owned. It shows an unpretentious house set in its garden and orchard; and, on an elevation about fifty yards from the main building, a Pavilion, where East India Company visitors were occasionally accommodated. Many distinguished soldiers and civilians passed through St Helena on their way home, or to India, and availed themselves of the Company's hospitality and William Balcombe's garden rest-house. It was a pleasant break in a long journey to be among hills and surroundings accepted as lovely by all visitors, with both English and sub-tropical flowers growing in profusion. Somewhere in St Helena's archives there must be a record of those travellers — names of merchants and soldiers of many nationalities, of their ships and regiments. Perhaps descendants still remain in England who treasure relics of that period, and can hand down some family historical gossip, as in the case of the Beales of Greensborough, Victoria, who wrote to me as recently as 1957:

"Is there any relationship between you and a child named Betsy Balcombe who was a friend of Napoleon on St Helena? I am related to a grandchild of Major Anthony Beale who lived at St Helena at the time of Napoleon's exile and is mentioned in the table of precedence at Plantation House."

If this can happen in Australia — how much more in the old country, to which most of those people returned?

In 1805 Sir Arthur Wellesley took passage for England on the Company's ship, *Lady Jane Dundas*, after a 'glorious' victory at Assaye, a name that finds no echo in twentieth-century minds, and gratefully slept five nights in the Pavilion. He used the simple blue china and piled his papers and travelling gear upon the round teak table that ten years later was to be used by his great adversary.

It is said that Wellesley, like Napoleon, spent his first night on St Helena at Mr Porteous's boarding-house in Jamestown and, as did Napoleon, went to the Pavilion next day. Was it a coincidence, or had the hardness of Mr Porteous's beds something to do with it, since Mr Porteous, doubling the role of boarding-house keeper with that of Government Botanist, probably possessed a soul above creature comforts?

When the *Lady Jane Dundas* anchored in James Roads, two boatloads of passengers, anxious to see the island, put off to the landing-steps — among them the General. A sudden squall, whipping up the customary long-spaced rollers, upset the boat in which he was sitting and left the passengers struggling in the water. Three people went under immediately and were lost, while Wellesley, unable to swim, was disappearing when a sailor from the other boat dived in and held him up, and eventually towed him, exhausted, to the steps, "on his left arm and shoulder". The seaman was not then aware that he had rescued the "illustrious hero", seeing only a man about to drown. After Wellesley recovered sufficiently on the landing-stage, "he rewarded him by a cordial hand-shake, promise of 6 bottles of rum, and a warm invitation to come and see him in England". The narrative states that the sailor subsequently settled in Rotherhithe, where he was known by the townsfolk as "the saviour of England", which he took in good part. The fact that Wellesley spent several days at the Briars is accounted for by this accident and the necessity for an inquest on the drowned passengers, for though many visitors stayed there during the brief period of their vessel's re-victualling, few ships lingered in the open roads longer than was necessary. Nowadays a modest notice hangs at the Pavilion door stating that the Duke of Wellington once lived there and later Napoleon.

In Jamestown in 1806, Mr Saul Solomon erected the St Helena Press, which subsequently the East India Company took over, and in due course he brought out a printed sheet called The St Helena Monthly Register. Progress was on the march. Nowadays his descendants are influential in South African life; one of them still remains on the island.

Contemporary books hold records and pictures of several pleasant homes outside Jamestown, among the folds of the hills and in steep little valleys, sheltered from the south-east trade winds. There was Plantation House, one of the residences of the Governor, then Colonel Mark Wilks, who also had a town house, the Castle, where, in approved colonial fashion, Mrs Wilks set the social tone for Jamestown's activities. Mr Porteous's three-storied establishment stood on a corner, whitewashed and severely plain. (It has now been demolished to make way for a motor garage.) Sir William Doveton, Member of Council, owner of Mount Pleasant and a true 'yamstock', as St Helenians term themselves, was something of a figure. A story is told of him that, when in London to receive his knighthood, he met a friend in a crowded street and asked "that the conversation be deferred until the procession passed by".

As an offset to the gentler way of living on the island, there is a note in one book that "inferior habitations are occupied by people who subsist principally by the fleets and mostly keep wine-shops for the accommodation of soldiers and sailors". Rum was a favoured tipple and in good supply. It also seems certain that rum was the spirit in which the surgeons preserved Napoleon's heart after its removal from his body.

Among homes to which reference can be found are Alarm House, the Wynyards and Knollcombe, occupied by Sir George and Lady Bingham; and round about the district others with the pleasant English names of Rosemary Hall (still standing), Prospect House, High Knoll, Rose Cottage, Geranium Cottage, High Pasture Farm, Arnos Vale.

In my own recollection the family have spoken of friendships with the Skeltons, the Wynyards and the Wilkses; and there was a special link with Colonel Beatson, the Governor before Colonel Wilks, who was godfather to William's youngest son, my grandfather, born on St Helena four years before Napoleon's arrival.

Alexander Beatson, a noted engineer and soldier, but at heart an agriculturist, came to the island with ideas that bore some fruit; he dabbled in guano export, aloe fibre, crops, kelp and lichen gathering, but being in advance of his time he achieved disappointingly little. At least, however, he built a granary and cleaned up the graveyard, which he described as "having more the appearance of a common for dogs than a burial-place for deceased Christians".

There might have been good commercial results from the gathering of guano, but today the snow-like islets rise unexploited from an ultramarine sea and still remain the favoured nesting-place of myriads of wide-awake gulls (Antarctic visitors) and black-winged sea-birds that wheel and complain above a concentrated mass of lime.

In all, when Napoleon arrived at St Helena in 1815, there were approximately seven hundred white civilians, one thousand soldiers, fourteen hundred slaves, and four-hundred-and-fifty 'free people of colour', an uneasy minority in the political structure of the island. Jamestown possessed a Freemasons' Lodge and a theatre, besides merchants' houses, sundry other dwellings, drinking-houses, a church and the graveyard. It was, in fact, a prototype of any Anglo-Indian garrison town of the time, and social life followed the same pattern.

To deal with Napoleon's captivity, the military camps were enlarged at Deadwood, Francis Plain, Lemon Valley and Jamestown; and bugle-calls, heard in the quiet mornings and at sunset, were possibly not unpleasing to the ears of the Emperor. Military life had outweighed all other preoccupations, and he came to linger in thought more constantly on this than on all other phases of his turbulent years' existence.

CHAPTER 2

The Exile's Arrival

On the day the *Northumberland* anchored in James Roads, Dr Warden, the ship's doctor, and Mr O'Meara, Napoleon's surgeon, called at the Briars to tell my great-grandfather about their illustrious prisoner.

They were amused at the fear the young members of the family held of him, instilled into them by servants and hearsay. "He is only a man now," said Dr Warden comfortingly, "and will charm you; there is nothing about him to alarm." As Dr Warden was a close friend of William Balcombe, and Mr O'Meara an acquaintance from past naval days, they were made very welcome and stayed to lunch and talked all the time of the strange overwhelming personality that was now to share the life of the little island. Mr O'Meara had been disposed to like him from the beginning, said he was a docile patient, interested in medical matters and one who could discuss the circulatory system. He experienced days of depression when he remained in his cabin, but the doctor considered that this was his reaction to past events rather than from any physical cause. "Of course, he is too fat for his age — 46," he added.

He talked of the seventy-day voyage, uneventful as far as weather was concerned, of Admiral Sir George Cockburn (who commanded the deportation) and Tom Pipes, his dog, of the Bertrands and their children. Count Bertrand, Grand Marshal, they found quiet, efficient and likeable. His wife was part-Irish, her family name Dillon. They were a devoted couple. Napoleon once said to Dr Warden that Bertrand was the best engineer-officer living. The doctors both remarked on his devotion to the Emperor. His determination to accompany Napoleon had been fiercely but unsuccessfully combated by Madame Bertrand, who in the end gave way, packed up and came too. She was a most engaging and fascinating woman, they said. Tall and commanding, she stooped a little to diminish her height. Her eyes were black and animated. She was a distant relative of Josephine's, a Creole, with something of Josephine's immense charm. Accustomed to courts and their ways, their luxuries and intrigues, Madame was appalled when it became known that Napoleon's exile was to be spent in St Helena. She knew the barren life would destroy them all by its ennui and she made a final hysterical scene, flinging herself into the Emperor's cabin and even attempting to drown herself by half-climbing out of the cabin-window until her husband hauled her back by the legs, while Savary, who was watching, shouted with laughter and said, "Let her go, let her go." The surgeons told William Balcombe that Captain Maitland of the *Northumberland* after several brushes with her had been so sorely tried that he told her, with some rudeness, not to speak to him again, declaring that she was a very foolish woman. Later when they were approaching the island she asked him to shake hands, "as God knows, we may never meet again". No one of Bonaparte's entourage had made a greater sacrifice to his cause than Madame Bertrand had in accompanying her husband. Mr O'Meara was very well aware of this and related to the Balcombe family incidents in which she had been peacemaker among the exiles. "She is unafraid, outspoken and a great lady," he told them.

Count de Montholon, next in importance in the suite, was closely identified, with the career of Bonaparte. Of an ancient family with some English blood, he had in his youth received lessons in mathematics from the young Napoleon when Captain of Artillery. Montholon was fated to know him in his young days of obscurity, to be associated with him in the magnificence of his empire, to follow him into exile and watch him die, hearing his last indistinguishable words. In spite of all that was demanded of him, he remained his blind devotee. Madame de Montholon had two divorced husbands living when she married the Count. Napoleon, hearing of the proposed wedding, promptly forbade the banns, but afterwards gave permission for Montholon to marry the 'niece of President Séquier' — the same lady, but otherwise described. Captain Maitland summed her up as a quiet, unassuming woman who gave no trouble, followed her husband happily and provided music by strumming on the piano and singing Italian songs in a little voice. The St Helena climate never agreed with her and at first she played only a minor role in the household's activities.

The two doctors gave shrewd descriptions of the characters and personalities of the remaining members of the suite — seventy days spent in the close confine of a sailing-ship leave little to the imagination. They spoke of the Bertrand children, their high French voices calling the dog, Tom Pipes, of the valets, the servants and those surrounding the Emperor.

William Balcombe and his two guests were interrupted by the arrival of Admiral Cockburn, a former shipmate of Balcombe's, who was intent on ventilating his annoyance at the inadequacies of the Longwood accommodation. "Even the printed maps show Plantation House as Napoleon's residence," he grumbled. He had hoped for the Governor's house, but Sir Mark Wilks, the Governor, studiously avoided any mention of a change. He went into the garden and sniffed the air appreciatively. William Balcombe was putting him up and he looked forward to the days on shore. The men smoked and talked, bridging gaps in the news made by a slow voyage; the French as yet remained on board.

At dusk the family rode down the valley to Jamestown, where most of the island's inhabitants had already gathered in anticipation of a sight of the most feared figure in the world — a small man in a green uniform and a cocked hat — who was now to share their island life.

The Balcombes were eager to see him too, and waited opposite the Castle gate near the East India Company building. Sure enough, the French party disembarked at sundown, and one by one came up the landing-steps to the jetty. They passed between parallel ranks of soldiers while the crowd jostled for a glimpse; the silence was so profound that Betsy remembered the sound of the exiles' feet on the cobbles. Napoleon they distinguished by his cocked hat, and long topcoat half-concealing something that twinkled on his breast. Betsy concluded the coat must have been open but more she could not make out; only the bobbing hats of the passing group, and Sir George Cockburn's tall figure bringing up the rear, and Betsy noted that he appeared harassed and preoccupied.

The newcomers were lodged in Mr Porteous's white, box-like building with its little garden in front, on which the crowd settled, still silent, still curious even though the quick tropical twilight had almost gone and the blinds had been pulled down. The family returned home through the scented night, and heard later that Napoleon had lifted a blind. Surveying the scene he demanded a bolt on his door, and had his valets sleep on the threshold, himself not stirring till daylight. His appearance at the window was the signal for a wild scramble towards the house. Admiral Cockburn agreed it was insupportable, but pointed out that anything was better than another night on board ship.

He arranged for the Emperor to ride with him to Longwood next morning. Longwood had no pretension to anything more than a farmhouse used as a summer retreat for the Lieutenant-Governor and his family. It was cool, however, and might possibly be made adequate.

Aboard the *Bellerophon* Napoleon after his surrender had abandoned himself to rage on hearing, through public journals, before it was officially announced to him, that his destination was St Helena — 'the barren rock'. At first he furiously declared that he would never be taken from the *Bellerophon* alive, but later when a calmer mood prevailed he began to show himself to the crowds who came out from Torbay in the little boats and circled around the ship. Curious but not hostile folk, their numbers gave the authorities some concern. On one occasion the Emperor was observed to throw a handful of torn papers into the sea, "which drifted towards a gentleman's boat. Gathering them and carefully drying the scraps he pieced together a portion of a letter to the Empress Marie Louise".

"Madame, my dear and honoured wife, attending once more solely to the interests of France, I am going to abdicate the throne and in closing my own political career to bring about the commencement of the reign of our dear son. My tenderness for you and for him impels me on this step no less than my duties as a Monarch. If he ensures as Emperor the happiness of France, and as a son the happiness and the glory of his mother, my dearest wish will be accomplished. Nevertheless if even in his most tender infancy I can give up to him all my authority in my capacity of head of the State, I cannot, and it would be too painful to my heart to sacrifice also, the inviolable rights which nature gave me ..."

The remainder of the letter was not salvaged.

An officer's description of the Emperor's first days on the *Northumberland* tells that he ate a "very hearty dinner", amused himself afterwards on the quarter-deck by listening to the band of the 53rd Regiment, and asked them to play national airs for him — 'Rule Britannia' and 'God Save the King'. He spoke to those of the officers who talked French, and they remarked his commanding attitude, a legacy of Talma's tuition and one he adopted when giving audience to his marshals. At other times he was completely natural in demeanour.

The next day he breakfasted at eleven o'clock on meat and claret, followed by coffee. At dinner he ate a mutton cutlet with his fingers — later he played whist.

When the vessel ran into rough weather he became seasick and retired, but later appeared on deck "very unsteady on his feet". He asked many questions — when was the gale likely to subside, how many leagues did it travel an hour, what strange sail appeared on the bow of the vessel? He asked a midshipman how long he had been in the Service and, on being answered, "Nine years" remarked that it was a long time. "Yes," the officer replied, "it is so; part of it was passed in imprisonment in France. I happened to be at Verdun when you, Sir, set out on your expedition for Moscow." Napoleon shrugged his shoulders and dropped the conversation.

The Emperor's two camp-beds had come aboard with his luggage. They were two yards long and one yard wide, with steel frames and green silk curtains. One he used, while the other went to Madame Bertrand's cabin.

Shown papers expressing the opinion that he would commit suicide, Napoleon commented, "No! I am not sufficiently a Roman to destroy myself." His health on board was excellent.

Something must be said for Admiral Cockburn's tact that the preliminary adjustments necessary at the beginning of the long sea voyage had proved adequate. The Admiral overcame Napoleon's objection to long-drawn-out meals by a routine which included willy-nilly the general departure of all the French on deck when the Emperor rose, after which the officers of the *Northumberland* resumed their chairs and, as was the custom, lingered over port and cheroots after first drinking the loyal toast — sitting. The habit of remaining at the dinner-table appeared senseless to the exiles. That men should smoke and circulate the port while their female dinner companions waited gossiping in the drawing-room never ceased to intrigue and perplex them.

Their strange, dynamic leader, hands in pockets, his brief meal ended, leaned against a gun to gaze at the passing rollers, oblivious of the seamen working around him or the creaking blocks that answered to the press of sails overhead, or of the periods of silence when the ripple of the bow wave might be plainly distinguished. It was a moment when the rancour of the undelivered letter to the Regent stirred his soul anew. The carefully chosen sentences requesting asylum "in the English country a few leagues from London" reformed in his mind. It had been a dignified appeal; monarch spoke to monarch, and the return of Gourgaud with the report that an official veto had blocked its passage astounded his ears. Later came the interview with Lord Keith (no mention of the Prince Regent) and the subsequent transference from the *Bellerophon* to the present vessel. He saw the incidents as steps slowly descending to the farthest corner of the earth, to a fortified windswept rock.

It is difficult to absolve the Prince Regent from some share of the blame for the treatment of Napoleon after Waterloo. The Prince remained supine, glad to shelter behind the Cabinet's and the Allied Powers' decisions. After reading the Emperor's letter throwing himself on his mercy, he simply remarked, "Upon my word, a very proper letter! Much more so I must say than any I ever received from Louis XVIII. He addressed me as 'Altesse Royale' instead of 'Monsignor'."

Betsy's part in the final phase of Napoleon's life was more complicated than that of the four-year-old Alexander Beatson, her brother. The self-crowned

Emperor, once controller of Europe, a man of arresting personality, had, when she first spoke to him, stepped down from world-domination into the anti-climax of a garden and an English family, his lodging a Pavilion in their grounds, his surroundings the bare hills of St Helena, the horizon a stretch of the South Atlantic Ocean. The charger that brought him to the gate of the Briars on that first day was the final expression of the pageantry of the past — a brief moment, fading like the sunset behind him. He represented to her a symbolic picture of the mighty Napoleon; it was all there, the green coat, white breeches and tricorn hat, the red saddlecloth and gold trappings; Admiral Cockburn walked beside one stirrup, Count Bertrand by the other, orderlies and horses behind. William Balcombe and his family watched him ride down the straight path later to be called by him the Avenue of the Philosophers, the jingling of accoutrements and the ring of horses' hooves the only accompaniment to a fateful entrance. Earlier in the day they had seen the cavalcade ascend the road above the valley; the uniforms making a conspicuous patch of colour above the stone barrier wall, but at such a distance they were unable to ascertain the identity of the riders. So many brilliant uniforms had come suddenly to the island during the past day or so. A regiment was even then disembarking and James Roads had been occupied for the past week by a fleet riding at anchor. William Balcombe had heard nothing further in Jamestown than that the Emperor had slept at Mr Porteous's lodging-house.

Now they wondered at this unexpected visit. The afternoon sun was losing its heat, perfumes were beginning to rise from the garden and Toby, the slave, his tools collected, could be seen plodding off to the quarters. A gleam of silver marked the waterfall that fell endlessly into a valley behind the home. The trade wind blowing strongly above the peaks was diverted by the shoulder of the hill, and St Helena's best time of day gave an added appearance of well-being. Jamestown lay, a white lime-washed town in the cleft of the mountain, calm and drowsy and content.

The Balcombe family little knew that on this day they had come to a turning-point in their lives, hitherto spent in peaceful anonymity, comfort and prosperity. For a brief time they were to enter the orbit of Napoleon's star, receive his friendship and confidence as well as the approbation and disapproval of officials; suffer gossip, censure and suspicion, face retirement and poverty and, when finally officialdom was appeased, receive a Government commission in a new land, Australia. They were to be divided, shaken and disturbed; and, in the case of Betsy, over-young to be caught in political whirlpools, shadowed by the memory of one she had loved passionately, as a tomboy adolescent, and later with even deeper feeling. But to Betsy and her sister, standing behind their mother on that afternoon, the cavalcade only ushered-in a new and exciting world, differing from the stereotyped small-town existence they had hitherto been living, a way of life in keeping with that of any English colony — the Governor calling the tune, the officials following in accordance with rank, the merchants coming after. In their case, their father combined the qualities of the last two estates, being at once the representative of the East India Company (which still owned the island) and Naval Agent, as well as a partner in business with William Fowler and Joseph Cole.

The Emperor dismounted, awe-inspiring and unsmiling, and came forward. "I have heard of you," he said abruptly, addressing Balcombe. As Mrs Balcombe curtsied, his eyes swept over her and back to his host. "You have a beautiful wife," he announced. His gaze passed on to Betsy as she made her best school-taught obeisance. "And a beautiful daughter," he added.

In the meantime Admiral Cockburn had explained the purpose of the visit: that the Emperor wished to remain at the Briars; he had no inclination to return to the town, which was stuffy and where he found it impossible to maintain the privacy he demanded. William Balcombe immediately placed the Briars at his disposal, with its servants and all its possessions. The family would move immediately to Jamestown. Napoleon declined this offer, saying he had heard of the Pavilion where East India Company visitors were accustomed to stay. He would sleep there, order his camp-bed to be put up — anything but return to Jamestown. Dubiously Admiral Cockburn agreed, feeling the Briars house to be a more workable proposition. The Pavilion was furnished, but its dimensions made it hardly suitable — a fifteen-by-seventeen room with two attics and a few offices. However, Napoleon made up his mind to remain. The charger was led away by the orderlies and messages were despatched to Jamestown for necessities, and for Count Las Cases. It had already been arranged for Admiral Cockburn to stay at the Briars and sleep in William Balcombe's dressing-room. The Emperor's servants went to the quarters; Las Cases and his son, the page, were allotted the Pavilion's attics. "Marquees can be erected tomorrow for the kitchens," William Balcombe promised. "In the meantime, Sir, will you do us the honour of dining here tonight?" The details settled, Napoleon moved to a lawn, where, in accordance with his wish, a chair had been placed. It was a wide stretch of green with shrubs masking the paths that led to the Pavilion on a rise fifty yards away. A grape arbour, heavy with fruit, stretched from a little wooden gate, which the gardener Toby kept locked, to a tangle of pomegranates and lemon trees. The sun in its waning strength cast long, indefinite shadows as evening approached from behind the mountains. It was the time for tropical flowers to spill their sweetness.

Betsy's comment later on Napoleon's appearance was shrewd. She said he looked deathly pale, stern and tense. Even his hands were colourless. His uniform, the bottle-green coat, high boots, nankeen waistcoat and white breeches, so famous in pictures, were well-worn but scrupulously valeted; a glittering star and some orders shone in a beam of the late sun. He had removed his hat and held it on his knee. She noted that the band had left a dark mark of sweat on his fine hair with its reddish undertones. His eyes travelled over the garden to the orange trees planted in rows beyond, and to the grape arbour.[1]

Betsy sat quietly, without fidgeting, her school training restraining a temperament that did not allow of tranquillity for long, her mind focused on the man whose face was turned towards the breath of coolness from the mountain. He seemed fully alive to the surroundings and their implications, and to have accepted the fact that here in this island-fortress he had come to his journey's end, the end of thirty years of struggle, of triumph and disaster. A fierce longing awoke for the bustle and pomp of the so recent past, for the edicts and pronouncements, the Councils of State, the battles and the intoxication of risk; even the sharpness of defeat, in the movements of men and guns, and the complications and intrigues surrounding Imperial existence. Here around him was the empty aftermath, the anti-climax to splendour, not even the ship's movement to distract thoughts that, wherever he might be, would crowd and beat against the door of memory. The cycle of his life was complete: from an island to an island he had travelled the full circle, returning to the simple regimen from which he had sprung. The hills and encircling sea, the sound of goat-bells, and the glimpse of people at work on the land confirmed the realisation. He was to spend his later days in writing an apologia, an assessment of his actions, groping for the set of circumstances over a recent past that had precipitated the ignoble present, this being the last and final act of his career.

He considered that he might not remain on this barren rock for ever; but it was only a faint stirring of hope, lost in the silence of the dying day. His physical lassitude overrode mental activity, the past only lingered rather as we hear today a playback of a well-known tune. Where had been the error? Increasing lethargy perhaps, periods of inaction when energy was demanded, too great a multiplication of interests, the imperial crown, the weight of majesty? Josephine had begged him not to assume the diadem of royalty. Disaster would follow, she had said, and her prescience had usually been remarkable. Dead Josephine, she had found her ease at Malmaison among her roses — another garden, infinitely more formal and magnificent than this, bathed in the morning of the sun that was passing to its evening here. He recalled her features. Mrs Balcombe's features had reminded him of her. Had the loss of Josephine deprived him of some vital element?

The scent from the jasmine bushes against the house roused him to glance at the girl sitting, in attentive silence, one foot tucked under her skirts in an attitude typical of youth. Something in her demeanour prompted him to take more notice. There was an unafraid awareness, a forthright challenge in her eyes. No coquette this, a hoyden perhaps, definite in character and with the promise of beauty; not in the French but in the English style. The fine skin and rosy complexion overlaid now by sunburn, the unruly, pale (*cendré*) curls, the small capable hands. Her hat hung on her neck by a ribbon, pantaloons extended down to the flat shoes and made Napoleon glance a second time at the one visible leg — not a French fashion this, he thought, and an unbecoming one. Only when Betsy's skirts were let down finally to adult length did Napoleon approve of her appearance.

"You speak good French, better than the others," he told her abruptly. Betsy was tempted to say that this was the only reason she had been left to entertain him. Instead she informed him that she had once had a French nurse and had learned to write the language while at school in England.

"It is very quiet," he remarked, inconsequently, glancing at the mountains.

"We are in the country, Sir, you will hear the farm animals and the fowls in the morning. They may disturb you."

He grunted, a habit she grew to expect when he was inattentive or irritable.

Domestics passed along the path with linen and candles for the Pavilion, and the lamp-lighter, one of Napoleon's servants, followed with a lantern. Fresh curtains had appeared in the windows and there were sounds a-plenty of activity within.

"You will have more air up there, it is always a little cooler," Betsy told him. "By dinner time your room will be quite ready. It is only a mile and a half from Jamestown, and your things, and bed, will soon be here." She emphasised 'and bed'; the implication that her mother's feather mattress was not good enough for him warranted some slight comment. Above all else Mrs Balcombe was a housekeeper.

"I hope you will be comfortable," she added primly. "Most visitors like the Pavilion. Of course they are usually soldiers or sailors."

He looked at her quizzically, "And what am I, pray?"

"An Emperor," she answered promptly.

Betsy was remembering that, hitherto, the most illustrious occupant of the Pavilion had been the great Wellington. She cast a glance at the brooding countenance, and decided not to volunteer this item of information. Instead, she added, "Our visitors mostly have been on active service."

"I, too, have been on active service," he reminded her tartly. Meanwhile Admiral Cockburn and William Balcombe were inside with Las Cases, making further arrangements for the visitor's comfort. After tonight the marquee would be erected for kitchen quarters, with yet another in front of the Pavilion to enlarge the living-room. The Briars kitchen would serve for the moment, and there the water would be heated for the Emperor's bath-tub, which even then was being carried up the road from the harbour in company with the famous camp-bed. Chickens were ordered for breakfast, which Napoleon himself carved next morning, an unusual occurrence which he commented upon, remarking that he considered he had done it very well for so little practice, food being usually cut up outside and served on silver platters. It is generally accepted that at first Napoleon's meals were cooked and sent up from Jamestown, which was not the case — certain prepared provisions may have been delivered from this source, but the actual cooking of the meals was undertaken in the kitchen of the Briars, where there was adequate staff in fact Le Page, the Emperor's chef, habitually worked in the kitchen of the Briars even after the marquee had been erected, until the Emperor left for Longwood.

As was his custom when he met anyone for the first time, Napoleon asked personal and direct questions. In Betsy's case he had been distracted by the events of the last twenty-four hours, but now he roused himself and examined her about her studies in England, particularly about geography.

"What is the capital of France?"

"Paris."

"Of Italy?"

"Rome."

"Russia?"

"Petersburg now, Moscow formerly."

He turned abruptly and Betsy felt for the first time his direct stare.

"*Qui l'a brûlée?*" he demanded, his voice changed and cold.

She remained dumb. Moscow and its burning had been discussed at the time with appropriate expressions of horror but she could not remember which side had actually set it alight. He repeated the question and in desperation she replied, "I do not know, Sir."

"*Oui, oui,*" he replied, laughing violently. "*Vous savez très bien; c'est moi qui l'a brûlée.*"

Betsy said, "I believe, Sir, the Russians burned it to get rid of the French." He again gave a high-pitched, violent laugh, rose from his chair, dismissed the subject with a gesture and commanded Betsy to show him the garden.

William Balcombe and the Admiral presently joined them among the orange trees, and the former, with the politeness he accorded to the Emperor at all times during their association, again suggested he might honour them at dinner. Later Napoleon closely examined the drawing-room furniture, which happened to be French, and told Mrs Balcombe that he approved of the room, its comfort and its elegance, which he was evidently pleased to find. After dinner, swiftly served and brief in deference to the Emperor's habit of quick eating, he said to Betsy:

"I suppose you are too young to play the piano?"

The implication of youth was too much, and she informed him she could both play and sing.

"Let me hear," he demanded, seating himself to listen.

'Ye Banks and Braes' was the vogue at the time and so, spreading her skirts, Betsy settled herself to render the simple melody as well as she was able. Napoleon pronounced it "the prettiest English air" he had ever heard, to be told by Betsy it was a Scottish ballad. To this he remarked, "I thought it too pretty an air to be English. Their music is vile, the worst in the world."

He enquired if she could sing 'Vive Henri Quatre', Grétry's work, which she had not heard. He commenced to hum violently, leaving his chair and marching around the room in time to the song. Presently he asked for her opinion of the tune and she quite candidly admitted that she did not think much of it as it was difficult to make out. Napoleon's voice was extremely unmusical. He had no ear and it was pure guesswork to attempt to recognise any tune he was rendering. He volunteered that he considered French music to be almost as bad as English, his southern background responding to the more voluptuous outpourings of Italy. He talked of the operas he had attended in Paris, of the glittering stage productions, crowded tiers of spectators, the upholstery of rose-red and the heavy gilt walls. The silence of the St Helena night swallowed his voice and the little group listening appreciated the depth of the abyss that opened between the past and the present.

From the galaxy of wealth, of magnificence and beauty, of which he had been the focal point, this little rotund man, with the piercing eyes and sudden sweet smile, had travelled far to be entertained by a simple Scottish ballad, presently to sleep in the Pavilion on his camp-bed, his valet stretched across his door as his only guard. Yet at that moment Napoleon was not actively unhappy; amidst the normal flow of activities, the food and the scent of flowers, the tinkling piano, and the sound of the waterfall, the shock of the forbidding rock prison was forgotten, as were the pressing crowds around Mr Porteous's house. As he bade the family good night, he pinched Betsy's ear, a token of approval, glanced distastefully at the pantaloons, and again complimented her on her song.

CHAPTER 3

At the Balcombes'

Napoleon made no adverse comment on his inadequate abode. The marquee, connected with the main room by a covered way, was now divided into two parts, the inner being the Emperor's bedroom, holding the small camp-bed with the green silk hangings of his campaigns.

On the lawn by the marquee, and just where he must tread, a servant had cut a crown in the turf. No flag might fly, but the symbol was there, nevertheless, at his feet.

Napoleon lived simply; he had no great liking for food at this time and ate quickly, although later at Longwood food became all-important. Cipriani, the *maître d'hotel*, made a punctual appearance and with reverence intoned, "*Le diner de Votre Majesté est servi,*" then backed out of the presence, followed by the Emperor and suite. When he was not himself dining in the homely atmosphere of the Briars household, Napoleon more often than not sought the girls at dinner. He teased them about the English fondness for *rosbif* and plum pudding. Betsy retorted by producing one of the toys belonging to the little boys, a wooden figure of a Frenchman with a frog that jumped down his throat. *A Frenchman's Dinner* was the legend inscribed underneath. Napoleon remained unruffled, frogs'-legs being a delicacy to him; Las Cases's son on the other hand was deeply affronted.

Betsy showed the Emperor another toy brought to young Alexander by Captain Edmund Denman, with whom Napoleon later dined at the Briars and afterwards played whist in the drawing-room.

It was a wooden figure of the Emperor, with green coat and cocked hat, mounting a ladder only to topple to the ground. He worked it reflectively for some time, watching the little caricature of himself ascend and fall. "*Eh bien,*" he said, with a half-sigh.

Lampoons, broadsheets of abuse, animated toys, caricatures — they now took the place of loyal pronouncements, court portraits and eulogies — cheap

backwash of a storm that had wrecked him and wiped away the future of his
son. Affected by the silly toy's crude demonstration of defeat he at length
dropped it with the favourite word when annoyed, *canaille*, and a look of
disgust came over his face. Betsy saw with surprise that he was disturbed
— usually he laughed; it was one of the few moments when she felt contrite.

Napoleon talked sometimes of his early life, of his mother's struggles to
keep a large family fed and clothed on insufficient means. He admired her
courage and bore her a deep filial love, and told Betsy that during one period
at Brienne he had cooked for himself and his younger brother "Two meals a
day, not much to eat." These early struggles held no nostalgic memories for
him — sentiment died behind a tightened belt.

Meanwhile the rest of the staff, Count and Countess de Montholon and
their child, Baron and Baroness Bertrand and theirs, with the servants, settled
in Jamestown in Mr Porteous's prim house, bearable now because the crowds
no longer congregated, and authority, in the persons of Governor Wilks and
Admiral Cockburn, commenced to function. Longwood, which both men
inspected on the day preceding Napoleon's landing, was found impossible by
any standard of living.

The Admiral discovered that the bedroom intended for Napoleon was too
small to hold a bed of ordinary dimensions. They decided there were only four
rooms habitable, with sound roofs. Napoleon, riding to inspect his prospective
home on the day after his arrival, was definite in his description of the site.
"Frightful" was the word he used. He found the view barren, the position
exposed and windy and the clouds from the mountain-tops "conducive to
rheumatism in the human frame and mildew in clothing", and he took an
immediate and active dislike to the Barn, the mountain that hid most of the
view of the sea. There was no vegetation but a single gumwood tree (still
standing today), a few stunted shrubs and a variety of inhospitable grass
that somehow survived the ever-blowing south-east trade and the alternating
periods of cloud and burning sun. The Barn, a barren mass, gave some shelter
from the wind, while, down below, the sea stretched in a flat waste, too far
off to show any surface movement. Admiral Cockburn, aware that it was
customary for official and distinguished visitors to be housed at Plantation
House — maps of St Helena had already in fact been printed. showing it as
Napoleon's residence, was informed that Governor Wilks, acting on explicit
instructions, could volunteer no counter-suggestion to Longwood.

Later the Emperor harped upon the conditions with bitterness. He regarded
Longwood with its ramshackle buildings and wretched inadequacies as a
crowning insult. 'General Bonaparte' never entered the Castle or Plantation
House, nor did he recognise the appellation 'General' in responding to

invitations from the Governor, replying that, as far as his knowledge went, General Bonaparte still remained in Egypt!

Of his suite, Las Cases and his son became indispensable to him. Las Cases, a comparative newcomer to the Imperial circle, was classed offhand by William Warden, the *Northumberland*'s doctor, as a secretary. In this, Warden showed lack of knowledge. Las Cases, a marquis, his title of nobility dating from the eleventh century, had served in the French Navy and possessed all the best attributes and manners of the eighteenth century.

Small and of insignificant appearance, Las Cases was a man of the world. He had fought, gambled and travelled, and observed the Empire and its court with independent eyes. Moreover he knew much about England. Napoleon found him immensely useful and, in turn, he said simply, "Napoleon is my God." He was even shorter than the Emperor, and made an unimpressive figure dressed in civilian clothes and a beaver hat, with scanty hair that blew about when, bareheaded, he waited on his Imperial Master. Once he disgraced Napoleon by being violently sick on the deck of the British man-of-war. He handed over to him, at a time of need, what was probably his whole fortune, £4,000, and insisted on joining him in his exile.

Aboard the *Northumberland* Napoleon had displayed great interest in the ship's routine. He questioned any officers who understood the French language, exclaimed upon the general cleanliness, tasted the issue of rum, and commented upon the severe discipline demanded. There were times when he paced the quarter-deck with the Admiral, usually in the half-light of evening, re-living the vital years of the immediate past; each achieving a substantial personal appreciation of the other in the canvass of the lively topics of the time.

Napoleon's reconstruction of the Battle of Waterloo displayed a thorough knowledge of the alignment of troops on both sides. His opinion of Wellington's strategy was uncomplimentary. The blame for his own downfall he heaped primarily on Fouché — Fouché, Minister for Police, Fouché the traitor, the unfrocked monk — whom he openly regretted not having shot; though he also railed against others more nearly concerned with the battle. If the truth be known it was Napoleon's lassitude and lack of energy, the first symptoms of the disease that eventually killed him, which had already begun to sap not only his physical powers but his genius, and which in the last analysis certainly saved Fouché's life. Once to Betsy he admitted to an over-powering fatigue and apathy on that day and to submission to some weightier force, even though he rode all through the early hours of the fatal morning of Waterloo and showed himself among the soldiers. Even the battle he watched with apathy. "*Il paraît qu'ils se sont mêlés,*" he remarked, as he rode off the field to Paris and a hot bath. But when later the full implication dawned he gave way to despair. It wrung from him his high, rasping laugh, a pacing to and fro, appeals to God, until numbness and indecision returned, to show him Fouché, a traitor! He recalled the mechanical signing of the abdication and the sudden emptiness of a palace. Malmaison, once Joséphine's, awaited him, her roses in the formal gardens, her spirit and personality still warm in the well-remembered rooms, her gaiety and elegance reflected in the placing of the furniture and the trivialities of service and food, the little jewelled singing-birds that waited to be wound up; Napoleon searched for a novel to read. It was not long before he received a direction from Paris to leave the country, and presently he left France for the last time.

The Admiral had heard most of this as he paced with his prisoner on the ship; moreover he had personally witnessed the agony of Napoleon's last view of France. At dawn when the ship was making Ushant, the Emperor came on deck and, taking his telescope, stood motionless, gazing at the grey shadow of receding coastline. Respecting his manifest distress, no officer or sailor approached him. It was his supreme hour of despair. From seven o'clock to nearly midday he remained gazing fixedly. At last the outline faded, and the tumbling sea surrounded the ship. Napoleon turned away and, concealing his emotion as best he could, was helped by Las Cases to his cabin. Apart from his other qualities, Admiral Cockburn had the gift of tact; he allowed the torrent of bitter reminiscences of calumny and blame to pour forth, purposely forgetting some of the more unguarded utterances and, when possible, directing the prisoner's thoughts to less intimate channels. The love of the sea was deep in them both, and the order and cleanliness of the British ship elicited many tributes from Napoleon, as did also the qualities of the marines — "Give me ten thousand of these men and I will win any battle."

His admiration for the British Navy in general was unbounded and that William Balcombe had been a naval officer counted with him. Admiral Cockburn, reverting to the present situation, felt that if the Emperor decided to accept the limited accommodation to be found at the Briars, he would be satisfied in other particulars with the treatment he was accorded. The transformation of Longwood could then proceed without interruption. He had not then contemplated Napoleon settling for the Pavilion, which was even smaller, but later he came to the conclusion that the proximity of the family was preferred to solitude.

As yet the spate of Government edicts and instructions was not swollen to full flood, but Napoleon's mind had already travelled around the situation and appraised the extent of the boundaries and communications. He knew his prison to be a formidable natural fortress. He repeatedly voiced his regret at not meeting the Prince Regent. Lord Keith, speaking of the Emperor's wish, said, "Damn the fellow; if he had obtained an interview with His Royal Highness, in half an hour they would be the best friends in England." In Napoleon's belief, it was all-important to reach the fountain-head, monarch speaking with monarch without intermediary. He dwelt in retrospect on the Admiral's gossip about the Balcombes, of the equerry brother at the Regent's elbow. Finally, he cast a trial balance of the character of the man who lived in the cottage down the valley and, as he turned into the gate after the Longwood inspection, he had already come to the conclusion that here was a possible channel by which he could reach the Royal ear without the formal representations demanded by any Governor. Perhaps the future was not going to be so formidable as it had appeared. It is from subsequent incidents remembered and repeated by the family that we have grounds for believing that this was in his mind, and in the Hudson Lowe Papers in the British Museum there is evidence that William Balcombe, when the situation became insupportable for the exiles, transmitted letters to the Regent and to others, and in doing so incurred a serious risk of dismissal and perhaps worse.

For the first few weeks at the Briars, Napoleon set about arranging a routine for living, and commenced a daily dictation to Las Cases of the continuation of his memoirs which he had begun on the *Northumberland*, a task which he never completed. The teak table became crowded with papers, and the silver ewer and basin were conspicuous in the marquee, as was the crown incised in the turf and tended by Toby, who had become already attached to the royal visitor. Napoleon on the day of his arrival had enquired about Toby, noticing the bent black figure of the slave, at work among the orange trees, and had subsequently questioned Betsy as to his life's history. A passing sea captain had put Toby ashore sick, flotsam in the traffic of the sea between the Orient and the island, and when the Malay had recovered he was detailed to the Briars as gardener. No tyrant ruled his domain with a more rigid severity. Toby watched for footprints among his seedlings and the children robbing the fruit trees learned to know his wrath. "I have asked Father to buy his freedom," Betsy told the Emperor; "he has a daughter my age in the Malay States."

Napoleon spoke to William Balcombe and expressed a wish to pay for the man's emancipation, but was informed, after the request had been transmitted to Sir Mark Wilks, that the Government would not accede to it. He endeavoured to persuade Balcombe to free the slave by personally purchasing his release. Balcombe eventually repeated the request, under pressure, to Sir Hudson Lowe some months later, to be again refused; the Governor, it appeared, feared that to grant Napoleon's wish might gain for the Emperor the sympathy and support of the coloured world! To Toby it made no difference — his life was centred on the Briars garden. His native land had become a nebulous image, and his family a memory; to uproot him from his present peaceful state would invite disaster; he continued to dig and plant and to scold the children when he thought it necessary.

It was warm in the Pavilion, so Admiral Cockburn caused a small shelter to be erected in the arbour, under the vines, and a chair and round table placed there for the Emperor's use. Here he remained many hours of the day, sometimes sleeping, sometimes gazing fixedly at the frowning mountain, sometimes pacing to and fro, dictating so swiftly that Las Cases was hard put to keep pace. In those early days he possessed no books of reference, a deprivation which irked him greatly, and he had to rely on a retentive memory. It was not until much later that he received boxes of volumes from London, but by that time the determination to continue writing had begun to flag. His hours of dictation were respected by the children up to a point, but at times an influx of (to Las Cases's mind) unwelcome visitors ran up the path and made demands for a game. Betsy on several occasions in her memoirs noted the sweetness of the Emperor's expression on hearing the young voices. Her memory seems deeply inlaid with his welcome of them, the ever ready smile and the kindliness; she recollected with equal vividness Las Cases's scowls. Napoleon's manner, when he wanted it to be, was disarming and delightful; and he liked most the moments when Betsy arrived or the little boys clambered over him asking questions about his sword and medals. His teeth, small and regular, were stained with the liquorice he habitually chewed, probably finding it helpful to his digestion, which was, even then, giving him periods of discomfort. The children chewed also, fishing pieces of liquorice from his pockets, but they did not find it so palatable as Napoleon pronounced it. Like most men of the day he also took snuff and his waistcoat was dusty with it.

Admiral Cockburn's dog, Tom Pipes, a large shaggy animal, caused daily interruptions to Napoleon's programme Having travelled with him on the *Northumberland*, he knew the Emperor well and naturally paid him periodic visits. Tom Pipes felt the heat and there is a note in a diary that Betsy, after swimming him in the fish pond, let him run and shake himself over the Emperor and the papers on the table, in a muddy and affectionate greeting. Las Cases, blaming Betsy, scolded her furiously for her carelessness, to be commanded to be silent by a master who had commenced to enjoy such informality.

The Emperor's dictation began with the campaign in Egypt and the history of the Consulate, and Las Cases proposed that the other members of the suite, living in boredom at Jamestown, should make it an everyday practice to attend and transcribe in turn. The Emperor was pleased at the suggestion and one or other of them took down his quickly spoken words, remaining to dine in the marquee. Gourgaud, the least tractable, was made to sleep in the marquee, an arrangement that, though agreeable to the A.D.C., aroused feelings of jealousy in Montholon and Bertrand, who perforce had to return to their families in the boarding-house.

Gourgaud was volatile and amorous. He sought the company of women and bewailed that there were so few of his standard on St Helena. Jane, an older and more serious girl, displayed no interest in him and he considered Betsy an adolescent tomboy. Finally, Laura Wilks, the Governor's daughter, captured his heart, and his too clamant expression of bereavement at her departure a few months later exasperated the Emperor into a mimicry of his doleful tones.

Like Las Cases, Gourgaud suffered from a lack of humour. He brooded over fancied insults and upbraided the Emperor, who, strangely passive, soothed him as if he were a fractious child. "My dear Gourgaud, how glum you look. Have a cold rub down, that will do you good. Do you fancy that I don't have terrible moments? At night I wake up and think of what I was and to what I have come."

Betsy avoided the aide-de-camp; she considered him a nuisance, a watch-dog, unnecessarily standing guard over his master. Napoleon, in a mischievous mood, commanded her to dance with the young man, and to be nice to him. But Gourgaud's tastes habitually leaned to the more sophisticated, and the flying skirts, the pantaloons, and general untidiness of Betsy did not conform to his conception of charm in woman.

His devotion to Napoleon was "hysterically fantastic in its intensity", and it was considered that he watched him with a jealous fervour that reacted violently to a chance word of commendation by the Emperor for any of the others, or indeed to reference of any kind to their virtues or their attributes.

"He loved me, as a lover his mistress," Napoleon exclaimed when Gourgaud finally left for England. "He was impossible!" The Emperor bore with him, however, tolerating his tantrums and supporting his outbursts with a moderation almost out of character with his own fiery spirit.

Betsy disliked his appearance as much as his personality. She wrote that he was a spare, swarthy man, rude, impatient and querulous. He complained that the restricted quarters dismayed him, but that as he had clamoured to be allowed to remain there rather than in the boarding-house, he had to be reconciled to it. He was not particularly polite to William Balcombe, and did not except Admiral Cockburn himself from his discourtesy.

CHAPTER 4

A New Napoleon Bonaparte

Betsy wrote of the Emperor's daily routine. He rose at eight o'clock, took coffee and breakfasted or lunched at one o'clock, dined at nine and retired at eleven. He took a liking to a Nankin china mug and habitually used it for coffee; its great size intrigued him. (The coffee was so bad at first that on the day of his arrival he had thought himself poisoned) His manner was completely unaffected and kind, and soon the children watched for his appearance and included him in their games and daily activities, which mainly took place in the garden or around the farm. He became 'Boney' to the younger ones; no longer the ogre, but a willing playmate, which nonplussed and displeased his staff. In their eyes, majesty still clothed the rotund form and, as men who habitually walked backwards from his presence, they were appalled by the sight of little boys clambering over his person and the familiarity of Betsy's commands.

After the first morning greeting and curtsy, Betsy habitually called him 'Boney' and when the Emperor asked once what it meant, Las Cases literally translated it, "a bony person". Napoleon, laughing, patted his stomach and said, "*Je ne suis pas osseux?*" in a puzzled tone.

Napoleon enjoyed this total lack of inhibition; he responded to the children's candour and encouraged them, relaxed in their company and joined in their careless fun. Betsy became the lodestar of his affection and, from the beginning, a deep attachment sprang up and remained. From the first day of meeting he had noticed how she was different from the women he had associated with in the past; something of the adolescent with formed judgment and mature decision intermingled with the tomboy's quick predilection for mischief. He had probed her mind, witnessed her reaction to games and teasing, appreciating her approach and now finding much to satisfy him in her company. It was a carefree, teasing intimacy that, after the formality of the first morning, slipped naturally into the human relationship of people oblivious of rank. The faithful Las Cases, resenting the Emperor's manifest preoccupation with the girl, attempted to prevent her approaching him; but he was unsuccessful, for the Emperor habitually set off in search of her. The whole staff, devoted Frenchmen, voluntary exiles for the sake of their master, were frankly disapproving of the fun and chatter that took place, surrounding the man whose every word they held in awe, and adjudged the careless acceptance of his presence as an actual affront. In their subsequent journals they castigated the youngsters, calling them unmannerly, which was probably correct, recollecting that they had to suffer in grudging silence when screams and shouts rose from a game of hide-and-seek and the Emperor trotted 'home', perspiring and out of breath, but greatly diverted because he had managed to outwit the seekers. Little Las Cases, the thirteen-year-old page, inhibited by his court upbringing and by an earnest-minded father, and at the same time inherently devoid of humour, was instructed in the current games, but either lost interest or became offended at the combination of shoving and shouting and he only joined in when Napoleon commanded it.

Betsy's matter-of-fact acceptance of royalty was all the more irritating to the staff because of the attention he paid to her. Jane, older, more respectful in her attitude, was admired for her elegance and reserve. The little boys had no approach other than that of one playmate to another. Napoleon was well aware that, for all her uninhibited demeanour, Betsy was a shrewd evaluator; pantaloons and short skirts, hat off and hair untidy, she gathered the gifts of the day, entering into its interests and activities and along with her brothers included him also. It gave him a warmth of feeling and a sense of wellbeing that he was part of them, not as the privilege due to his royal state but for himself.

Jane became friends with Madame Montholon and Madame Bertrand, and spent time with them in Jamestown, helping with their shopping and gaping at their magnificent clothes, probably the first Paris creations ever seen in St Helena. Their lovely flowing skirts and colours played havoc with the appearance of the St Helena ladies, and Jane began remaking her own wardrobe and brushed her coiffure into a high structure such as was worn by Madame Bertrand. Emperors and romps in the garden were all very well for children, but the 53rd Regiment arranged periodic dances and the young officers were compliant partners. (The family considered Betsy as yet too young to attend these functions.) Jane also had her hands full in other directions, in the housekeeping duties imposed upon her by her mother and by her own personal affairs. She was kindly disposed to the little Las Cases, but he appeared too bewildered to respond. In the play of human tragedy and comedy enacted over that period, perhaps the Las Cases boy was one of the more pathetic figures. Without a mother, isolated in a group of erupting 'foreigners', sheltered behind a precise and narrow-minded father, he was shown no special favour by Napoleon; Betsy actively disliked him, her disregard diverting the Emperor, who laughed and teased and, with his malicious streak well to the fore, prophesied that they would one day get married — a remark which Betsy countered briskly.

At the beginning of his stay at the Briars, Napoleon took a great deal of exercise, exploring the valleys and walking about the mountainside that backed on the Briars farm, sometimes by himself, a meditative figure plodding along goat-paths and across fields, at other times in company with both the girls or with Betsy alone. General Gourgaud made an unwilling fourth on occasions; he felt uneasy with two frisky young women who were firmly established in his master's favour.

Beyond the rows of orange trees, the Briars milking herd grazed close to the farm sheds, and on one occasion a cow, disturbed by the strangers, put down her head and charged. The Emperor happened to be nearest and, quick to notice, he ran for cover and leapt a wall with great nimbleness, only seconds behind the girls, and from safety called encouragement to the less nimble General. Gourgaud stood his ground, drew his sword and, facing the cow, shouted, "This is the second time I have saved the Emperor's life." Napoleon burst out laughing and shouted back, "Put yourself in the position to repel cavalry!" The cow, however, lost interest and commenced to crop grass. Betsy remarked that she became tame the moment she lost sight of Napoleon. Greatly amused at the sword-play and still out of breath, he pointed towards the cow and said to Gourgaud, when he joined them on the wall, "She only wished to save the English Government the expense of keeping me." To Betsy and Jane he added, "You vaulted like the goats on the mountain."

The staff living at Jamestown rode daily to visit the Emperor, the seeds of discontent already sown among them that later were to grow into disagreements, childish altercations and situations that he was to settle personally, sometimes harshly, at others in a manner, for him, astonishingly temperate, for he was by nature intolerant.

After their first exclamations of disapproval at his cramped quarters, they began to envy him the garden and the prospect of walks about the fields and in the hills. Periodically they went up the winding road to Longwood to survey its unlovely growth, while the two married men, Bertrand and Montholon, sought to procure cottages adjacent to the Longwood boundary. William Balcombe owned Ross Cottage nearby, named after a friend, the Flag Captain of the *Northumberland*, and Montholon cherished a hope of acquiring this, small as it was, while the Bertrands coveted Hutt's Gate, lower down the road and overlooking Geranium Valley.

Meanwhile the rehabilitation of Longwood itself continued and a series of barrack-like rooms took shape, devoid of grace and comfort. It was a haven for rats, the island at that time being infested with hordes of these, successive parting gifts from visiting ships.

The problem of wild goats did not engage Longwood particularly, but the island as a whole suffered their depredations and its treeless condition was directly attributable to them. Even the Government plantations had to be abandoned, the majority of the young trees either ring-barked or broken off.

The British Government laid down explicit orders on expenditure. William Balcombe had a budget to adhere to, liberal enough in the beginning to meet the exiles' moderate demands, but later whittled down to such an extent as to involve measures of unnecessary stringency. At the commencement of his exile, the sum of twelve thousand pounds allocated for Napoleon's annual expenditure was presumed to cover the needs of all members of his suite, which, counting the children, made a household of twenty-one. It was intended to provide for food, wine and clothing, horses and horse-feed, wages and repairs. Certain of Napoleon's moneys were held by the Governor, but records are vague on this point. He was not allowed to draw on funds from abroad. Members of the suite could draw upon their own resources overseas, but all communications to Europe had to pass through the Governor's hands, a matter tactfully dealt with by Wilks and Cockburn, but it became the subject of bitter quarrelling with the advent of Sir Hudson Lowe.

In the custody of the worldly-wise Cockburn, Napoleon was treated with consideration. No guards surrounded his quarters at the Briars. When he desired he met the residents of the island and, within bounds, led a normal life.

At the Briars, when riding, he cheerfully accepted the presence of the orderly officer, Captain Poppleton, almost the only condition the regulation required; and he made a striking figure that caused a moment's stir as he rode by the island homes or cantered on the ill-made roads to the mountains, where ravines and waterfalls provided interesting, if dangerous, diversions. Betsy often spoke of the Emperor's imposing appearance on horseback, and his perfect hands and seat, which made him as one with the magnificent animal he rode. Captain Poppleton, a cheerful young officer of the 53rd Regiment, though equally well-mounted, was overshadowed by the green-coated figure in high boots and cocked hat. Captain Poppleton's orders from Admiral Cockburn were explicit: he was not to lose sight of the Emperor. This seemed superfluous since, riding with Bertrand, Gourgaud and Montholon immediately behind, he had Napoleon constantly in sight, and, on occasions, remained for long periods beside him in order to describe the terrain and the oddities of the island's volcanic structure, so different from the unrelieved greenness of France.

Napoleon made the outing a daily habit, stopping sometimes to speak to people on the roadside, sometimes to question the Chinese employed on the Longwood alterations, as they passed. On one occasion he met Mrs Balcombe with a pretty Scots woman, Mrs Stuart, newly arrived from India. Following his usual practice with a fresh acquaintance, he asked her innumerable questions, openly expressing his admiration for her and her clear complexion. As they were held in conversation on the road, Mrs Balcombe motioned a party of slaves laden with materials to make a detour around the Emperor. He stopped her with the injunction, "Consider the burden, Madame", and himself drew aside for the party to pass. The occasion made a great impression on Mrs Stuart, who had been influenced by the popular conception of the man: "Heavens," she whispered, "what a character and what an expression of countenance; how different to the idea I had formed of him!" It was the Emperor at his best. In conversation he dwelt on the trials of a long voyage for women-travellers and discussed Indian customs, and, discovering that she was a Scot, he quoted Macpherson's *Ossian*, which he held in high admiration.

Occasionally, when contrariness took hold of him, he made the going hard for the staff, and for Captain Poppleton. Once, without warning, he swerved his mount violently to the left and, applying spurs and whip, urged him up the precipitous mountain-side, causing a cascade of stones and boulders to roll to the depths below. This sudden impulse struck his companions aghast, for they feared for his life, yet hesitated to follow as he disappeared over the shoulder of the mountain. Eventually they sensibly rode home by the bridle path. Captain Poppleton had lost his charge, however, and, agitated at the prospect of censure, galloped to the Briars, where Admiral Cockburn was lunching with the family. Scarlet and excited, the Captain burst in on them. "Oh sir, I have lost the Emperor!" he announced. He proceeded at once to give a description of the incident. The Admiral, drinking soup, was not impressed. "Have you looked in the stables for his horse?" he asked. "I'll lay abet with you Napoleon is at lunch. My dear Poppleton, he is just having a game!" Napoleon, full of glee, welcomed the Captain, quizzed him on his want of nerve and remarked that, captive though he was, he still had power to disappear at will.

He was extremely proud of the figure he cut on horseback. He asked Betsy did she not think he rode well, and she in turn declared he looked better mounted than anyone she had ever seen, adding impishly he looked far better than when he was on foot. Being in a mood to demonstrate his prowess, he called for a horse and forced it to perform tricks that made Archambault, the groom, quail for the animal's safety. "Once I rode a grey charger a hundred and twenty miles in one day to visit my mother when she was dangerously ill," the Emperor told Betsy. "There was no other means to get there. The horse died before the night was out." Archambault led off his mount and returned to his job of breaking-in a young Arab, which had been bought for the Emperor's requirements at Longwood. The youngster, plunging and rearing, could not be induced to approach a white cloth on the ground. Archambault, clever horse-master that he was, found difficulty in handling him. Napoleon bade him dismount, took his place and after a few minutes rode the Arab past the cloth and then over it. Archambault was of two minds, pride and humiliation struggled in his rather simple mind, but, after all, it was the Emperor! "You could have been a horse-breaker," Betsy told him. "Men and horses have a similar mentality," Napoleon replied.

On another occasion in the garden, when, to avoid some newcomers invading his private domain, the grape arbour, he sprang over a high hedge into a patch of prickly pear, Dr O'Meara's assistance was required to extract the spines from his plump posterior, and the children displayed a healthy amusement at his inability to sit down with any comfort.

Betsy relates a story about Alexander, the youngest boy, who contributed to the Emperor's discomfort one day with an offer of bonbons. As Alexander had already half emptied the box and did not consider it looked very nice, he substituted some pills he had found on a garden seat and gravely presented the box thus replenished to the Emperor, who could never resist the child. He helped himself to the contents and the coughing and spluttering that ensued brought Las Cases running from the Pavilion. Napoleon, again fearing that he had been poisoned, was violently sick. Retribution overtook Alexander at the hands of his father, whose feelings were not at the moment lenient owing to an untimely onset of gout.

Rousseau, the little lamplighter, a gnome-like person attached to the Emperor's household, had a rare talent for constructing toys and balloons. His antics became an amusing after-dinner diversion when he let a hundred coloured balloons float into the still warmth of the garden around the marquee. As a kind of appeasement for Alexander's punishment — according to Betsy — Napoleon encouraged the lampiste to make a tiny carriage, a model of her brother's goat carriage, to which were harnessed four mice. The children crowded around entranced when invited to see what was waiting on the carpet and made ineffectual prods at the little animals to start them off. Napoleon, on his knees, finally pinched the tails of the two leaders and away they scampered over the floor, the Emperor and the boys, the grown members of the family and the suite equally diverted. The lamplighter had a *succés fou* amid spontaneous laughter such as perhaps never again touched them all.

Betsy, when she gave herself time to analyse the Emperor's appearance, was struck by the fact that his features were extremely good although the overall impression was not striking and in fact "the effect of his physiognomy was hardly an agreeable one". Yet she reiterated that his smile was the sweetest in the world and his charm spellbinding to those he desired to attract. He had a large head measuring twenty-two inches in circumference, a short neck, broad chest, neat feet and calves. He took great care of his hands. When meditating sometimes he developed a curious habit of shrugging the right shoulder, an involuntary nervous gesture of which he was quite unaware. Once or twice, when she placed her hand upon his arm, the movement immediately ceased. This nervous habit might have been a late development. He ate quickly and, in her words, "not very tidily" and he had a taste for fricasseed chicken. He also liked lamb and bitterly complained at the gaunt legs of mutton provided on the island. They noted that, while at the Briars, he ate and drank with moderation and daily commented, with heavy pleasantry, on William Balcombe's attacks of gout and his nightly glasses of port. Betsy remarked that the Emperor's mouth was "well cut", his nose "faultless" and his sense of smell "intensely acute", specially when the night-blooming lilies spilt their fragrance, causing him discomfort. The valets used eau-de-Cologne in quantities for his toilet. There is an item in the accounts to Balcombe, Fowler and Cole: "12 dozen bottles of eau-de-Cologne for Longwood". When subsequently the Cologne did not arrive with any regularity, he missed it.

One day, while at dinner, Napoleon seized a silver dish from Pierron, the butler, and gave a surprised exclamation. The arms of the King of France had been engraved on it. "How they have spoiled that!" he exclaimed, and observed that the King had been in great haste to take possession of things that certainly did not belong to him. He went on to tell his hearers that in a small cabinet of his, in which were kept medallions given him by the Pope and other potentates, he had found very private letters of the mistresses of Louis XVIII, which in the suddenness of his departure the King had forgotten and which he had apparently hidden there himself.

Napoleon remarked how strange was his experience in walking to his desk in the Tuileries after his return from Elba to find a mixture of his own personal belongings and papers and those of the King, strewn together as one tenant had hurriedly vacated for another.

Memories of the Tuileries suggested further reminiscences and, as was usually the case, his conversation turned to the days before he had attained the throne. He re-fought battles, and spoke of Josephine. It seemed as if the later years were as yet too near to be spoken about, although at times he discussed with General Montholon the battle of Waterloo. He had once said of Josephine elsewhere that "she was extremely fond of luxury, disorder and the spending of money, qualities which are peculiarly characteristic of the Creoles." Another of Josephine's traits he was wont to quote was her continual habit of denial; no matter what the occasion was, or what the question was, her first impulse was to negation. Her first word was 'no', and this 'no' was not exactly a lie, but simply a measure of defence.

On one of her visits to the Briars, Madame Bertrand produced a miniature of Josephine to show Mrs Balcombe, and, taking it to the Emperor, put it in his hand. He was filled with deepest emotion; to her knowledge there was no picture of the former Empress in his possession on the island, and the painting vividly highlighted the memories that would return to him more and more as time passed. At length he exclaimed that it was the most perfect likeness he had seen and begged Mme Bertrand to let him have it, which she did. Until he died the miniature was before him always, hanging on the Pavilion wall and later above the mantelpiece at Longwood.

He often gazed long and earnestly at Mrs Balcombe and apologetically excused himself by saying how like Josephine she was, how forcibly her manner reminded him of Josephine. She was amiable, full of tact, a necessity with a family of children such as hers and with William Balcombe strong-tempered and prone to definite opinions, who equally took handling.

It was evident that Napoleon held her in high esteem. He spoke to her repeatedly of his son and Josephine, and dwelt on Josephine's sweetness of disposition; the most truly feminine woman he had ever known.

He thanked God she had died before his final miseries and misfortunes. Josephine, he said, had never acted inelegantly in her life. Glancing at Betsy's appearance, he declared with emphasis that Josephine's toilet had been perfection and added, "She resisted the inroads of time to all appearances by the exquisite taste of her *parure*," but admitted she did not smile much; her teeth were bad and she showed them as little as possible.

Small unrelated notes in diaries combine to give an overall picture of Napoleon's daily life, rather than Betsy's actual statements, which, in the form they have been preserved, appear to have been edited. As the weather grew warmer, he rose as early as four in the morning and commenced his writing in the arbour, where coolness still lingered from the night and the shadow from the mountain held off the sun's rays longer, and where always the distant sound of the waterfall obtruded. There, too, he had complete privacy; a key locked the little gate across the path, and not even the children dared enter without his permission, except Betsy. By his direction, she was exempt and he welcomed her at all times, even though awakened from sleep by her calling him to unlock the gate. He had resumed his habit of dozing at odd moments, a characteristic that had persisted over the years and which he had forgone in the last few months.

He told Betsy that this faculty for sleep and immediate awakening had enabled him to retain the almost incessant activity which marked his life. Now the lessening of tension and the recourse to regular exercise, both on horseback and on foot, were having a beneficial effect. The first sharp agony of his fallen state had passed, and although possibly he himself did not appreciate it, he had begun to adapt himself to the rigours of this last phase of his adventurous career, a phase lit by a waning star of hope — for not until illness made it impossible did he really give up hope that some day he might be allowed to live in England.

As was anticipated, William Balcombe's appointment as purveyor to Napoleon necessitated many conversations between the exiles' staff and himself. One of the first duties that devolved on him was to improve upon the unappetising meals served at Mr Porteous's boarding-house, and so to the hands of Balcombe, Fowler and Cole was entrusted the task of purveying for the entire French household. Items of a widely divergent nature appeared in the Company's books, beginning with a memorandum, "Bullocks and carts, three trips carrying Napoleon Bonaparte's luggage to the Briars ... Three guineas". After a week the washing bill registered £23 15s. 7½d. and the porterage of stores to the Briars, £1. At the foot of every statement rendered to the Government a note was habitually added, "The above account is correct and just — signed W. Balcombe". Accounts paid to Porteous and sundry minor items appeared, but it was not until the party were installed at Longwood that the accounts were submitted in complete detail. Letters passed daily between Plantation House and the purveyor. These established how the exiles lived, and what they ate, what wines they required, the allowance appearing to be liberal enough by ordinary standards. Sir George Cockburn, a factual and knowledge-able sailor, had a fair idea of the party's needs and he interpreted the regulations imposed upon them by the British Government in a reasonable fashion, using a fine discretion when conditions warranted it. Although at times Napoleon was critical — and on some occasions warm arguments ensued between the Admiral and himself — the Emperor was to deplore the replacement of Cockburn by Sir Hudson Lowe. Legally there always remained a doubt whether the British Government had power to hold the Emperor, whether the detention of his person was within their jurisdiction once the Peace Treaty had been signed. The situation was unusual and unexplored. To the majority in England, however, the 'menace to Europe', as many characterised Napoleon, had himself volunteered for asylum and a safe custody seemed the logical answer from the Allies — but not a prison sentence, and there arose confusion of thought. The new Governor, Sir Hudson Lowe, soon to take the place of Admiral Cockburn and Governor Wilks, turned their 'safe custody' into a shameful parody of police domination and austerity. That, however, was yet to come.

CHAPTER 5

Prison Society

While at the Briars, Napoleon to some extent shared with the island people their simple lives and the normal distractions of a small community, hardly aware of guards or jailers. Deference to his rank was accorded to him as far as orders from England permitted.

His title of Emperor was forbidden, an unnecessary regulation. Even to be called 'ex-Emperor' would have maintained a certain dignity and given a more truthful rendering of the position and, as he himself pointed out, "If not Emperor, then why call me General?" England had formally recognised his state, indeed had sent ambassadors to his court. The situation was absurd and created a great deal of resentment in the minds of the French exiles. Later, when Sir Hudson Lowe took charge, it was to be an instrument with which to insult and distract the prisoner. That practice Lowe was to follow to the Emperor's tomb, even disallowing the simple word 'Napoleon' to be placed upon it unless followed by 'Bonaparte' — so the slab remained unmarked.

In the meantime Napoleon was regaining repose and health. The parchment-like appearance had gone from his features; he began to put on weight and the periods of moodiness became fewer. The resilience that had stood him in good stead in former years was expressing itself again, and his capacity for mapping the future warred with his desire to commit the past to paper. The future he hardly dared think about — a draughty house on the hilltop, a circumscribed circle of people around him; the track of the eternal south-east trades, and the sun to usher in every new day, leaving him to wait only for the coming of darkness; and he not forty-six years old, an Emperor in whose ante-room once kings had waited. Sometimes he contemplated taking his life and with Gourgaud actually discussed suicide; he expressed bitter regret that a cannon ball had not put an end to him before Moscow. In his heart he knew the world had judged him and that he no longer counted in the eternal march — and, realist that he was, he tried again and again to analyse the reason.

It was a subject of heart-searching until he died. Lust for power? Personal ambition? Self aggrandisement? His marriage to Marie-Louise had made him foolhardy; trusting for Austrian support, he had overreached himself. Josephine knew that too, dear Josephine, somehow nearer to him now than in the past year. Their court had been a tumultuous gathering of the old and the new nobility, of soldiers and savants. Her grace had welded the inchoate whole. Josephine, with the lovely face and defective teeth; the extravagant habits and sound instinct.

Napoleon by now presented no complicated front to Betsy. Possessing a boyish streak that gave him immediate entry into the world of the young, he played their games with no grown-up reserves and did not hesitate to take toll in retaliation, to bump and run, pinch and hold, and end with a kiss on both cheeks and a tweak of the ear. Once he became 'Boney' to them, he had entered into a kind of secret world of fun and laughter which held no place for the suite — nor, indeed for young Las Cases, though later the Bertrand children were accepted.

Occasionally he would abruptly withdraw from the light-hearted talk and movement, and relapse into a moody silence from which none could distract him. Betsy on occasions wilfully endeavoured to intrude on his thoughts, shaking an arm and demanding recognition, but in response he would make a gesture of negation with the smile that all her life she was to remember as "the sweetest smile in the world", and she knew that for him had come a time of retrospect. After a while they recognised these moods as something that rose out of the past into which they had no entry. In later life Betsy wrote that she "trembled at her temerity, that in unthinking youth she had challenged the portals of his silence and sudden retreats, had held his hands and demanded attention, had called him Boney, had chased him in undignified games of hide-and-seek and run him, breathless, down the mountainside."

The nickname 'Boney', always an insult in Las Cases's ears, was an endearment which Napoleon encouraged and responded to, once he realised it carried no disparagement. He also encouraged their walks together and mutual silences, even sought the one-sided conversations with Toby — for the slave knew no French and Betsy's swift translations were too sketchy for him to catch the actual words, although their broad import penetrated. Napoleon, to him, was "the good gentleman", the recipient of the flowers and fruit from the Briars garden. These became a daily tribute from the slave gardener. For Napoleon, Toby had an affinity: because they were both prisoners, to achieve the slave's liberty turned into something of an obsession to the Emperor, so keenly did he desire it.

In reality the Malay could have returned to his native land long before. The East India Company had befriended him and probably the hut he lived in and the work of gardening ensured him better conditions than any he had experienced.

His later history is not known, but Lowe was to write to William Balcombe asking for an affidavit stating that he had never refused Toby his liberty. This was in 1822, when, after Napoleon's death, and his own return to London, Lowe was preparing a lawsuit to refute the accusations of Dr O'Meara.

It is probable that the slave remained until he died at the Briars estate, where he had become part of the establishment, and his slow-moving mind found sufficient interest to shut out memories of his past. He was certainly happy enough when the children raced about his domain and he could scold them impartially, and when he received Napoleon's presents — gold napoleons — not necessarily for their worth as money, but as something of a gesture to his prowess as a gardener. He died before the exhumation of the Emperor's body in 1840.

Betsy's conversations with Napoleon bore no historical importance, they were factual, the physical present uppermost to them both. The happenings of the day, the actual sights and sounds and emotions of the moment, concerned them; to be discussed, dropped and renewed in a camaraderie that grew deeper by its very unconsciousness. Never during the period of 1815-1818, after which she returned to London, was the thread of interest and affection severed, though for a while she became jealous and inattentive. It seemed as if their meeting kindled an immediate affinity. Betsy's mind could follow Napoleon only at the moment. The past lay closed to her, she could only dimly conceive the glitter and pomp, the vast movement of armies, and the immense power that once had been his. When all too soon she grew to be an acknowledged beauty, to his waning powers she became a fillip and a figure of much promise in a drab surrounding. Hers was a warming personality; with supreme disregard for protocol or policy she braved sentinels, feared no member of the suite, and met him without thought of appearance or of comment. The time came when the suite at Longwood welcomed her as a respite in the aching boredom of the prisoner's life. She was no more the 'rude hoyden', and when in 1818 she sailed in the *Winchelsea* store-ship for England with the rest of the family, the days were longer for them all. Much later the members of his suite were to meet her again in London, to talk interminably of their master, of the time at the Briars, of the Emperor's illness, of the petty policies of Lowe and Longwood. Even Bonaparte's brothers came to glean from her such scraps of information about him as she could give them. As her family were by that time in Australia, she alone remained to talk of St Helena.

Las Cases's diary contains some reflections on the family that betray his own prim reserve. The Balcombes habitually shattered his sense of fitness and formality, their light-heartedness hurried him into situations and left him to extract some meaning of his own. His beaver hat intrigued them, whereas the show of swords and medals worn by the suite had no significance to girls surrounded by the officers of Waterloo and Trafalgar, and their own father's Royal Navy background.

Las Cases wrote on the 18th April, three days after their arrival, "We had hardly entered the garden [at the Briars] when we were joined by the daughters of the owner of the house. They were about 14 and 15 years old; one was bright but empty-headed, without respect for anything, the other more sedate but very naïve; both of them spoke a bit of French. Soon they were flitting around the garden gathering things right and left to offer the Emperor whom they also showered with questions which were either bizarre and weird or ridiculous. The Emperor was highly amused by the girls' familiar ways which were something new to him. We've just been to a masked ball he told me after the girls had left.

"That evening the Emperor decided to call upon his neighbours the Balcombes. The head of the household, suffering from gout, was in his dressing-gown and lying on a sofa; his wife and the two young ladies we had met that morning were beside him. We were once again at the Masked Ball, and the conversation dwelt on many subjects. We talked about novels; one of the young ladies had read *Mathilde* by Mme Cottin and was delighted to hear that the Emperor had known the heroine of the book. A fat Englishman present, square-faced and a true *vacuum plenum*, it is said, who was listening intently in an endeavour to put to use his slight knowledge of French, was bold enough to ask the Emperor, with a show of diffidence, whether the Princess, a friend of Mathilde's, whose very excellent character was the subject of his great admiration, was still alive. The Emperor solemnly answered, 'No, sir, she is dead and buried,' and was amused to notice that, on his announcement, tears sprung up in the eyes of the face of the enquirer. (The princess was a fictional character!) One of the little ladies showed similar simplicity although, in her case, it was more pardonable; however, I had to conclude that none present were very versed in chronology:— Reading Florian's *Estelle* to show she could read French, she struck the passage concerning Gaston de Foix and, noticing that he was addressed as General, she asked the Emperor whether he was satisfied with him as a military man, whether he had suffered in battle, and whether he still lived!" (Gaston de Foix lived 250 years before Napoleon!)

The Balcombes gave an evening party so that it would be possible for Napoleon to see and meet, without the necessity of official approval, most of the island's inhabitants, especially those who lived in the houses he rode past during his daily exercise. He came to the gathering and made himself charming, as only Napoleon could. The spell of personality, strong in him, caused distrust and enmity to disappear; indeed the island was to become, to a degree, proud of him, possibly as a regal exhibit, certainly as an object of curiosity and commiseration; and, to a few, an honoured friend. It was later stated that Sir Hudson Lowe did not fear his actual escape, his obsession being with the power of attraction the Emperor exercised over everyone with whom he came into contact.

When first presented to Napoleon, newcomers were subjected to close interrogation about their family, profession and circumstances, and he immediately entered into conversations concerning their sphere of work, with a knowledge of the subject that astonished them. With a visiting medical man, he withdrew to a corner and he reasoned, argued and advanced theories which the astonished doctor called 'heterodox'. Napoleon announced he had no faith in medicine for himself, his specific being starvation and a hot bath. He possessed a high opinion of surgery and considered the profession of healing, as a whole, the greatest of all. On the practice of law he passed some stringent comments, holding it a severe ordeal for the human under-standing and declaring, "He who habituates himself to the distortion of truth and feels satisfaction at the success of injustice will ultimately hardly know right or wrong," finally remarking that "a lawyer must possess a conventional conscience". Of the Church he spoke harshly also, saying that too much was expected of its members, turning them into hypocrites. (He was himself a believer, calling on God as the Creator.) Soldiers he castigated as "cut-throats and robbers". (This comment surprised both William Balcombe and the doctor.) But surgeons, he went on, were neither too good nor too bad, their mission being to benefit mankind, not to destroy, mystify or inflame. They had an opportunity to study human nature as well as to acquire science. He went on to speak of Larrey, a man he pronounced to be of generous and impeccable integrity.

One feels a certain exasperation on reading the old diaries. Betsy wrote at length of inconsequential incidents but omitted matter that would today have been of extraordinary interest. On only one occasion did she quote her father, and then it was in a brief résumé of what had evidently been a long and serious conversation between Napoleon, the doctor and himself. She did not mention the doctor's name. Of subsequent incidents complete corroboration is found in other books, with the names, occasions and, in some cases, dates. Her facts were astonishingly correct but all too few, and written, strangely enough, with neat precision. She made a brief reference to newspaper reports of the childish games that were shared at the Briars by the Emperor, omitting the name of Marquis Montchenu, the French Commissioner, as the author, calling him Mons. M., who, having circulated canards in English, French and German journals, had not hesitated to slander both Betsy and her sister. Napoleon was incensed and wrote an indignant commentary in his journal. Balcombe, a hot-tempered man, "wished to call the Marquis to an account," but Mrs Balcombe stepped in and obtained an ample apology. Montchenu, a grotesque personality, later provided some lighter moments for them all. When his housekeeper, Mrs Martin, a women of spotless virtue, complained that Montchenu tried to kiss her, Napoleon, on hearing of the incident, remarked, "I suppose the old ram wanted to violate her." Captain de Gors, Montchenu's secretary, Betsy mentioned briefly once or twice. She could well have enlarged upon the Hudson Lowe disagreements; instead she left them sandwiched between trivial incidents, remarking that she did not care to dwell upon them — evidently as too recent an occurrence and for this reason perhaps dangerous.

The month of the exile's landing was the season of balls and entertainments, and although Napoleon did not attend, he questioned Betsy closely as to what went on and how his staff enjoyed themselves. The French ladies, by their manners and magnificence, made a tremendous impression. They were amiable women, anxious to please, and Madame Bertrand, who was partly British by birth and spoke without accent, knew the score; Mme Montholon, being quieter and less approachable, and moreover in bad health, did not excite such a lively interest. Jane divided her allegiance between Mrs Wilks and Madame Bertrand. Mrs Wilks, a typical Governor's lady and having a fund of gay spirits, joined in all the social activities. From Betsy, Napoleon learned the kind of dancing they indulged in. Newly admitted to grown-up dances, Betsy described the quadrilles and country measures in detail; the latter he considered unsuitable for Government House. She told him of the new waltz — refrains imported from London by a young exquisite, the Hon. George Carstairs, the greatest beau that ever came to St Helena. Carstairs fascinated Betsy on his first appearance at Plantation House, and, round-eyed, she watched him as he floated over the ballroom floor, contriving to make his partner appear as graceful as any ballerina. She was told he would sit for an hour with his feet propped up over his head before dressing for a ball so that he might squeeze them into tight shoes.

He wore epaulets that almost fell to his elbow. His sword belt was heavily embroidered with golden oak-leaves; an embroidery duplicated around each knee, seen from a short distance, resembled the Order of the Garter. He also affected perfume.

Napoleon strode rapidly up and down while Betsy described the young man's attire in an awed voice. Never had he seen her so impressed. She went on to describe Carstairs's scorn when he learned that the St Helena ladies knew nothing but, as he described them, "kitchen dances and reels"; he began to organise classes so that they might master the intricacies of the waltz. Mrs Balcombe, one of his pupils, unceremoniously put her foot on his heel when he bent in front of her in an exaggerated bow to Mrs Wilks and poked his sword and stiffened swallow-tails in her face; as he had difficulty in replacing his foot in the two-sizes-too-small shoe, he never forgave her. Napoleon demanded to meet the young man and Betsy accordingly arranged for her mother to invite him to dinner. Napoleon gave him, in Betsy's words, "a comical look" and then, with a show of affability, told him he had heard from Betsy he was a great dandy, which disconcerted Ensign Carstairs considerably, for he had assumed the honour of the interview to have been accorded by reason of his birth and social circumstances. Napoleon went blandly on, admiring the cut of his coat and saying, "You are more fortunate than myself, for I am obliged to wear my coat turned." This was the simple truth, for at the time there was no cloth on the island of a similar shade of green to that the Emperor customarily wore. Lieutenant Carstairs, nevertheless, gave Napoleon a degree of diversion and entertainment, for he spoke French fluently and could relate many happenings in fashionable London and Paris that were disregarded by men less accustomed to the social round. Afterwards Napoleon said to Betsy, "Do not consider that young man as a husband. He is too aristocratic." Unthinkingly she retorted, "You are jealous because he dances with me." Startled at her own rudeness, she stammered an apology, but he pulled her ear and turned away towards the Pavilion without answering and for once unsmiling. It was then she suddenly understood how much he depended on her for fun and laughter and the cheerfulness she created. It was a frightening admission that such an insignificant contribution as her unsophisticated youth and simplicity of approach could maintain normal balance in a man such as he, and impulsively she ran after him and put her arms around his neck, contrite, uncertain. He held her close and kissed her on both cheeks. This playmate caught by the glamour of a scented dandy with sham epaulets and tight shoes, how young she was, and to him precious now, for she brought a return of youth and freshness, something of spring.

CHAPTER 6

Betsy and the Emperor

The routine of the establishment at the Pavilion, now set to pattern, continued in unbroken calm. Admiral Cockburn took up residence at the Castle; Napoleon rode daily — the English orderly officer, Captain Poppleton, in attendance; William Balcombe took over the Emperor's personal affairs as well as those of purveyor; the members of the suite paid their visits and transcribed his dictation; Le Page cooked; the Las Cases watched for misdemeanours on the part of the children, while Toby made his daily call with flowers.

On 20th November, Admiral Cockburn in return for the hospitality accorded by the island residents, gave a special ball at the Castle. The next day the Emperor, very amused, gave imitations of the dancers, singing the tunes in his unmusical voice and reproducing with great faithfulness the efforts of one lady at a sarabande, turning and pirouetting. Though he did not admit it to Betsy, she had a shrewd suspicion that, incognito, he had been there watching outside the windows. Betsy was included in the invitation to the Admiral's ball, and with the help of the maid, black Sarah, contrived an evening dress trimmed with pink calico roses, the most important gown she had ever possessed and a source of innocent pride. She showed it to Napoleon one evening, before they sat down to a game of whist, spreading the skirt and displaying the bunches of roses for his approval, afterwards laying the garment on the sofa. The pack of cards set out for use were new and did not shuffle easily, so Napoleon availed himself of the opportunity to ask questions about the forthcoming ball, to enquire who might be there then, and surprisingly demanded what stakes they would play for: usually it was for sugar plums, but tonight he wagered a Napoleon with Betsy. Her sole possession of any value was a 'pagoda' brought to her as a present from India, but not to be outdone she matched it against Napoleon's stake.

Napoleon and Jane drew together and Las Cases partnered Betsy. The Emperor's impishness continued, and he played outrageous whist, peeking at the cards as they were dealt to him and then distracting Betsy's attention as he showed the hand to Jane. Finally Betsy caught him in the act of revoking, accused him flatly of cheating and pounced on his hands, holding them tightly as he tried to mix up the pack together on the table — Las Cases registering, as usual, horrified disapproval. Napoleon laughed until the tears came, and, having created one of the disturbances he so enjoyed, insisted he had played fair, that it was Betsy who had cheated, and that she should pay him the 'pagoda', maliciously telling her she was *méchante*. Jane attempted to restore peace, but further argument and disorder brought in the family, and Betsy was severely reprimanded, Napoleon not troubling to defend her as was his habit when she was in disgrace. Instead he picked up the ball dress and ran out of the room. Betsy gave chase up the path to the Pavilion, through the marquee, but he reached the inner room and locked the door. No entreaties in English or French would persuade him to restore the frock, and she had the mortification of hearing him laughing on the other side. She knew he was enjoying her anguish, while the most heartfelt appeals only provoked him to more intense amusement. He announced that he intended to keep the dress and so prevent her from going, or at any rate from wearing the gown to the ball — her first big function — as punishment. Remembering the simple evening dresses she possessed, he calculated that female psychology would cause her to stay at home rather than suffer from comparison with the *décolleté* creations of the others.

The psychology of women always interested Napoleon: he once remarked he regretted having so little contact with them, especially at court, for his way of life had thrown him almost exclusively into the company of men and he felt he could have learned much. He liked to talk in a detached way of his loves. He had had seven mistresses in his life, he said, and added, "*C'est beaucoup*." With the staff he had once talked of love in the abstract. "What is it?" he demanded. "A passion which turns aside from everything in the whole world just to get a sight of the loved subject I neither wanted to nor was able to fall in love. It is made for other characters than myself." He believed women had been a bad influence on both Henri IV and Louis XVI and he had not wanted "a house full of women in his court". Now he felt he had overlooked something.

At one stage he imagined he was sincerely attached to Madame Walewska, but to disconcert Gourgaud he slyly told him, when they were setting out for St Helena, he would have given her to him for a wife but that he learned she had re-married. "She is rich," he said complacently, "and has probably saved." "Your Majesty," replied Gourgaud stiffly, "paid Mme Walewska ten thousand francs per annum." Napoleon, who was in turn disconcerted, flushed and enquired how he knew the sum.

Sometimes at Longwood, out of pure boredom, the exiles would talk after dinner of their conquests. The Emperor might remark, "Now we shall talk of women," but the theme was stale and the discussion without enthusiasm. Napoleon once described adultery as "a word of enormous meaning in civil law, at bottom only an act of gallantry, a joke behind a mask. It is not by any means a rare phenomenon, but a very ordinary occurrence on the sofa".

He mentioned, among passing female attractions, Madame Duchatel, who refused any presents, even a diamond necklace — although he prudently recovered a few of his love letters from her — and Madame Mathis, who accepted presents. One of his Generals had introduced him to a transient flame who spoke no French, while he had no German for her. He classed her as one of the most agreeable women. "She wore no perfume. When day came she woke me and I have never seen her since. In 1809, however, the Chief of the Vienna police told me she was a Judith, a Jewess."

The day following the whist game, Betsy sought her dress again, and sent him several heart-rending appeals, only to be told that the Emperor slept and could not be disturbed, an excuse Las Cases presented with ill-concealed satisfaction. Betsy was at last feeling the hand of discipline, he told himself, and he was glad she had incurred the displeasure of his master! In the evening the saddle horses were brought round, this being the usual means of travelling over the poor roads and goat-paths, and the little black boys picked up the tin cases packed with evening finery, shoes and make-up, preliminary procedure to nearly every evening entertainment on the island. The lights had just begun to twinkle in the house and the kindest moment of the day was at hand, yet there was no ball gown for Betsy! A simple garment had gone into the box, an adolescent's frock, high on the shoulders, short and revealing the pantaloons. With no swirling skirts or bare shoulders, such as marked the débutante, she would appear as a child at a party; just what Napoleon manifestly desired to happen. As they proceeded to mount, and were moving off, they saw the Emperor running down the lawn to the gate with the ball gown in his arms, shouting, "Here, Betsee! I have brought your dress!" Breathless, he handed it over. "I hope you are a good girl now and will dance as well a little with Gourgaud." The implication was understood — young Carstairs and the epaulets still lingered in his thoughts. General Gourgaud had attached himself to Laura Wilks, and Betsy knew she would probably not even receive a glance from his direction, but she let the remark pass and seized the dress. Napoleon told her he had ordered the roses to be pulled out and arranged so that they would look perfect. She examined the silk and lace lying across the saddle; the calico flowers in pink bunches showed evidence of Marchand the valet's attention just as Napoleon had said. "No harm has come to it," he assured her earnestly, the impish mood gone, the kindly friend returned once more. He walked in the dusk beside the horses until they reached the bridle path that led from the Briars to the valley. There was to be no ball for him — though mainly by his own decision.

The fact that he must officially appear as General, and not as Emperor, debarred him from formal entertainments, and the dispute over his status became more bitter as time passed. He appreciated, but did not accept, the reason that, out of deference to the French nation, British recognition of Louis XVIII prevented any recognition of him as royalty.

He stood where the path divided and, wishing them a happy time, remarked on the appearance of a house below in the valley, asked the name of the owner and said he would walk down with Las Cases to look at the garden, which he did, meeting a surprised Major Hodson, who happened to be judge Advocate of the island, and to whom Napoleon had immediately taken a liking. He was tall — more than six feet — and the Emperor nicknamed him 'Hercules'. They stayed talking until late in the night, finally returning up the mountain in the dark, Napoleon riding the Major's Arab pony.

The Admiral's ball remained the topic of conversation for some time. Apart from the setting, the beauty of the French ladies' dresses and the brilliant uniforms, Ensign Carstairs surpassed himself as "the life of the party". He and some fellow ensigns backed a farm cart into the Castle archway, effectively blocking the entrance for all comers, while Carstairs, standing on top, shouted, "Lord W.'s carriage stops the way."

A full moon rode over the sea and even the exiles felt its romance as it lit the broad iron staircase, the long windows open to the breeze and the anchored ships close in-shore, while the softened trade wind carried the voices of the dancers and the new waltz music to the listening sailors.

All this was described to Napoleon the next day by the half-contemptuous, half-amused members of the suite. The girls, they said, looked nice in their white blouses and skirts![2]

It was then that Betsy contended Napoleon had been there himself, watching from the shadows. He did not contradict her.

The Emperor met Carstairs again when, on Admiral Cockburn's orders, the Ensign set sailors to work to erect a studding sail as a marquee for the Emperor in the Longwood garden. Napoleon remarked that this was one of the very few instances in which he had observed high birth coupled with intelligence.

There was no comment on Admiral Cockburn's ball in Betsy's record of the day, 20th November 1815, nor whether she enjoyed a triumph in the new frock with the pink calico roses; or if she danced with Ensign Carstairs of the epaulets and tight shoes. If General Gourgaud ignored her for the lovely Laura, or if they returned as the dawn broke, she neglected to say; and it was left to other pens to reveal that the fabulous attire of Madame Bertrand astonished St Helena's female society.

Small additional comforts and even luxuries now began to accumulate at the Pavilion. The blue and white set of Nankin china cabinet pieces, by reason of their historic associations, did not appeal to the taste of Cipriani. At all times he extended himself to uphold the majesty of his master's estate. As china from the East held no recommendation in his eyes, it was only grudgingly that he complied with the Emperor's demand for the old blue mug for his morning coffee. He welcomed the arrival of part of a magnificent set of Sèvres plates and dishes, once presented by the City of Paris to Napoleon. The pieces had been decorated and painted by the foremost artists in France, and Napoleon invited the family to be present at their unpacking, telling them complacently that each plate had cost twenty-five napoleons. There were hundreds.

The subjects depicted were his campaigns and a few episodes in his early life. Napoleon was shown in triumph, waving an encouraging sword to his troops as he rode past piles of dead and wounded enemies. Wrecked gun-carriages and discarded equipment and victorious National Guards decorated several pieces.

"During that engagement," he remarked, indicating an unusually spirited flight of imagination that showed him viewing a battle from the back of his grey charger, "I did not leave my carriage."

One plate made an impression on Betsy, mainly because it depicted a young Napoleon, a slim youth standing alone, dead and dying soldiers falling around him as he cheered on his distant companions to further assault. "I was rather more slender than I am now," he said, putting his hand on the corpulence that was beginning to become noticeable. The Sèvres version of the Battle of Leipzig, one of Napoleon's most disastrous failures, showed him to great advantage, the figure majestic and the likeness admirable. Betsy heard her father enquire why, of all his engagements, Leipzig should receive such heroic treatment; Napoleon replied drily, "Probably the good citizens of Paris were not so well aware of the outcome then, as later."

The Egyptian scenes in particular stimulated the Emperor's memory, as he picked out one fabulous piece after another from the straw-packing that now lay strewn over the floor of the marquee. He pointed out ibises (which he called "birds of veneration"), pyramids, the sphinx and palms, telling long stories of adventures on the Nile. He advised Betsy never to go there, that ophthalmia was a scourge and would surely send her blind. She enquired if, during the campaign, he had really become a Moslem, her question prompted by someone less brave than herself, and put the question to him in Anglo-French, "Pourquoi avez-vous tourné turque?" It puzzled him sufficiently to enquire what she meant. One of the suite explained rather acidly that she wanted to know whether he had changed his religion. "Who was it prompted such a question?" he demanded. "What is it to you? Fighting is a soldier's religion. I never changed that. The other is the affair of women and priests. *Quant à moi*, I always adopt the religion of the country I am in." Nevertheless, it seemed he evaded the question. Napoleon had a sharply defined respect for religion; it was the personal application of its trappings and forms that he disregarded. At Longwood, however, Italian ecclesiastics were attached to the suite, and the priest Vignali was with him when he died.

The Egyptian pictures also prompted a recollection of anger at old *canards* of cruelty attributed to him, the butchery of Turkish prisoners and the poisoning of the sick.

From Dr Barry O'Meara, Betsy later received a faithful record of the Emperor's account of these incidents, in his own words, which O'Meara habitually transcribed immediately he heard them.

"Before leaving Jaffa, and when many of the sick had embarked, I was informed some were in hospital wounded beyond recovery, dangerously ill and unfit to be moved at any risk. I desired my medical men to hold a consultation as to what steps had best be taken with regard to the unfortunate sufferers, and to send in their opinions to me. The result of the consultation was that seven-eighths of the soldiers were considered past recovery and that in all probability few would be alive at the expiration of twenty hours; moreover, some were afflicted with plague and to carry these onward would threaten the whole army with infection and spread death wherever they appeared. On the other hand to leave them to the mercy of the Turks was unthinkable since they always made it a rule to murder prisoners with protracted torture.

"In this emergency I submitted to Desegnettes the propriety of ending the misery of these victims by a dose of opium. I would have desired such a relief for myself. I considered it would have been an act of mercy to anticipate a death of dreadful horror. My physicians did not enter into my view and disapproved of the proposal, saying it was their profession to cure, not to kill. Accordingly I left a rearguard to protect those unhappy men from the advancing enemy, and they remained until nature had claimed payment of her last debt.

"Not that I think it would have been a crime," observed Napoleon, "had opium been administered; on the contrary, I think it would have been a virtue. To leave a few poor creatures who could not recover, in order that they might be massacred, according to the custom of the Turks, with the most dreadful tortures, would, I think, have been cruelty, nor would any man under similar circumstances, who had the free use of his senses, have hesitated to prefer dying easily a few hours sooner rather than expire under the tortures of those barbarians.

"I ask you, O'Meara, to place yourself in the situation of one of those men, and were it demanded of you which fate you would select, either to be left to suffer the tortures of those miscreants or to have opium administered to you, which would you rather choose? If my own son, and I believe I love my son as well as any father loves his child, were in a similar situation, I would advise it to be done, and if so situated myself I would insist upon it if I had *strength* enough and *strength* to demand it.

"Do you think that if I had been capable of secretly poisoning soldiers, or of such barbarities (as have been ascribed to me) as driving my carriage over the bleeding and mutilated bodies of the wounded, my troops would have fought under me with the enthusiasm and affection they uniformly displayed? No, no. I should have been shot long ago. Even my wounded would have tried to pull a trigger to despatch me."

The Emperor drew Betsy's attention to the grey charger on one of the platters and said, "I ride a black horse now, but as his name is Hope I like him well." None of the exiles thought it extraordinary to eat from china painted with scenes of death and carnage. Heroics had become so interwoven in their subconscious memories as to be taken for granted. The magnificence of the service with its gold borders and 61 muted colours was an anachronism in the Pavilion and accentuated the reduced condition in which the Emperor lived.

Something strange came out of its arrival at the Briars, as if a foreign wind had blown through the now homely Pavilion, bringing impressions of past years packed with action, strengthening memories that had mercifully begun to fade. Napoleon became introspective and gloomy after the first spate of reminiscences, and once, when Le Page sent in creams for the children, he gathered them together on one of the ornate dishes, tied a napkin around it and handing it to the children said, "Eat the creams but keep the dish, it will be of great value one day."

CHAPTER 7

Admiral Cockburn —
A Kind Jailer

Proclamations issued by the Governor-in-Council regulated the movements of all the inhabitants after dark; passwords and countersigns, hitherto neglected, more often honoured in the breach than in the observance, now took effect. A virtual curfew was imposed near Longwood, even though the exile was not yet in residence, and it became evident that the prison was almost ready to receive its occupant. The routine at the Briars still remained unchanged. While Captain Poppleton accompanied Napoleon during his rides abroad, and while the staff busied themselves transcribing their master's dictation and voicing their own personal discomforts and complaints, William Balcombe judged them to be sufficiently occupied and Napoleon to be adequately 'insulated'.

Napoleon spent much time in the Briars home. He lingered after dinner in the drawing-room or outside on the square lawn, where they had Coffee, played whist, gossiped or listened to music. Visitors arrived almost daily, for the most part people he already knew: Major Hodson and his wife, the officers of the 53rd Regiment, Major Fehrzen, whom he admired, and occasionally Admiral Cockburn, eminently correct but now tending towards an official formality of manner, a change from the cheery sailor of the *Northumberland* days and one which Napoleon regretted. Some of the visitors who toiled up the road to the Briars were townspeople, ostensibly coming to discuss Jamestown problems with the representative of the East India Company, but glad to hold their conversations in the scented dusk of the garden, where Napoleon asked many questions. Human relations differed little in most communities, and he recognised in Jamestown the same interests that might arise in any French provincial town. He heard the same talk of husbandry and soil conservation, rotation of crops (the proportions widely differing, the island being ten and a half miles long by six and three-quarter miles wide). He realised that here the cycle of the seasons held tropical influence rather than temperate. He learned that the depredations of wild goats constituted an ever present problem. The condition of the roads, the sudden appearance of the white ant, which subsequently caused havoc, and the unexplained periods of fever came under review. Without his realising it the very diminutiveness of the problems assisted Napoleon, curtailing his wide horizons of thought to the narrow present, relegating the immensity of the past to something shadowy. He disliked the thought of his departure to the windy heights of Longwood, the more so after the Governor's refusal to allow him to purchase the Briars. That had been a brief hope entertained since his arrival. The climate was kind there, the flowers lovely and the waterfall cool; and it was a windless spot. He hated wind, and he knew Longwood was subject to the almost constant trades. There were sharp infractions of light and shade at Longwood, few flowers, sudden downpours from the clouds caught by the mountains, a steely sea spreading to a horizon where British ships disappeared, but where he must not. It was a place without hope. He hated it.

He postponed any conversation on the subject of departure from the Briars, saying briefly he would not entertain it until the house was made complete, free from workmen and the pervading smell of paint, to which he strongly objected; and for the time being nothing more was said. The soldiers and slaves continued to make their way up the path with increasing loads.

At Betsy's suggestion he agreed to what she termed 'a ball' in the marquee, but he then withdrew his promise, saying the space was inadequate. Instead he proposed that she and Jane give a young people's party, which he would attend. William Balcombe knew that once he left behind the informality of family life and the nominal guard, as represented by Captain Poppleton, the rigours of his life would not be confined to the climate. Camps and sentries, now absent, would become an ever present reality, bugle calls, now faint on the morning air, would sound strident and imperative. Longwood had its guardhouse; passwords would become compulsory; no excursions might be taken except in the company of a sentry. No longer would there be walks in the valley, greetings to the passing people or a gold napoleon slipped to a slave who opened a gate for his horse, no longer a stop at Toby's hut and daily flowers from the garden. Since his arrival Napoleon had shown a complete readiness to meet the residents of the island. He was interested in the visitors who came to the Briars, whether naval officers or townsfolk from Jamestown or William Balcombe's own friends. The women he complimented on their appearance and asked questions. One girl simulated fright at the sight of him, and, satisfied that she was only playing a game, he growled at her, ruffled his hair and howled like a Cossack, so that he really did implant terror in her heart.

Once, out of devilment, and knowing the Emperor had a great repugnance to ugly women, Betsy begged to present a lady whom in her diary she calls 'Mrs S.', the wife of one of the highest officials in India. Mrs S. had spent a day or two at Jamestown while her ship, homeward bound, lay in James Roads. Betsy adjudged her one of the plainest women in the world, though her airs and graces made it manifest she imagined her charm to transcend that of the most famous beauty of the day. She was overjoyed at the prospect of meeting "the great prisoner" and arrayed herself accordingly, in crimson velvet and pearls, her hair held up by butterflies of diamonds, rubies and emeralds. Napoleon, when she was presented, opened with the usual gambit — Was she married? How many children? — and so on, but his amazement was undisguised as he scrutinised her appearance, trying in vain to single out one attribute upon which to compliment her. Finally his observation settled on the coiffure caught up by the bejewelled butterflies, and, as he bade her farewell, he remarked, "Madame, you have most luxuriant hair," and retired precipitately. After that, Napoleon forbade Betsy to bring anyone to meet him. He was seriously displeased, knowing that a trick had been played, especially as afterwards he learned that the lady in question, on her arrival in England, had published in the newspapers a full account of the meeting, and reported that Napoleon had lost his heart to her charms.

The Emperor had certain favourite walks in and around the confines of the Briars. Fleet-footed Betsy, taking him by the hand, guided him down the steep side of the cliff on which the Pavilion was built, forcing a way through the dense greenery (which today has developed into mighty, aged trees — mohur and banyan, pencil pines and pomegranates, bound by briar, hibiscus and plumbago). It was easier going at the foot, darker too and quieter, and the gaunt hills towered in silhouette. Here there could be captured a measure of peace, even with the chattering Betsy beside him, retailing the simple island gossip. He remarked the strange mixture of tropical and occidental flowers, the goats in the hills, the rats, the patches of white dwarf-arum lilies in the sheltered slopes, the fruit trees, and conceived companionship with this matter-of-fact youngster who treated him as an equal in age — a tribute, on her part, to a mind that could adapt itself to her adolescent mentality. Her tricks he could always counter by equally juvenile play, and her modicum of information about the place and people he retained in his memory for contemplation. Her fair, untidy curls and careless dress he deplored, but knew could not be altered. These belonged to the make-up of her youth; later she would become 'a young lady', but now she was an unthinking, intelligent tomboy who said and did what came into her head, even to dragging him across the stones, over the damp of the waterfall's base, and calling him 'Boney'. He valued her uninhibited clasp and hand-in-hand they would return, flushed with exertion, up the steep incline to the comparatively level plane of the garden. Living from day to day, he had begun to re-orientate his existence.

For Napoleon, the valley always indicated shelter, and later, during his last illness, he expressed a wish to return to it. Not only did the rim of mountain divert the ever-blowing wind, but the waterfall lent a soft dampness that lingered on the hottest day. The roof under which he slept was just another bivouac to a soldier accustomed to a life of movement, the birds and farm noises taking the place of men and the clatter of accoutrements. Undoubtedly, of the whole six years he endured on the island, those months for Napoleon were the happiest. Admiral Cockburn had no mind to make the fact of Napoleon's imprisonment obvious to the captive. A fair-minded and generous sailor, he knew that the main deterrent to escape — should it indeed be contemplated — was the fleet that patrolled the waters; so the Admiral experienced no qualms and proceeded daily to direct Longwood's rehabilitation, in itself no small task, for general neglect had created a most melancholy picture of havoc. Originally built flat upon the ground over farm refuse, the floors had to be re-laid. Fortunately some of the rooms were tiled in black-and-white marble, and these became habitable once the window-panes were replaced. A kitchen range was installed and a bread oven. The water supply became a problem, and remained such until a pipeline from Diana's Peak was installed to give adequate fresh water; at the beginning all there was had to be carried in casks — wine barrels still holding the residue of the grape, which rendered the liquid within turgid and foul. Day by day a hundred Chinese and slaves toiled up the road, with its hairpin bends, to the plateau four miles from the Briars valley, carrying the timber, railings, tiles and all the necessary materials to remake the house. Goats had cleared the Deadwood plain below of shrubbery, and the sides of the Barn held no vegetation whatever, but, sturdy, ancient, defiant to the winds and goats and time, the single gumwood tree stood by the Longwood house.

The Admiral arranged for a fence, a hedge, a small garden, a guard-house some way from the residence, a sentry-box a little nearer, and then centred his attention on the lamentable state of the actual buildings. By this time he had planned a fair-sized, well-proportioned billiard room opening off a drawing-room of modest size. Napoleon himself would now have six rooms for his own use. The bath-tub — of copper and rather deep — was built in a room off his bedroom. Here Marchand passed in buckets of hot water, from a fire outside the window, for his master's ablutions. Here the Emperor sometimes reclined and ate his breakfast, served on a board across the bath. It was here the orderly officer, Nicholls, later peeped and saw him ministered to by the faithful valet, noting in his report to Lowe how ill Napoleon looked. (Standing by the side of the old tub more than a hundred years afterwards, one caught something of the man's domesticity and also the constant physical unrest that drove him to alleviate his pains with hot water; there was a place for soap on the worn sides where his hands had grasped — nothing glamorous or indeed even very clean, just a bath-tub in a cubicle with a little window opening on to what, in time, he convened into a garden.)

Cockburn did his best in the circumstances. Later, when Napoleon rode up to inspect the progress, he made strenuous demands to be allowed to remain where he was at the Briars, anything but be exiled on this plateau of solitude and wind. There was no prospect of evening whist with the family, no Betsy to tease and walk with, no visitors like those who came, without passes, but with a lot of goodwill. True, his suite would be reassembled around him. The Bertrands had specially asked to have Hutt's Gate as their home — a small cottage near the guard-house. Madame Bertrand, hearing there was a ghost in the ceiling at Longwood, said she did not wish to go there. "There are no ghosts," Napoleon told her shortly, but she prayed to live with her family in the little cottage, and got her way, her real reason being simply her disinclination to dwell in close proximity with the rest of the suite.

Admiral Cockburn, in the meantime, ordered the erection of a small house on the boundary of Longwood, so that Bertrand might reach his master quickly. This cottage is in good order today, though Hutt's Gate has fallen.

The servants at Longwood occupied poorer quarters, their rooms being small attics above the Emperor's apartments, heated in the day to an oven-like temperature. Some of the more fortunate, however, were given tents and Napoleon's valets slept near his person in a small room appointed to them on the ground floor. Madame Montholon, having no fear of ghosts, and also no objection to other members of the suite, took the three rooms with the black-and-white tiles leading to a stone veranda, where the inroads of rats were not so noticeable. The Admiral fought a losing battle with the rodents. They swarmed everywhere: "Like a flock of chickens feeding in the yard," said Le Page.

The Emperor disapproved of everything about Longwood. "They have collected all the crazy furniture on the island for my house," he told the family. "And probably said at the same time, 'We will gather all the rotten articles *en masse*; they are good enough for Bonaparte and the French.'" (He had just learned that the carpet in the bedroom had come from an officer's room in the barracks.)

He was passing through a phase of resentment against the Admiral, his soul irked by the prospect of the move and more realistic signs of enforced detention in the new quarters. "Were the Admiral to heap every kind of benefit on me, the manner in which he does it would make me conceive each and every one a bloody insult. Everything is given to us as if we were demanding alms. Let them at least not treat me with contempt, even if they give me nothing." He turned to O'Meara and Balcombe, to whom he was talking after dinner, "Tell them that it is not generous to insult the unfortunate." He worked himself up into a fit of anger, realising that the guards, the restrictions and the prohibitions were going to prove difficult to take after the easier interval at the Pavilion. "Who is this Admiral?" he demanded. "I have never heard his name mentioned as commanding in a battle, but it is true he rendered it infamous in America and is commencing to render it thus on this detestable rock."

When the time came, Admiral Cockburn was astute enough to modify the regulations under discussion. He was very sensitive to his prisoner's feelings, and under a bluff exterior felt sorry for him; the Regent had made a good choice when he sent for Sir George Cockburn. He tactfully allowed Bertrand to deal with the matter of passes to Longwood rather than from Plantation House, and in that Governor Wilks concurred. Later Napoleon was to learn that what he believed to be Cockburn's actions and prohibitions had been deliberately misrepresented by some of the suite — by Montholon especially, who at that time grossly and shamefully endeavoured to blacken the Admiral's character to the Emperor. Bertrand, on the other hand consistently declared Cockburn to be really an honest and good man. Napoleon was to know later, unless he already knew but would not admit it, that Montholon was not infallible.

CHAPTER 8

Ghosts

Admiral Cockburn, a stickler for protocol, and more experienced than Governor Wilks, proved the dominant factor in keeping the Emperor unobtrusively guarded. In his seaman's judgment, the presence of the British Fleet patrolling around the island provided sufficient security, without passwords, regimental guards and curfews; for Cockburn's attributes were in the best naval tradition.

Cockburn counted it a happy accident that Napoleon had elected to remain at the Briars and the decision had an added convenience in that it furnished an uninterrupted interval in which to complete the Longwood alterations.

Captivity in its full sense, the actual curtailment of movement to the perimeter of his own domain, was yet to come.

The Emperor lived in limited comfort and notable quiet in the valley, in the circle of an English family to which he had become warmly attached, and which gave him in return his only companionship other than that of his suite and a few chosen visitors. Family environment of this uninspiring but eminently normal type did much for him — how much, the Balcombes were not to know at the time. They learned it some years afterwards from Joseph Bonaparte, once King of Spain, and later still from Louis Napoleon III.

At the end of the third edition of Betsy's recollections, she intimates that Louis frequently questioned her about the personal appearance of his uncle. Did he, Louis, resemble him in any point? Had he a mannerism, 'a look'? He sought knowledge of any trivial attribute that resembled his own. Had his features at least the mould of Napoleon? Had he not the same bearing, the same air?

The resolutely truthful Betsy, unchanged even in later years, was compelled to disappoint him, to tell him plainly that in no way did he resemble the Emperor.... Not his eyes nor his figure, not his height ... Perhaps his hair? She fetched the lock that had been cut by Marchand and compared it; remarkably fine and silky hair, pale in colour, with a reddish undertone. Louis succeeded in achieving some slight resemblance by brushing his own in the same manner.

William Balcombe now began to experience all the difficulties of administering an insufficient grant Twelve thousand pounds did not go far and he put in an application for a further allowance. The island had always proved an expensive place, importing much of its meat and staple requirements, with service from the mainland so infrequent that it often created shortages. The English expatriates who lived there were nevertheless carefree, even prodigal. The light-hearted Mrs Wilks and the pretty Laura, the officers of the 53rd Regiment and a coterie of young people, made Plantation House a focal point of gaiety in the island society. The regiment held dances and there were races at Deadwood. The Hon. George Carstairs set an example of sartorial elegance which the officers at once derided and, in modified form, emulated. (Napoleon's comment that the young ran, "appeared to wear the Order of the Garter on both legs" went the rounds.)

Betsy and Jane joined in the social activities, as did the impressionable Gourgaud and to a lesser degree the other members of the Longwood party. Sometimes the girls were overwhelmed with questions from curious enquirers whose imagination conjured up dramatic situations out of the Emperor's quite ordered and even humdrum existence.

Betsy's face and figure created a jealousy that her careless manner did not help to assuage and she became an attraction to the younger men, mainly because she showed no inclination to attract. Years later Montholon's description of her gave some clue to her looks. He called her 'pretty', a lukewarm word, for he was always faintly hostile — and said she appeared older than her years and had a good neck and figure. She was soon to discover her own face. Napoleon's obvious preference created a situation that in such a small circle became unduly accentuated. To the visiting officers and naval ensigns she was an enigma, evincing none of the traits of the average young lady recently left school. They in their turn were small fry in contrast with the force of the Emperor's personality. His was a strong brew for an adolescent. Betsy became submerged in the cross-currents and shoal waters that flowed around the Pavilion. Light-hearted badinage followed graver moments; near tragedy, haunting sorrows came to be routed by a chance word created by temperaments fundamentally different from the normal English phlegmatic routine.

At the Briars the round garden-table with the marble top soon bore neat piles of books, papers and an ink-well. Las Cases's precise arrangement of documents took on a different aspect once Napoleon laid his hands on them. Although demanding order from others, he created immediate confusion himself when he searched among his notes, or in one or other of the volumes, for a confirmatory passage. At that period he had few books to refer to; later many came by store-ships and his library grew to some thousands of volumes, which were ultimately sold at Sotheby's after his death, the scarcely intelligible annotations and the comments in his own hand giving them historical interest sometimes of the first importance. Betsy more than once referred to "his bad calligraphy, impossible to make out".

A small travelling library habitually went with him on his campaigns, and it was examined with curiosity on the *Northumberland*, where it formed part of his luggage. It was of little use for reference, however, comprising standard works like Corneille and Voltaire, and a book of Ossian's verse.

The garden gate leading to the arbour remained locked on several mornings, and Napoleon's irritated tones could be heard when memory failed him and Las Cases could not assist. Ordinarily the Emperor's wishes were respected, and the family avoided the arbour, although Betsy was assured that her voice calling for admission would find immediate response; indeed sometimes she demanded entry in order to cause a diversion when Napoleon's impatience could be heard plainly, and on those occasions Las Cases cast her a glance of gratitude and relief. Once, to use Betsy's words, "During a morning's dictation a Miss C. arrived and begged to meet the great man." It was a day of oppressive heat, no sound came from the arbour, where earlier than usual Napoleon had retired to its comparative cool, and for a while Betsy hesitated, but the girl appeared so 'mortified' that eventually Betsy ran down the path and called; there was no answer. After several attempts to attract some notice, a sleepy voice demanded to know what was the matter. After a bad night, he had dropped off over his papers. The Emperor came slowly down to the other side of the gate and asked what she wanted. "Let me in and you shall know," she replied cheekily. "No, tell me first, then you shall come in." Betsy asked permission to present the young lady, which he summarily declined, saying he felt ill from the heat, but Betsy persisted, saying the visitor would be dreadfully disappointed, and added, as an incentive, that she was extremely pretty and gay. Napoleon groaned, "Not like the lady I was obliged to say agreeable things to yesterday?" Betsy earnestly assured him this one was different, really young and handsome.

With reluctance Napoleon unlocked the gate, remarking he was not inclined to meet anybody, it was too oppressive; but Betsy roused him to immediate activity by running to the table, seizing up his papers and crying, "Now, for your ill-nature in keeping me so long at the gate, I shall keep these and I shall find out all your secrets." Napoleon ordered her to put them down, and, alarmed for their possible fate, made a snatch, but Betsy was off down the path "flourishing her trophies", Napoleon following. At last he called that if she did not give them up he would not be her friend, and at that she returned and, taking him by the hand so that he could not escape, led him into the house, where Miss C., all agog, sat with Jane. Napoleon, always susceptible to a woman's appearance, found her extremely good-looking and delighted her excessively by his compliments. Retrieving the papers and with hair still somewhat ruffled by the interruption of his sleep, he presently walked down the lawn with her, helped her to her horse, which she had tethered at the gate, and leaned against the post, watching her ride away. His remark to Betsy afterwards was, as usual, to the point. "A very pretty girl, but she had the air of a *marchande de modes*."

Betsy heard the execution of the Duc d'Enghien freely discussed. It was still one of the most fruitful topics anywhere the Emperor's name was mentioned, and one in which people's sympathies were entirely in accord with the victim. The Duke became a symbol of romance — good-looking, thirty-six years old and a Bourbon, exiled from his homeland, yet still plotting for his family's rights and for its return to France. Arrested by a body of French Dragoons, outside French territory, he was dragged from his bed and carried away, half-dressed. To a tribunal he proudly confessed his plotting for the Bourbon cause, but denied knowledge of any proposed assassination of Napoleon. His British contacts (one at least shared his ultimate fate), stories of smuggler-caves, and frequent travelling to and fro across the Channel built up such a background of high adventure that eventually Europe solidly sympathised with the Duke in his misfortunes and mourned his death at the hands of a firing squad. Napoleon felt the cold breath of disapproval and accusation, from which his nature shrank. He had perforce to concede that his act had been not only savage but stupid. The story created the only pocket of reserve and distaste among the island people. By any standard, Napoleon's was an ill-judged action and one that set off tremendous repercussions throughout Europe.

On the eve of the Duke's execution, Josephine, never interfering in political issues, had made it her business to see the First Consul and dragged herself on her knees to him, begging for the young man's life as Napoleon made to leave the room. She warned him of the consequences and was left rebuffed and unhappy, with a curt intimation to mind her own business. Afterwards when it was too late, and possibly new light had been shed on the affair, Napoleon sought to justify his action by announcing that a letter from d'Enghien had been suppressed by Talleyrand until the execution had taken place. It was cloak-and-dagger stuff, an incident officially and laconically described as 'seven balls in the body', almost naïve in its matter-of-factness. More than fear of assassination had actuated Napoleon. Pangs of jealousy assailed him as well as a plebeian resentment of genuine royalty, and handsome young royalty at that.

In her more mature years Betsy still asserted she found no trace of cruelty in Napoleon's nature. Boundless ambition drove him to the lengths that had appalled the world. A tremendous self-sufficiency bolstered him in acts of audacity, but sadism or wanton cruelty were remote from his nature; his intelligence prevented the latter and the normality of his common reactions prevented the former. Later in the long days at St Helena, as he reviewed the past, she knew of his despair. With the heat of ambition extinguished, the stark result remained an accusation, affronting his intelligence perhaps more than his heart. In the phraseology of today, it had not been clever to get where he was now — captive, impotent and disregarded by a world that once had hung on his slightest pronouncement. For all the evidence to the contrary, Betsy likewise found it impossible to imagine him the cause of thousands of Turkish deaths at Jaffa, men who had surrendered on a promise that their lives would be spared, only to be butchered by his order. Youth contributed something to her disbelief, yet in later years she stoutly defended him.

The incident of the Duc d'Enghien came to be discussed through the accident of a song. The family were not in the habit of dwelling on past battles, political or otherwise. William Balcombe's naval career and his active service against the French fleet were never mentioned; too much devolved on the order of the day and he had, as purveyor to the French, an exacting assignment, apart from his duty to the East India Company and the commitments of Balcombe, Fowler & Co. It was the wife of a newly arrived army officer of the 66th Regiment, Mrs Baird, who introduced the subject of d'Enghien. She played and sang with more than average ability and one of the ballads she taught to Betsy happened to be a lament upon the execution of the Duke. Betsy in turn sang it to the Emperor, who, caught by the tune, enquired what the new song was about. She handed him the piece of sheet music, the cover of which bore a picture of a man standing in a ditch with a bandage covering his eyes and a lantern tied to his waist. Before him stood several soldiers, muskets levelled, unmistakably a firing squad. "What does it mean?" asked Napoleon, who did not read English well. Betsy told him it was intended to represent the murder of the Duc d'Enghien. "What do you know about it?" he enquired coldly. Betsy, unafraid of the chilly tone, replied with some flippancy that he, the Emperor, was considered by some to be the instigator. He gathered up the song in ominous silence, gazed at the engraved vignette and then threw it down and remarked, "It was no murder, but action accounted for under the rules of war." He asserted that d'Enghien was a conspirator and had landed troops in the pay of the Bourbons to assassinate him, then First Consul. A lasting deterrent to such conspiracies would be to destroy one of their own princes, and this he had done. To Mrs Balcombe, whose judgment and balance he held in great regard, he described the incident, "The prisoner was tried and executed under the existing laws of the Republic and not slaughtered in a ditch." He waved a hand towards the offending sheet on the piano. "France had been gorged with the Revolution, with the most horrible murders and massacres of the most terrible description. Now she was in comparative repose. It was best to let the law take its course and as the lesser of two evils to allow the execution to take place." He reiterated he had not received the Duke's letter. How stark it sounded in the quiet drawing-room, arresting enough for Betsy to remember and later write about.

For William and Alexander, the Balcombes employed, for want of a better, a tutor named Huff, a curious character who lived on the island for nearly half a century. Napoleon's arrival and subsequent kindness to the old and eccentric, though erudite, fellow had created such turmoil in his mind as to make it mildly unbalanced, his delusion being that he was the chosen instrument to liberate the Emperor. Reprimands and threats from the authorities and Napoleon's studious avoidance of him when he came to teach the boys at the Briars in the morning served only to stiffen the old man's resolve and some of the schemes he put to the suite became an acute embarrassment. Huff was considered deranged, but not to an extent that warranted his detention, for on other subjects he remained sane and eminently scholarly. One fatal morning he found a means to destroy himself. After an inquest, orders were given for his body to be buried on the spot where three cross-roads joined, not far from the Briars gate. Napoleon's curiosity drew him to the place, anonymous and trodden as it was by the feet of horses and slaves and marked by the infrequent traffic of farm carts and vehicles. It impelled him to talk to Betsy of the possibility of suicide as a means of his own release. On one occasion, he said, a chemist had told him that the easiest means to end life was by burning charcoal in a closed room. He certainly knew something of what he talked about and had once approached that fine edge of reason where it gives way to a tangle of despair, cowardice and pure misery. Even there the Grand Marshal Bertrand had been with him. Perhaps during the quiet period in the Briars garden they re-lived the night at Fontainebleau, the hurried call for candles to light the sleeping palace, the curious servants who listened to the groans and cries from Napoleon's bedchamber, the arrival and hurried departure of Dr Yvan, the faithful Constant, the valet, in attendance, and then profound silence.

During the retreat from Moscow, Napoleon had procured a small package of opium and other drugs, to be available in case he should become a prisoner.

This he wore in a bag around his neck, and, when the danger had passed, hid in a secret drawer, where it lay, its properties losing strength as time progressed but the knowledge of its existence still alive in the Emperor's mind.

A valet de chambre, who slept in an ante-room, heard Napoleon empty something into a glass of water, drink and return to bed: a few minutes later agonised shouts roused him to call help. The doctor arrived, learned what had occurred and, losing his head, fled from Fontainebleau, from the Emperor's groans, who declared the poison was not quick enough. Suddenly Napoleon fell into a stupor and a profound sweat, waking the next day unharmed — to his great astonishment. "God has ordained I shall live," he announced, and resigned himself to a new destiny — Elba, the Hundred Days, and now a garden in St Helena.

Later, during a walk with Betsy, the Emperor was to spy a tumbled heap of clothing halfway down the precipice by the waterfall. She could just make out the object, but the Emperor's glass showed more, and he sent her away to the house while a party assembled to recover what lay there — the remains of a soldier-suicide of the 53rd, caught on the cliff face.

After Huff's burial, Cipriani reported to the Emperor that the Briars black servants showed great disinclination to pass by the grave after dark and made a habit of walking in pairs along the road for protection. Betsy, fed by black Sarah's superstitions and stories of witchcraft in her native Africa, became equally apprehensive, and Napoleon, discovering this, played on her weakness and told of unquiet spirits that haunted battlefields, and of Corsican ghosts. When the family's bedtime arrived he would call from the Pavilion veranda, "Betsee, old Huff, old Huff," and so send her scurrying to her mother's room for protection. The others, not so susceptible, paid little attention, except to remark, "It's the Emperor again."

However, aided by Sarah's tales, he managed to implant in Betsy a genuine terror of the unknown to such an extent that she recounted it at length in her notes.

The story of 'Old Huff' reached a climax one night when the three women of the family sat alone on the Briars veranda, waiting for the light breeze that would later drift up the valley. William Balcombe had been called to a meeting by Admiral Cockburn, an occurrence that usually indicated a late arrival home. The little boys were in bed, even the servants in their quarters had become silent and the Pavilion showed no light. Probably Napoleon slept. He kept irregular hours and the staff took the opportunity to rest when he did, knowing that at his waking some of them would immediately be roused: Las Cases to take dictation of thoughts that had come to his master in the night, Marchand to help him dress, Ali to prepare coffee. When sleep deserted him he walked about the garden, an unapproachable and unquiet figure, hands behind his back, the shadowy trees surrounding him. At dawn he sometimes picked fruit from the trees — peaches, paw-paws or oranges — or watched the activities of the awakening farm behind the house and the rising sun creating shadows on the valley from the back of the old mountain. A faint, tropical, earthy breath created a few moments of magic. Usually he returned to bed after daybreak.

The town lights twinkled feebly down the valley and the quiescent mountain by some trick of darkness appeared closer than ever. The waterfall made no sound and the uncertain starlight accentuated the path's paler darkness against the grass.

Suddenly Betsy imagined she saw movement among the bushes. A white formless object drifted from the direction of the road and, pointing to it as it slowly advanced towards them, she screamed "Old Huff" and rushed inside. Her mother and Jane, startled, watched the formless object approach, until 'a low gruff laugh' was heard from the darkness, and Mrs Balcombe at once recognised the Emperor's voice.

Jane ran down the steps and pounced on the object to discover one of the little black servants, enveloped in a sheet and giggling delightedly, while the Emperor, the instigator, emerged from the shrubbery, equally diverted that he had routed the tormenting Betsy.

The sequel, however, provided a different ending, and the next ghostly visitant was carried to Jamestown Hospital.

A gardener-slave, Alley by name, absconded, and weeks passed with no trace of the missing man, notwithstanding a search that took in the Jamestown drinking-houses, the huts of the freed blacks, even the scattered little valleys and near-inaccessible heights. Alley had vanished.

Runaways were not unusual among the slave population — some contrived to reach a passing vessel, others drowned in the attempt, a few in despair leaped to suicide over the sharp precipices. The more fortunate hid among the freed families.

The yoke of slavery, although no heavier in St Helena than elsewhere, appeared less bearable because of the proximity of the African coast, which kept alive thoughts of home and hope of return.

The legend of Huff's ghost grew and reports circulated among the servants of a floating form seen in the darkness of the valley. It aroused William Balcombe, who, with help from Jamestown, constituted a series of watches, to be rewarded one night by a glimpse of a figure coming from the direction of the waterfall.

There was no answer to the challenge but the resultant volley brought forth a piercing scream and led to the discovery that the runaway had indeed been found and now lay seriously wounded. His hiding place, a cave in the mountain-side, was almost completely hidden from view by a large boulder.

Napoleon, who had taken part in the watch, climbed the mountain to see the pile of mean rags that constituted a bed, a tin of water, the neatly piled animal bones stacked against the side; it reminded him of the catacombs of Rome, he declared. Betsy loudly blamed the Emperor's prank for the incident and the staff, glad to ventilate their feelings, united in complaining to William Balcombe of his daughter's outspoken assertions. He administered a severe punishment and the inevitable repercussions followed almost immediately.

Napoleon and Gourgaud in search of a game of whist had entered the Briars drawing-room after dinner, the former in a particularly cheerful frame of mind, the moods of depression and irritability for the time being dissipated, and Betsy's *bêtise* forgotten. He was once more the indulgent companion who never resorted to rank or years or lost his temper as the consequence of familiarity. On this occasion, Betsy's resolution to be circumspect, as a result of her punishment, went unheeded; for Napoleon's voice calling her, and his so evident happiness at her appearance, meant a great deal and she responded unthinkingly and with rising spirits. She made a special note in her diary that if she approached him with gravity and gave a subdued greeting with the habitual curtsy, he would immediately challenge by saying, "*Eh bien, qu'as tu, Betsee?*" and pat her cheek with a perfectly kept hand, manicured nails on tapering fingers that dimpled on the knuckles. On this evening Betsy, clasping one hand, told him it did not look large enough to hold a sword. The mention of swords prompted General Gourgaud to draw his sabre from its scabbard and, pointing to stains on the blade, he announced proudly to Betsy that they represented the blood of an Englishman he had killed in battle. The Emperor immediately ordered him to sheath the sword, saying it was in bad taste to boast, particularly before ladies, and himself produced from a heavily-embossed case a truly magnificent weapon, the handle a fleur-de-lis shaped in wrought gold, the sheath of tortoise-shell studded with clusters of gold bees. Memories of the punishment, linked with the General's stupid boast, made the temptation irresistible. Betsy pounced on the sword, drew the blade and flourished it over her head, making passes at both men, but in particular the Emperor, who retreated until he became fairly pinned in a corner, Gourgaud beside him, furious but impotent to move. Betsy announced that their time had come, and that the Emperor had better say his prayers. Gourgaud, for his part, would die for the Englishman he had killed; and she forced their hands above their heads. Jane, hearing the tumult, ran to restore order and found a half-anxious, half-laughing Napoleon, dodging the unwieldy passes Betsy was impartially directing. General Gourgaud's spare figure was stiff with disapproval and fear every time she gave a lunge in his direction. In due course the weight of the sword told, and out of pure exhaustion Betsy desisted and finally she returned it to Napoleon, hilt foremost in the approved manner. He took the weapon with a deep breath of relief, pulled her nose and her ears and kissed her on both checks, his good-humour unimpaired.

Gourgaud consulted the rest of the suite the next morning and in consequence further retribution fell upon Betsy. The Briars cellar, recently stocked with wine, also maintained a fair colony of rats, and there, by her father's orders, she sat locked every day among bottles and rodents, her world apart from the others, only a scrap of the sunlit garden visible through the window-bars close to the ground. There had been a scene surpassing all scenes. Harassed as he was by the tightening of regulations, and his efforts to preserve a measure of freedom for the Emperor, William Balcombe knew the story of the 'incident' would circulate in no time and have a bearing on the exile's well-being. It was an unfortunate affair, made the more so by the complaints of the French. So Betsy sat, holding on her lap a piece of needlework brought by a sympathetic Sarah, her face blotched with crying. A whole day had gone by in solitude before her absence was remarked by Napoleon, who, on the morning of the second day, as usual, went in search of her, but to no purpose. Las Cases remained obtuse, the morning dictation, taken by Gourgaud, commenced, but went haltingly. "*Où est Mademoiselle Betsee?*" demanded Napoleon suddenly.

Las Cases led him to understand she was in the house. There were no sounds of voices, the garden had suddenly become empty, no dogs, no Toby. Napoleon stamped down the path and made a hasty search, calling, "Betsee, Betsee!" Presently he spied a face behind the cellar bars set almost flush with the ground. "I am being punished," Betsy told him in a small voice, "I was rude to you, Sir, but I did not mean it — you know that." Napoleon knelt on the ground and peered below, seeing the stocks of bottles behind her in the dank interior, bottles of port, her father's tipple.

Bars separated them with uncompromising finality, bars reminiscent of the intangible barriers that surrounded his own person. "Betsee, see we are both prisoners and you cry. I don't cry."

"You have," she told him flatly.

"Yes, I have," he admitted, his voice losing its bantering tone, "but the prison remains nevertheless, so it is better to be occupied and cheerful."

Betsy mutely held up her sewing, a dress in the early stages of completion. Napoleon laughed suddenly. "You must be very bored sewing," he commented; "but cheer up. I shall see your father immediately. You have been punished enough."

He rose, dusted his knees, and Betsy saw his neat white legs and buckled shoes disappearing down the path that led to the front of the house. It was some time before he returned and knelt again before the grating. "Your father is a very hard man," he reported; "you are to stay for your full period of punishment, I cannot move him; I am very sorry, Betsee."

"Count Las Cases and General Gourgaud were the cause," she burst out. "They spoke of *lèse-majesté*. I really didn't mean to be rude, I love you too much." The tears were falling again, dripping on to the grating. Napoleon leaned close and passed his handkerchief through the bars.

"Do not cry," he pleaded. He mopped her face and pressed his own close to hers, the cold iron intervening. "Remember, Betsee, I love you, I understand all you say and do, perhaps more even than your parents. When you are liberated, come to me and we shall have Pierron make some bon-bons, and we shall laugh again." The sweetness of his tone and his tenderness caused her to sob all the more; he changed his tactics and endeavoured to restore her cheerfulness by banter, calling her half-made dress the 'prison livery'. "I shall ask your mother to keep it specially and show it to you in warning when you are *méchante*," he told her.

Once more mopping her face, he left with her his handkerchief and the promise of a reunion when the term was over, not, however, humming 'Vive Henri Quatre' as was his custom. Gourgaud would know the reason when he returned to the Pavilion.

Again and again Betsy's reports closely coincide with the records of other contemporary writers. Even the version of the Marquis de Montchenu, Commissioner for the French, and not a Bonapartist, revealing a certain bias against the Emperor and a malicious inclination to highlight such incidents, tallies fairly closely with her story of the sword.

Montchenu's journal tells:

"I met the members of the Balcombe family. The two girls speak French, the younger called Betzi, is quite extraordinary and says whatever passes through her head. She is the one Bonaparte is courting, if rumours circulating in Europe are to be believed. I said to her, 'I am not surprised, Mademoiselle, at your mastery of the French language. Bonaparte has been giving you lessons.' 'Lessons? He is not gallant enough for that.' 'But I thought that with your lovely eyes you had tamed him.' 'You don't know him. I detest him.' 'Why then, he must have frightened you.' — 'Frightened me? I should say not, it is I who have frightened him.' 'How is that?' — 'I found a sword in his bedroom. I unsheathed it and charged at him. He shrank into a corner and shouted for help. Las Cases came behind me and wrenched the sword out of my hands.' 'You wanted to kill him then?' — 'Not really. Just puncture him slightly for fun!' She is quite capable of doing such a thing, for, if necessary, she would stick needles into one's calf or bite one to the bone. Her sister told of their last meeting. Bonaparte pinched her ear hard and said to her, 'Well now, little girl, are you a better girl these days?' 'Yes, it's quite true,' said Betzi, 'he was pinching me hard.' 'Well, what about this pretty hand of yours? Did it not serve your purpose?' 'Oh, you can be sure that it did, for I boxed his ears. He was so put out that he pinched my nose very hard indeed and it stayed red all day.'"

Montchenu added as a footnote, "The two girls became very friendly, and their straightforward attitude seemed to entrance the General, especially that of the younger, who was the General's favourite, and who would tell him everything that passed through her flighty head. She would ask him the most untoward questions but he answered them all without any apparent hesitation."

Betsy's diary about this period sets down an un-reconciled sequence of incidents, some dating from earlier years, others interlaced with brief comments on personalities that remain anonymous to us today. 'Tasks' were itemised. Their father evidently expected the girls to study geography, and to memorise portions of the Church service. Betsy writes of the lessons and collects, and her history 'task' takes the form of St Helena's colonisation.

She painted in water colours, the accepted accomplishment of the young lady of the day. One of her pictures is extant, a washy presentation of the Briars, showing the garden not yet in its adult growth, the two sentinel trees by the house slim in dimension and the wall intact between the Pavilion and the main building, behind which lay the orchard. Aloes, today a feature of the island, had not appeared on the scene.

On one page, she notes, "Give B. a book," later, "To Jamestown, Lord Amherst's arrival — of fine appearance. Great echo of guns in the valley." (She alludes to the sound of the salute fired from Ladder Hill in his honour.)

She goes on to discuss the habits of the French women, and the "advanced" fashions they wore.

Lord Amherst is mentioned again, his "courtier-like manner and charming address". She quotes Napoleon as saying, "The Ambassador must have been fascinating to have impressed your youthful fancy."

She describes Lord Amherst as "British Ambassador to China" and repeats a story which raised considerable mirth, arising from the Ambassador's official reception by the Chinese Emperor. She claims Napoleon contended that the representative of any country must conform to the court's regulation; if the Emperor of China insisted that the visitors approach on their knees, the visitors must acquiesce.

They 'kissed hands' on their reception by a British monarch (Napoleon remarked the French disliked the habit), embraced the Pope's toe when in Italy, and if the Chinese Emperor desired a deep obeisance it must be given. When the English plenipotentiary arrived, he found the doorway into the Presence to be so low as to make it impossible to enter except on hands and knees, so the Ambassador crawled in backwards, presenting a massive posterior to the Emperor, and thus created a new problem in protocol.

Napoleon was delighted with the story.

CHAPTER 9

The Friends are Separated

On his return to the Briars after a visit to Major Hodson in the valley, Napoleon passed Betsy on the lawn, and invited her to the Pavilion to dine. Betsy said she and the family had already finished their meal in the house. "Come up and see me eat, then," he told her. When the meal was announced by Cipriani, she went with Napoleon and Las Cases into the marquee, where the Emperor habitually took his meals. It was only pleasantly warm and the view towards Jamestown and the sea showed ever-changing colours as the shadows lengthened. Novarrez, spying Betsy, brought in some creams, her favourite sweets. Notwithstanding she had already dined, Napoleon made her eat one, her partiality for the creams always a source of amusement to him, and when she refused a second, he insisted. Here was an opportunity to tease, and crying, "More, more," he commenced to feed her "like his little bambino," in gales of laughter until, not able to bear it further without being sick, she ran away, pursued by his gleeful cries, "You like creams — have another!"

The next day Marchand, smiling broadly, brought a quantity of Pierron's bonbons to the household with the message that the creams were only for 'Mademoiselle Betsee'. Pierron, who daily supplied the Emperor's table with sweets, was supposed to be the most accomplished *confiseur* in the world, and on the barren rock he performed miracles of sugary designs of palaces, shapes and gardens, reminiscent of his former triumphs in Paris. Betsy's diary is dotted with admiring tributes about them, for Napoleon often sent the fairy castles to the house for the children to play with and eventually to eat. To Betsy they came, from Napoleon, with appropriately sugared words, "To make these sweet things sweeter," he wrote with great gallantry. On New Year's Day, after he had left the Briars, the Bertrand children arrived from Longwood, with a selection of bonbons for the Balcombes. Napoleon wrote he had sent his "Cupidon to the Graces". The bonbons were in crystal baskets on Sèvres plates, covered with white satin napkins. It pleased him to make little gifts as it did to pay compliments. He liked talking to women. Perhaps that arose from the rigours of his early life, which did not permit of women's company, so that any associations he had with them were transitory. Towards the end of his stay at the Briars, the temperature in the valley became changeable. The sheltered warmth of the mountain was transformed into a damp and clammy mist and, notwithstanding barricaded windows, Napoleon caught a violent cold and retired to his camp-bed, with its green drapes. Mrs Balcombe visited him with household remedies, camphor, steam inhalations, honey and orange drinks, but Napoleon refused all. No cures for him, but bed and Marchand's ministrations. The children were kept away and he coughed himself to recovery. It was his only illness while he was at the Briars. The symptoms that manifested themselves later did not show during the first months of his exile, though Constant, his valet in Paris, wrote of disturbances before he had left France, of unaccountable vomitings and upsets. Mrs Balcombe first remarked on his altered appearance when she saw him after the move to Longwood, and the change must have been pronounced, for Betsy specially noted her mother's remark in her recollections.

One last prank of Betsy's occurred to rock again the fortitude of Napoleon's suite. The Balcombe family had been invited to dine at the Pavilion, where, under the spreading tent that caught the cooling night airs, the little *lampiste*'s lanterns bobbed and glowed. Napoleon essayed a remark, one that had become well-worn with usage, that when Betsy grew up, Emmanuel Las Cases would make a good husband for her and keep her in order, but this time demanded that Las Cases kiss her — '*gage d'amour*' — and when she dodged a rather reluctant attempt on the young man's part, the Emperor held her still for the proffered embrace, whereupon the page got his ears soundly boxed.

It was one of the Emperor's 'moods'. He enjoyed the turmoil and ear-boxing and the juvenile confusion, his malicious streak, equally infantile in its impishness, uppermost. Here was the same man who had slapped bearers of unpleasant news, who took the fire-tongs to the shins of reluctant Generals and who actually kicked one of the Empire's philosophers in the stomach. It was evident that force played an appreciable part in his psychology. This was no court circle, however, where retaliation could never be indulged in and where such attacks were borne in silence.

At the end of the meal, William Balcombe and his wife left for Jamestown; the intention of the others was to go to the main house for whist. The party walked from the Pavilion down the steep path in the dusk, the Emperor leading the way, humming his unmusical rendition of 'Vive Henri Quatre'. The older Les Cases followed, then his son, then Jane, with, by design, Betsy last. She allowed them a small start, when, throwing her full weight on her sister, she pushed her off balance on to young Las Cases, who in turn cannoned against his father. The older Las Cases, not nimble, fell heavily upon the Emperor and caused him an undignified tumble that culminated in apologies and protestations and much dusting of clothes. Las Cases, seeing the laughing Betsy and realising the 'accident' had been intentional, was incensed at the insult to his master. He shouldered her violently against the rock and forced her backward over the ledge, behind which was a considerable drop. Alarmed at the vicious anger in his face, she struggled and cried out for help. Napoleon, on his feet once more, took in the situation and immediately called, "*Ne pleurs pas*, Betsee, I will hold him while you punish him." This he did and the little man was pinioned with a swiftness that took him by surprise and his ears rang with resounding blows from Betsy's hands until he shouted for mercy. At length Napoleon let go and told him to run for it and that if he were caught he deserved all he got. Greatly diverted, the Emperor pinched Betsy's ear, dusted his clothing again and then went on to the house for the game of cards. Las Cases's dislike for Betsy mounted. He resented the Emperor's attention to the girl more than did the other members of the suite. As a devoted servant and close associate, he followed his master's every word and gesture, his high spirits, and the passing moods of depression. Napoleon's response to her distant voice, let alone her presence, was ever a matter of jealous concern — more so to him than to General Gourgaud, who by this time thought only of the lovely Miss Wilks. As far as Gourgaud was concerned, games were games; if the Emperor found relaxation in being playful, so much the better.

Betsy's memoirs, written in 1844, were of necessity guarded, but her daughter, Mrs Charles Johnston, elaborated them and filled in gaps that politics and the exigencies of the time made it expedient for her mother to leave unfilled. It was evident, she remarked, that Napoleon never ceased to be the preoccupation of her mother's life. Suddenly thrown into close proximity with the most dramatic figure of the age, she was ill-prepared to withstand the resultant repercussions, glamorous, disturbing and even sinister; intimate as well, for Napoleon lived closely within the circle of the household and was greatly at ease. Later, after he had gone to Longwood, he was to perceive the gradual change that had transformed her from the hoyden of the early days into a young lady of more thoughtful mien and deportment.

Not that these moods lasted for any length of time. The old flamboyance frequently returned, the careless word and quick action, the fun of living, alternating with the serious moments like a pendulum swinging. It took adversity, time and memory to damp her courage and, of these three, memory made the deepest imprint, recollection of the rotund figure of the Emperor, his invincible charm, the metamorphosis from majesty to teasing companion. It appeared as if in his youth he had never been given an opportunity to play. Work, poverty and ambition had been the preoccupation of those days, subordinating the normal outlets of childhood. Now he possessed all the time there was to be amused by little things, for want of others greater, to laugh at foolishness albeit rather desperately, and to play pranks. Probably, he sensed, it was that, or lose his reason.

On the 8th December, Admiral Cockburn announced that Longwood was ready for occupation, the furniture in place and the smell of paint no longer noticeable. This last had been the subject of controversy, Las Cases declaring the Emperor would not move until it was completely dissipated; the odour made him ill. The other members of the suite told Napoleon the place still smelled vile, and he had willingly delayed his departure on that pretext.

Finally the Admiral, feeling the strain, did not beat about the bush any longer. "Shall I have to bring a guard of soldiers, Sir?" he asked bluntly; after which Napoleon, with a shrug, offered no more objections. It was now a matter of a few days before the final move was at hand. In the gathering dusk he and Las Cases walked towards the Briars house; evening sounds from the farm buildings and from the valley lower down, and the unforgettable tropical scents, met them on the little path leading to the square of lawn below where he had walked, and ridden and sat over coffee. Lights showed in the windows, There was no cloud-top on the mountain peaks, no travellers on the road, only the domestic sounds and movements, muted by distance, and the flowers' perfume filled the evening. "This is a peaceful spot," Napoleon said. "Let us remember it thus." He stopped and surveyed the surrounding setting of steep rocks, the silver streak of the waterfall behind, and the faintly marked paths stretching below him. The house lay spread in lighted comfort. "A shelter for the blest," he said, half to himself, as he walked on. "I find the family middle-class and unambitious," was Las Cases's prim response.

They had eaten a quiet evening meal in the Pavilion, served, however, in customary state, Cipriani in evidence, a little more tractable than formerly because he had been allowed to choose the provisions in Jamestown himself, and it gave him added freedom of movement. Most of the suite were, in fact, in Jamestown engaged in packing. With young Las Cases dining with the family and Gourgaud invited to Plantation House, the Emperor and Las Cases had the Pavilion to themselves. There would be whist presently in the Briars drawing-room, now plainly visible, the windows wide open to the night. How ordered a routine it presented, where the days passed quietly, but all too quickly. Napoleon recollected his unexpected arrival over two months before. The setting sun had made riding unpleasant. They had left the derelict Longwood behind them in the gathering cloudbanks, after spending several hours in dismayed discussion. It seemed a long time ago. He remembered the first uncomfortable week, adjusting to the cramped quarters, the cessation of the ship's movement (for the ship had proved lively); and the time before that in Europe, hurried comings and goings, the uncertainty and the crushing decision of battle, the turbulence of imminent disaster, sudden death, the confusion of regiments, and the final débâcle ... a sombre picture that would remain with him always, an immense canvas in the gallery of his mind, far removed from the peaceful scene spread in the waning light.

A warm, human atmosphere met them at the door. William Balcombe, hearing footsteps, came in from the dining-room. "Two bottles only, Monsieur, tonight," he announced, holding up two fingers — the current joke on the port session. The Skeltons, a cheerful pair, happened to be dining and the drawing-room became pleasantly alive with voices as the younger children came in before bed-time. Someone proposed a game of blind man's buff before they disappeared upstairs and chairs were pushed back. Napoleon threw off his sombre mood and, on request, produced a cambric handkerchief heavily scented with eau-de-Cologne and prepared to take part, although he had no idea what form the game would take, Betsy being ignorant of its French name, *colin-maillard*. When it was described to him he tried to withdraw, telling them he had once played it at Malmaison, but eventually acquiesced, insisting, however, that lots be drawn for the role of blind man, and that he should prepare the slips of paper, on one of which he wrote, '*la mort*'.

Betsy was convinced that, as it fell to her to become the first victim, the Emperor had in some manner contrived it. He took the cambric handkerchief and bound her eyes demanding could she see. "I cannot see you," she replied, evading the fact that a little gleam of light filtered in at one corner. Napoleon waved his three-cornered hat, in which had been the paper slips, and its shadow made her flinch. "Ah, little monkee," he exclaimed in English, "you can see pretty well!" He brought out a second handkerchief and proceeded to close up every ray of light, tying it with his agile hands in tight knots behind her curls. She was turned about, and left in the middle of the room, there to be guided only by the sounds of breathing, the excited squeaks of the youngsters, and the starchy rustling of the women's skirts.

The Emperor administered some sharp ear tweaks, leaning over Jane's shoulder to do so, and then, bounding to another position, contrived a quick nose pull through the layers of handkerchief, while Betsy stalked another assailant. There arose a confusion of voices and laughter as the luckless 'blind man' was pushed and spun about. Sudden stampedes on the part of the younger ones avoiding capture swept Napoleon along with them, gay as any child, and quicker than most to bait the 'blind man' at every possibility. The sound of falling chairs brought the servants running to watch at the open windows. Happiness united youth and age in the simple game.

Betsy's diary comments that it was "fast and furious" and "the uproar great". The Emperor proved elusive: he sheltered behind Mrs Balcombe and the other ladies, who nimbly fronted for him, or he crouched with the little boys while Betsy's questing hands passed over their heads, to snatch at her curls with the glee of a boy when she turned away. Presently above the noise rose the sound of horses' hooves on the drive. The servants at the windows drifted off in the darkness. Archambault, the groom, went to the entrance in readiness to hold the mounts and William Balcombe passed into the porch to receive the visitors. Over the babel of voices within sounded deeper tones, and Admiral Cockburn, Count Bertrand and an A.D.C. from Plantation House stepped into the room.

The game ceased, quelled by the formality of the arrival. Betsy pulled down the handkerchiefs and, seeing the newcomers, understood immediately that this indeed was zero hour. The captive, a man to whom she had, in fun, issued perhaps more orders than any individual before, was now to receive an official intimation that he must move.

Napoleon, still breathless, turned about to face the group at the door, his carefree mood replaced by an imperious sternness, a sudden majesty dwarfing those in the room. For a moment he was the old Emperor, a compact, vital figure. The women watching, however, felt a sudden inclination to cry. His level gaze held dignity as he waited, and Admiral Cockburn, as spokesman, found his composure curiously shaken by the sudden termination of the joyous scene, as if he and his companions had spread a blight on its brightness. He bowed stiffly to the Emperor and, after an appreciable moment of silence, formally requested permission to transmit a message from His Excellency the Governor. Napoleon's cheek-bones became accentuated by pallor and the muscles at the back of his neck corded and bunched, a familiar manifestation when emotion gripped him. He had recovered his breath. "I will receive you in the Pavilion," he said shortly and, bowing to the ladies, turned to the door. By the time he reached the Pavilion Napoleon had his emotion under control. He glanced back at the lighted house, set in its shadowy garden, at the horses bunched by the door, and for a moment he paused as if to memorise the scene before he went to learn his future, to hear the details of the real captivity. It seemed as if he said good-bye to the pleasant living and the fun that had unexpectedly come his way during the last two mouths, to the balloons and childish games, to the sight of Betsy playing 'blind man', to the unaccompanied walks and chance meetings. He turned to Las Cases and said, as he had often done before, "I feel I have been to a masked ball."

The next morning Napoleon appeared earlier than usual and in a black temper. Las Cases's assurance that the smell of paint was gone from Longwood had been contradicted by General Bertrand, who, coming from a final inspection, equally insisted it still permeated the whole house. Napoleon then refused to have his household pack any further, and worked himself into a fury. Again and again he declared he did not want to leave the Briars, was happy there, indeed he did not think he could ever have been so content; the hours had proved "more endurable than he had even thought possible on such a horrible rock as St Helena". He walked up and down the lawn gesticulating violently, declaiming that he would not inhabit a house "polluted by smells". If the Grand Marshal's reports were true, he would send for the Admiral and refuse to enter Longwood until it was gone. The luckless Las Cases was despatched again for a further report. Practical Mrs Balcombe suggested sundry housewifely specifics to remove the offending odours, suggestions which Napoleon, if in his agitation he even heard them, disregarded. Betsy ran out to enquire what had caused him to be in such a rage, and one of his swift changes of temper occurred. Calmness of manner replaced the torrent of invective. "I was perfectly amazed," she writes, "at the power of control he evinced over his temper. In one moment, from the most awful state of fury he subdued his irritability and his manner became calm, gentle and composed." Las Cases returned later to confirm that the offending smell had indeed almost gone, that Bertrand, to whom the move was unwelcome, had exaggerated. The situation was beginning to tell on everybody's nerves; tempers were short and Napoleon walked up and down continually, and a general uneasiness pervaded the scene until the following morning, when the Emperor finally took his leave. Admiral Cockburn, accompanied by the whole suite, rode to the Briars to escort him.

"You must not cry, Betsee — you must come and see me next week and very often," Napoleon told her, observing the signs of distress. She at no time hid her emotions, which were usually stormy and on the surface. "Balcombe, you must bring both of them to see me soon. When will you ride up to Longwood?" It was like a family parting, homely, human, far removed from artificiality and pomp, acknowledgment of love and affection between people who, for a short time, had become close.

Napoleon then asked for Mrs Balcombe, who happened to be in the throes of a bout of fever that, at certain periods of the year, claimed them all, and, hearing she was in bed, darted off upstairs before anybody could warn her of his approach; and, seating himself on the bed, talked with great feeling of her attention to his comfort, her tact and her unfailing kindness to himself and to the suite. He repeated that he would have preferred remaining always at the Briars if it had been permitted. He had been happy. Not often was he to say that at St Helena. The children came in and hung about, a playmate departing; and tearfully Jane held a golden trinket he gave her to wear as a souvenir of himself. They made a forlorn little group and Napoleon wept with them. To Mrs Balcombe he presented a gold snuff box for her husband (it is now in a collection of Napoleana in America), and to Betsy, whom he held close to him as he tried to stem her tears, he presented a little bon-bonnière — something he habitually used, and which she had admired — saying with a flash of his old teasing manner, "You can give it as a *gage d'amour* to *le petit* Las Cases." That was more than she could support, still harbouring a hearty disregard for the page; and she ran off, filled with tears and emotion, and from her bedroom window watched the cavalcade presently file out of the gate to blend into the background of mountains.

For her a period had passed — it could never be the same at Longwood. Bleak mountains and mists would take the place of a garden. The interludes in the grape arbour, the evening at whist, the small-town gossip after dinner, the rides and the frequent visitors to the Pavilion, all were things of yesterday. Instead there would be a guardhouse and sentinels, regulated comings and goings, protocol would take the place of informal routine — distance would lend difficulty in meeting.

William Balcombe returned to report that Napoleon had made no comment on his new residence. The Emperor appeared out of spirits and, retiring to his dressing-room, had shut himself up for the remainder of the day. He said, moreover, that, since he was purveyor to Longwood, they all had a general order to visit there as often as they chose.

Inevitably a new pattern of events began to take shape. The Pavilion, the old shell, remained silent, still redolent of the occupant as if awaiting the ordered sequence of daily events, the servants' movements to and fro, the gurgle of milk from the farm pouring into the Pavilion pitcher, the glimpse of the lamp-lighter with his grotesque walk and coloured balloons, Le Page (who slept in the Briars quarters and did most of his cooking in the kitchen there, holding forth in voluble broken English on the inadequacies of the English cuisine, the echo of Archambault's provincial patois as he called to his brother in the stables, the sight of Napoleon himself pacing the arbour, his nimble legs and brisk movements so characteristic in their impetuosity, the harsh voice raised in demands for Las Cases. Betsy makes reference only once to the Emperor's voice; she speaks of its strongly masculine tone, not deep-pitched nor specially attractive, a harsh utilitarian voice, "his English pronunciation very bad". He told her that although he spoke bad English he did not regret it; he had learned to follow swiftly even the nuances of conversation held in that language, to which remark she did not agree.

The stables now held only their own horses. Captain Poppleton had seen to the removal of the Emperor's mounts the day before, and had gone with them. Napoleon himself had ridden Hope, with the Imperial saddle-cloth, the gold embroidery, and his green coat with its red facings noticeable even among the be-medalled and magnificently uniformed officers by whom he was surrounded. He rode one pace ahead, the Star of the Legion of Honour on his breast catching the sun's rays. The track up the mountain slope opened to him a *via dolorosa*, for, in his soldier's conception, it was another retreat.

Betsy went to the Pavilion; the silence made the empty and untidy marquee unbearable. Tufts of straw and paper littered the ground. The main room had the appearance of a hotel bedroom after the occupant had vacated it; only the bare furniture remained, the round table and inlaid desk, the chairs and the Indian rug showing signs of recent packing, everywhere the scent of eau-de-Cologne, of soap and the mustiness of snuff. The window was still boarded up where, on the first night, Napoleon had fancied there came a draught; the silver basin and ewer were gone, and also the green-curtained bed. A piece of china met Betsy's eye, a plate, one of the Sèvres set, broken across; one bearing not the portrait of the young Napoleon, however, but an Egyptian scene. She picked it up and went over to the spot where the blue and white Nankin set stood stacked on a shelf. The mug was there, Napoleon's mug, Cipriani's *bête noire*.

She lifted it down and held it with the broken plate. She saw the bare nails over the fireplace from which Josephine's miniature had hung along with the Consular watch, bearing the cypher B, attached to a plaited length of Marie-Louise's hair. Other people would come to rest here, other visitors. Life would go on in the Pavilion which briefly had sheltered the greatest man in the world. As the East India Company continued to play its part in history, so would William Balcombe play host to more and more newcomers.

The disorder of discarded packing papers, abandonment and departure started her suddenly to tears again, and Betsy ran outside, to find Toby engaged in re-marking the incised crown in the lawn, which the comings and goings of many feet had damaged. As far as Toby was concerned, it would remain there for ever, one of the garden's features.

Below, the house drowsed in the sun. She walked slowly down the path, carrying the pieces of china.

CHAPTER 10

Longwood Prison

Some days later the older members of the family rode to Longwood. They found Napoleon seated on the steps of the billiard room, a bored and lonely figure, putting in time talking with little Tristram Montholon. The moment the party came in sight he ran towards them, extravagant in his demonstration of pleasure, kissing Mrs Balcombe and the girls, pinching Betsy's ear and crying, "*Ah, Betsee, êtes-vous sage, eh, eh?*" He then waved a hand towards the house and enquired what they thought of the palace; he would personally conduct them over it. They considered his bedroom small and cheerless. He used the little camp-bed with the green hangings. In place of wallpaper, brown fluted Nankeen with a green paper dado made a drab covering and there were no skirting-boards; the only decorations were the portraits of his family, the only note of past magnificence the silver basin and ewer. In an ante-room was a set-in bath. Next came a dressing-room, strictly utilitarian; a dining-room, rather dark; a drawing-room eighteen feet by fifteen feet, and the billiard room, the only well-proportioned room in the house and built for him to Sir George Cockburn's specifications. The kitchens were adequate only for the needs of a small family. Pierron, the confectioner, was discovered at work, producing creams and bonbons, which he presented with his usual flourish. Napoleon showed every miserable shortcoming of the house, the ill-fitting boards, the rat-holes, the places in which he believed there was a possibility of draughts.

Then he unceremoniously invaded the rooms set aside for the Montholons and insisted that the six-weeks-old Montholon baby be produced, holding it with such inexperience that the women were in terror as he pinched its nose and behaved with all his old-time impishness. When entreated to give the child back to its mother, since he was such a dangerous nurse, he airily assured them that he had often held the King of Rome when he was much younger than the little Lile. Said Betsy, "Who knows but you didn't drop him?"

88

The Las Cases' quarters, a bedroom and sitting-room, were built so low that the ceiling could be touched with ease, and there was no room for a chair between the beds.

Marchand, Cipriani, St Denis and Josephine slept in the garrets over the old building. It was impossible to stand upright except in the centre of the rooms, and the heat sometimes became insupportable. "However, we eat well," remarked Napoleon to William Balcombe, though he added, directing his attention to a sheep hanging up in the larder, "*Regardez; voilà un mouton pour mon diner, dont on se fait une lanterne.*" And, sure enough, it was so, the French servants having placed a candle in its lean carcase through which the light shone. He then proceeded to show the garden. "After all, I am not at liberty to leave these grounds unguarded," Napoleon told them with bitterness. "There are now double sentinels passing backward and forward. There are even sentinels on the goat-paths."

The view from the windows presented a canvas of supreme desolation; rugged mountains cut by ravines and apertures, evidence of some vast volcanic eruption, gave a spectacle of unbroken sterility. No vegetation covered the sharp angles where a shoulder of rock, called the Barn, afforded shelter from the trade winds.

One or other of the family went to visit the exiles every week. Betsy notes the Emperor appeared to "suffer more depression of spirit" than when formerly he had been "under the spur" of an uninhibited family of youngsters. Once she found him in the garden at pistol practice. He made her fire a shot, which by luck went near the target, called her his *petite tirailleuse* and said he would found a corps of sharpshooters and she would be captain. Evidently his spirits had brightened and he felt glad to see her — any diversion in this desert of existence.

Holding her hand, he took her to examine the billiard table newly built by Thurston of London, which had just been installed; a handsome piece of mahogany with Regency-type legs. Betsy told him billiards was a childish game — marbles on a large scale — and made very little progress under his teaching, aiming at his fingers instead of at the ball, but when she hit them she caused him to laugh, which was her intention, for his depression tended to become alarming. Her mother remarked frequently on the change in his appearance after his arrival at Longwood. He looked drawn and ill. It was not the cold that affected him — that could be cured by simple remedies; but something much deeper and fundamental. His buoyancy of spirit had flagged, his interest and awareness, always part of him, were dimmed. Much of his condition they ascribed to the disagreements with the Admiral over the house, but not all; a physical change was taking place.

The Christmas of 1815 (for the exiles, their first at Longwood) brought other guests to the Pavilion — the Younghusbands, of the 53rd Regiment. Housing on St Helena had become a difficulty, and the influx of soldiers and families created something approaching a major crisis. The Younghusbands, mother and family, had already spent some weeks at Plantation House and still searched for a small cottage in which to live permanently. In the meantime, for the Christmas season, the Pavilion was made their abode.

In most narratives of the time there is mention of tents. Napoleon had recourse to one at the Briars. Longwood housed several of the staff in the same manner, the army at Deadwood and elsewhere lived under canvas and many families added a canvas room to the inadequate cottages they rented. As the weather lent itself to an outdoor life, however, the conditions were not quite so bad as might be inferred. Mrs Younghusband makes it sound almost pleasant in her subsequent letters to relations in England. She writes of Christmas spent with "the kind and hospitable friends, the Balcombes". It was a milieu that suited her high spirits and temperament and she said with some pride that she "slept in the late residence of Bonaparte". She describes the "grand dinner on Christmas Day, with Admiral Cockburn there and Madame Bertrand and all the grandees". One notices how the person of Madame Bertrand is accentuated. She must have held the attention of all women on the island, for, as one of them remarked, she had once presided over a court in Europe and, born to that social sphere, it would be hard to subdue her natural air of consequence.

Mrs Younghusband notes that the season was the height of summer and she mentioned the myriads of birds and the view of the garden and valley.

To her it must have presented a more attractive picture than it does today, for she speaks of roses, pomegranates, myrtles in profusion and ripe peaches on the trees. The myrtles have reproduced their type in the present wilderness and possibly there are pomegranate trees to be found, but briar, straggling plumbago and creepers hold together only an illusion of a garden.

Mrs Younghusband goes on to gossip about the Christmas festivities and, to judge also by Betsy's account, there must have been balloons and presents and, for the Balcombe girls, special gifts from the Emperor, although he did not himself attend the Christmas party. The French children, with the Younghusbands and the Balcombes, played the time-honoured seasonal games. It was a Christmas of sun and flowers such as the Balcombes would come to know in Australia.

Mrs Younghusband continues to write of Madame Bertrand and her distaste for the apartments allotted to her at Longwood. It was the ghost she objected to, and she spoke of Hutt's Gate at the top of the hill as a small building, which, inadequate as it was to the needs of the family, would make nevertheless a welcome if temporary alternative. Mrs Younghusband dwells on the "incompatible state of a woman born to luxury, shifting for herself in the abnormal conditions" and she depicts Madame Bertrand as interesting and amusing, "most flattening and caressing." The years have shown how well she dealt with the situation in which she was placed. The tightly-massed trees now surrounding what was Hutt's Gate demonstrate that she tended the garden with the object of shutting away the wind and gaining shelter from the sun. The camellias, strelitzia and plumbago she planted in both Hutt's Gate and the later garden on Longwood boundary are a memorial to her, as are the sweet alice and periwinkle and a host of old-fashioned border flowers still blooming there. The luxury of foreign courts had evidently not damped Madame Bertrand's active Irish spirit, although the influence of Napoleon always aroused in her a tendency to resume the formality of court etiquette. Once at Hutt's Gate Mrs Younghusband and her daughter were being shown a jewel box of trinkets and miniatures by the Countess, when a servant came running to say the Emperor was riding from Longwood, two miles away, to visit her; in the confusion and dismay that the Emperor should visit so small and humble a spot, she left by the back-door, Mrs Younghusband records, but not fast enough to succeed in escaping unrecognised, and Napoleon, dismounting at the front of the house, remarked that he was very vexed at her departure. He made a general survey, looked at the ravine directly in front of the little home (he was later to scramble down there to find the spring beside which became the place of his burial) and made a thorough inspection of its interior. Mrs Younghusband and her daughter, looking back as they walked home, saw him examining the Hutt's Gate pigsties.

For a brief time, Geranium Vale, below Hutt's Gate, was let to the Younghusbands (afterwards they lived in camp in a tent). The Bertrand children played with Emily, and Madame once came scrambling down the mountain "through mud and briars", to see them.

She records that Sir George Bingham, Major Fehrzen, the Bertrand family and their own family group went to gather blackberries together — a berry unknown before to the French, the name, Bertrand thought, being that of a horse in *The Vicar of Wakefield*. Of Bertrand, her impression was that "He spoke little English, looked about so, and was the best of the whole party."

Stormy weather was in store for Mrs Younghusband. Gourgaud reported, "... almost a duel with Captain Harrison and her husband", a fine of 300 pounds because she had aspersed the moral character of Mrs Nagle and, later, trouble with Lowe because a letter of hers had been found among the papers of Las Cases when he was arrested. Nevertheless, she was a woman of high spirits, who could amuse and was a happy companion, and, from what the Balcombes left on record, they at any rate liked her. History has it she was a great-granddaughter of Oliver Cromwell.

* * *

Napoleon sometimes rode outside his boundary limits but avoided the main roads, avoided also the red-coated sentries, who now became a feature of the landscape. "*Toujours le chapeau,*" he said, indicating his raised hat to passers-by.

His dictation was hampered by insufficient reference books, and he awaited the store-ships and frigates with impatience. The library accumulated books with the arrival of every incoming vessel.

Sometimes he watched the seventy-fours beating up the trades to the anchorage and the staff left him alone with his spy-glass, a solitary figure breasting the wind, seeing in the might and significance of the vessel a symbol of supreme power.

During these first days he still had a capacity for keen feeling. Later illness and physical distress dulled the poignancy of his lost estate, though never the thoughts of his son.

In the measure of dreams and reality, of miserable living and an even more desolate prospect of death, the boy alone became the focal point of the Emperor's thinking. It was always to his own family that Napoleon looked at last for help. He trusted that they would act in concert to alleviate his condition if they did nothing more. Although he was under no illusion as to their characters, he cherished the hope that the clan instinct uppermost in the Corsican nature would influence them sufficiently to take combined action and ventilate his reiterated demands for removal to another place with a kinder climate in which to live — and greater opportunity for a normal existence. Some members of his family, he knew, were impoverished, but Joseph lived in America in grandeur and luxury, while others had found shelter under the protection of Pope Pius VII. Madame Mère, with a considerable fortune, was domiciled in a gloomy palace in Rome, where the Pope, a pious and admirable man, manifested his high esteem for her. They talked of Napoleon. The prelate's religion taught him to look beyond the present scenes and pictures; perhaps he saw the final apotheosis of a great and complex spirit, understood the Gethsemane through which Napoleon was now passing. He met Madame Mère sometimes when out driving, she surrounded by the green and gold of Napoleon's Imperial livery. In his great simplicity he would alight, go to the carriage door, greet Madame Mère and, walking a short way with her, ask, "Have you received any news from our good Emperor?" Madame, limited as to education but immensely shrewd, would tell him all she knew, which was little enough — word-of-mouth messages, third-hand reports, sometimes a smuggled letter, the whole too scrappy a basis on which to formulate any true picture.

"Everything I have," she reiterated, "belongs to the Emperor, from whom I got everything," but she made no move to call on the family to speak with a united voice. Perhaps in her astuteness she appreciated how improbable was the prospect of success. Cardinal Fesch, a halfbrother, looked after her affairs, and she felt safe in the kindly atmosphere the gentle Pope engendered. It was he, finally, who wrote to intercede with the Prince Regent in favour of Bonaparte.

"We must both remember," wrote the Pontiff to his Minister, "that next after God it is Napoleon who was chiefly responsible for the re-establishment of religion in the great Kingdom of France. It would be an unparalleled joy in our heart to have had a part in lessening Napoleon's sufferings. He cannot be a danger to anyone; we wish that he might not be a remorse to anyone."

The Minster translated the sentiments to the Prince Regent, who did not acknowledge the receipt of the letter.

Although he avoided the roads, Napoleon sought distraction on horseback and took to circling the boundary until he remarked he felt it had become a riding school. He knew every aspect, every tree (there were not many), the changing face of the Barn, the mountain in the foreground, the bugle calls from below. He continued intermittently to learn English (a language he never conquered), and Las Cases became his teacher. Betsy conscientiously helped, but the language was completely strange to him and it seemed impossible to render his thoughts into the English idiom.

He wrote a letter to Las Cases:

"Longwood, this morning, the seven March, Thursday, one thousand eight hundred sixteen after nativity the yors Jesus Christ. Since sixt week y learn the english. Sixt wek do fourty and two day. If might have learn fivty word for day i could know it two thousands and two hundred. It is [Italian *C'è*] in the dictionary more of [Italian *di*] fourty thousand for knows it [percio si sa] on hundred and twenty wek which do more two years ..."

He never did try very much after that, though later at Longwood Jane and Betsy again endeavoured to instruct him.

Longwood House must have come as a shock to the exiles, even though for the last twenty years Napoleon had alternated between fabulous palaces and wartime billets; the leaking roofs, rotting floors and rats, added to the cessation of nearly all physical and mental activity, could have been nothing less than soul-destroying. He saw ahead a future bleak as the Barn and a loneliness as inevitable as the tides.

From the throne with the golden bees to the sofa with the shabby white drape, from the magnificence of the Tuileries to the tar-papered roof, the water-stained walls, of Longwood — there was no counterpart in recent history for this hideous metamorphosis.

Napoleon once described the throne to Betsy. It stood on a dais of twenty-two steps, half as high as the little knoll on which the Pavilion was built, and it was covered in blue with golden bees. The canopy of red velvet and the throne itself offered immense lighting effects in the Tuileries garden on the night of his Coronation. He talked of it while the little *lampiste*'s lanterns bobbed around the Pavilion veranda in the night breeze, and a few lights twinkled in Jamestown down the valley. He told her of the garlands of lights, orange trees of fire, voices, crowds, the breath of a multitude. "A huge star hung above the Place de la Concorde. The palace looked like a tremendous fire. Four outdoor dance floors were crowded with jugglers, singers, Merry Andrews of every type, and fireworks — such fireworks! — continued through the night. It surpassed in splendour all previous displays of the kind."

After a short period of confusion, a certain routine evolved at Longwood. With the exception of Madame Bertrand, the suite, now all together under one roof, were briefed as to their duties. To the Grand Marshal, Bertrand, was confided the general superintendence, to Count Montholon the domestic details; Las Cases was to take care of the furniture and property and General Gourgaud the management of the stables. Dr O'Meara, Gourgaud and the orderly officer shared a tent; not very happily, however, for the suite had ceased to be members of one family, the spirit that moved them to face exile with their master having died in personal strife. Admiral Cockburn maintained that the Emperor was the most good-natured of the lot.

The Campaigns of Italy being finished, Napoleon spent time correcting the manuscript and commenced to dictate on other unspecified subjects. Anything served to kill time, now his mortal enemy. Dictation was his morning occupation, the afternoon still lay ahead and after that the evening, when the hours dragged by. The Longwood household dined together between eight and nine o'clock, Madame Montholon seated on Napoleon's right, Las Cases on his left, Gourgaud, Montholon and the page, Las Cases's son, opposite. More often than not Count Bertrand remained in the Hutt's Gate cottage, where his wife and children coped with leaking roofs and sundry other inconveniences to create finally something approaching a comfortable little home. The Montholons had not acquired Ross Cottage from William Balcombe and elected to take the rooms available at Longwood House. In the Longwood dining-room the smell of paint still lingered, in consequence of which ten minutes sufficed for the meal, dessert and coffee being served in the adjacent room.

Las Cases, in his book, records that once during dinner their talk centred on the two young ladies (the Balcombe girls) — one of them rather beautiful and very alluring, the other taller, much less attractive but 'sweeter' in manner, possessing perfect grace and poise. Opinions were divided. The Emperor firmly voted for the younger — he had known and liked her from the first day and was definitely on her side. Someone took the liberty of saying he would change his opinion if he knew the taller one as well as he knew Betsy. Napoleon asked them to express their individual views about the girls. The speaker remarked that he too preferred the younger sister, which seemed contradictory, and when asked for an explanation said, "If I wanted to marry a slave, I would settle on the first, but, if I wished to become a slave myself, I would address myself to Betsy." "That is to imply," retorted the Emperor, with some spirit, "that you think I am acting in bad form?" "No, sire, but I suspect Your Majesty to have the same feeling as mine." Napoleon laughed and did not contradict him.

The exiles struggled with *les convenances* — after dinner, if not at other times. The meal now became a kind of penance — the little dining-room sweltered from many lighted candles that set the silver a-shine. It was filled with serving-men who moved behind the silent diners. St Denis and Novarrez stood at the back of the Emperor's chair. The suite spoke in whispers. Bonaparte ate in silence; normally twenty minutes would be the average time spent at table, but now, owing to the paint, it was much sooner when he abruptly pushed his chair back and led the way to the drawing-room.

Conversation occupied them, old themes recurred to be talked out once more, incidents were revived, controversies and rash statements stirred past antagonisms, and all the while protocol demanded the wearisome period of standing. A gape from General Bertrand caused glances of reproof, and when Las Cases leaned against the wall the Grand Marshal in turn made clear his disapproval, so narrow had become their orbit. It was the Emperor who showed a disposition to lift the scene from utter boredom. He required that books be read aloud — Molière, Racine and Voltaire. Sometimes he played reversis, a favourite game remembered from subaltern days. The thoughts that accompanied it were pleasant, and he endeavoured to concentrate on them, but found himself unable to do so for long; the only emotion remaining was the will to win, which by itself kept his interest while the game lasted but left the interludes between its close and bedtime hard to face.

Certain people known to him before he moved to Longwood came to dine. It was quite an event welcomed by everybody. Usually the suite were in a state of extreme weariness, stifling yawns, unutterably bored, yet as obedient to court dictates as if Paris and the magnificence of the Tuileries still surrounded them.

The days passed, unmarked by seasonal change, merging one into the other. Habits were formed, the times of eating, of rising, of writing, only to be altered in an effort to make the hours pass a little more speedily. The quasi-royal state was maintained; the servants, a trained band under Montholon's supervision, were nevertheless ill-controlled; he was not adept at keeping a household in order. Sometimes Napoleon had to administer reprimands owing to some oversight like the omission of buckles or a general untidiness in demeanour or duty. Marchand and St Denis (Ali), the two valets perhaps the closest to him of all the followers in his captivity, took premier place in the hierarchy below stairs. Cipriani and Pierron came next in seniority. They wore the green livery bordered with silver, white vest, black silk knee-breeches, white silk stockings and buckled shoes. Marchand and St Denis wore a similar uniform, but with gold trimmings. Pierron struggled with the kitchen. Le Page, a mediocre cook, aided him, together with local assistants, and the other servants fulfilled their duties in a generally haphazard manner.

At nine o'clock sentries entered the garden and surrounded the actual building. Nobody could enter without a pass. No one could leave except under guard.

Rats continued to run everywhere; thoroughly disturbed by the alterations, they congregated under the house, fled across the rooms between the Emperor's feet during dinner — on one occasion jumped out of his hat, left uppermost on the table — squealed and scurried behind the pine walls. One bit a servant on the leg and Bertrand, at Hutt's Gate, was nipped on the hand when asleep. Notwithstanding all this, the royal state was upheld. At night the ladies would appear in décolletage, hair dressed as if for some formal function. The officers wore full dress. Etiquette continued to keep them standing in the Emperor's presence, though he invited the ladies to be seated.

Fifty-one persons dwelt in Longwood House, in itself no more than a medium-sized building with rooms and outhouses barely answering to the demands of ordinary living conditions, all very inconvenient and unsuitable, not to say insanitary. The kitchens were too close to the Emperor's bedroom, and the smell of food drifted into the passage with the wood smoke from an ill-built chimney. Pierron finally departed on that account, declaring the fumes had made him ill, and a later chef, who came out to assist the limited Le Page, likewise complained bitterly. How the immense amount of cooking required could have been undertaken with success from such primitive conditions is remarkable. I have recently seen the stove. Although now unused, it remains in place and unchanged, the small bread-oven beside it.

Sometimes Napoleon talked to Las Cases of his early years, of his schooldays at Brienne, where as a poor stranger he learnt what it was to be a boy without pocket-money. He said, "At Brienne I was the poorest of all my school fellows. They always had money in their pockets, I never. I was proud and was most careful that nobody should perceive this. I could neither laugh nor amuse myself like the others."

It was from Brienne he wrote a letter to the British Admiralty requesting permission to enter the British Navy. He took it to an English boy (who later became Lord Wenlock) to read, and made the remark that his religion might prevent him from gaining his objective. The boy answered he didn't think Bonaparte had any religion, whereupon Napoleon replied that his family had, and he would probably be disinherited by them if he became a heretic. His letter is still in the Admiralty Archives. Perhaps he remembered it when he stood, very moved, at the farewell the sailors on the *Northumberland* accorded him. Some changing fate might have made him one with them.

Reverting to his early days, he recalled that he was known as 'The Corsican'. He knew that to be "a little boy neither more nor less distinguished than his fellows, poor, and struggling to learn a new language" was sometimes almost more than he could support.

The members of the suite functioned in their respective fields of activity, if not with amity, at least with a show of indifference to one another's shortcomings, Gourgaud being the only real disturber of tranquillity.

Madame Montholon, in bad health, spent much of her time in bed and it was common practice for Napoleon to cross from his dining-room over the black and white tiled floor that marked the division of their quarters to sit with her and gossip of the day's events and enjoy the scent of the roses he had planted outside. Little protection was needed from flies or insects on the island, and the night air came in faint drifts through open windows, a pleasing aftermath of the brisk trades of the daytime. Island gossip had it that one of Madame Montholon's children — Napoleone by name — who since lived to be an old lady of more than ninety — was Napoleon's. Montholon's moral cowardice was recognised by the more stalwart Bertrand, who bore with him with fortitude, though not so Madame Bertrand; and it was as well for the peace of the little community that the Bertrands, with their family, dwelt apart from the main home.

The appearance of the billiard room now suggested a kind of common-room. There were books galore, more and more arriving in crates from the store-ships, their contents examined in the Customs Shed, some of the volumes detained there merely because they carried the Imperial cypher. Those he received gave absorbing pleasure to the exile, who personally unpacked them and spent hours skimming the pages, dropping some around him on the floor and piling others beside him for further reference. Two great globes on ebony feet stood on either side of the door. He had shown Betsy the extent of France on their surface, turning the spheres with slow deliberation, "a pretty Empire with Paris and Rome as capitals".

Mischievously he pointed out little England — only an island, certainly bigger than St Helena ("but quite safe," retorted Betsy, conscious of her naval background). His conversations on world affairs had begun to educate her undisciplined mind and a liking for politics in later years was born of those hours, though at the time her scatterbrain thoughts were more often than not occupied with other things. She had stood behind him when, spyglass at the peep-hole cut in the shutters, he had first seen the Allied commissioners pass into the garden, or Lowe himself, with his regimental officers, ride by. She had heard Napoleon's comments, and in turn proffered gossip about the Sturmers and Montchenu. It brought them together perhaps more than lessons at billiards or at the globes, or marking old battle formations on the hanging maps. It became a game — a bitter grown-up hide-and-seek played with the same rules.

Later, when regulations were tightened still further, dodging the sentries was also a pastime Betsy indulged in, in which the sentries played as well, for she found her way across the boundary whenever she wished.

When H.M.S. *Phaeton*, carrying Sir Hudson Lowe, dropped anchor, uneasy anticipation permeated the island. Bluff Admiral Cockburn had appealed to the Navy-conscious community; they understood him, and his lieutenants carried out his orders with a certain tact, and notwithstanding the fact that Napoleon clashed with the Admiral on several occasions, Cockburn acted in an impersonal and official capacity and did not allow personalities to intrude. The matter of the Emperor's status and the fact that his royal titles were disallowed by Government order continued to incense Napoleon and caused his suite to over-emphasise his Imperial majesty in the confines of Longwood. As a General he rode abroad — as an Emperor he entered Longwood, with his Empire half the world away under the dominance, if not the actual administration, of enemies. He remembered with bitterness to what heights France had risen, from a bloodbath of despair and hysteria. The time, the place and the person for its deliverance had indeed synchronised, and the later odium of failure which troubled his thoughts sent him pacing about moodily, turning over situations, incidents, conversations, in an overburdened mind, causing a mental irritant that rarely left him and probably contributed to the ulcer that finally brought his end.

William Balcombe, one of the first to receive copies of regulations and procedures in relation to the 'foreigners', as the exiles became known to the Jamestown shopkeepers, consistently chose the middle path, and sustained the level of deference the Imperial captive warranted. To his mind the fortunes of war did not alter the dictates of decent behaviour and from the beginning he constituted a buffer between Governor Wilks and Cockburn on the one hand, and the irritable French on the other, his actions actuated by anxiety to establish a good relationship before both were superseded by Sir Hudson Lowe. Sir Mark, a servant of the East India Company, was retired.

Balcombe endeavoured to curb the exuberance of his family even though he realised their nonsense and laughter eased Napoleon's moodiness, and that the Emperor had dwelt with anticipation on their daily coming to the Pavilion and now to Longwood. To him, experienced, dominant and the former controller of monarchs, cessation of activity had become soul-destroying and he grasped at any diversion. In Betsy he perceived the antithesis of the women he had known, with the possible exception of his own mother (Madame Mère). As was his custom towards women, he openly paid her compliments, which it amused him to see she accepted objectively and with casualness. Also he feared for her; knowing her to be peculiarly defenceless and that, for all her self-confidence, her appearance and personality would later give rise to difficulties. In that he was correct. But to Betsy the fate of kings, the aftermath of battles, meant little when applied to Napoleon. Her awareness at the outset focused on the strange, compelling man now divested of any mantle of greatness — and remained so.

An extensive library of the period has enabled me to compare incidents in chronicles each representing their author's point of view, yet all factual in essentials, any divergence being so slight as to be negligible, with one exception — Betsy's diary by inference made Piontkowski's first visit to Napoleon occur at the Briars. On returning to the notes after reading other descriptions, I realised its ambiguity, and put it down to the result of loose writing, for Napoleon had gone into residence at Longwood when Piontkowski first appeared, yet Betsy clearly stated they met at the Briars. She evidently knew more than she recorded, for she said after the interview, which was a long one punctuated with argument, that she found the Emperor thoughtful and uncommunicative. He told her he was grateful for the Count's devotion, but he said "he knew little of him", a statement which is open to doubt. She noted that afterwards he continued walking up and down in deep thought.

It is possible that Piontkowski, who had called at the Briars to request an interview, actually did meet Napoleon there and not at Longwood. During Cockburn's command, this was not unlikely, but Betsy's divergence from other reports, which definitely state that Piontkowski went to Longwood, is so unusual that notice must be taken of it, specially as Piontkowski still remains something of a mystery. Unbidden by Napoleon, he was allowed by the British Government to land at St Helena and to attach himself to the Emperor's household when others, such as Las Cases's wife and Gourgaud's old servant, were forbidden. That Napoleon did not see him again is also on record, although he hovered around the French staff for some months before finally leaving for Cape Town. It is generally asserted he spied for the British. The staff avoided him when possible, called him a 'Pole', and Gourgaud found him out to be a liar who "spread false statements about past campaigns".

Napoleon openly suspected him, mainly because he had plenty of money from unnamed sources. On Elba, as a poverty-stricken trooper in the Polish Lancers, he had been granted a lieutenant's salary and given a commission because of his supposed fidelity to the Emperor. Piontkowski was, and still remains, a mystery.

CHAPTER II

The General and his Jailer

His Excellency, Sir Hudson Lowe, the new Governor, became more than a name to the inmates of Longwood on the 5th May 1816. Accompanied by his wife, two step-daughters, and the Deputy-Adjutant-General, Sir Thomas Reade, Major Gorrequer, A.D.C., and Mr Janesch, the writer, he arrived armed with a warrant that invested him with complete powers over Napoleon's person. On hearing of his appointment in London, he had written to Sir Henry Bunbury, an Admiralty official, that, "in his opinion a law was necessary declaring it a felony to engage in any attempt to hold communication with Napoleon or with his adherents, except with the authority of the Government." That in a word epitomised his outlook.

From the first, the impact of Sir Hudson's exacting personality was felt by the exiles at Longwood. By hearsay they knew him as a Colonel of the 'Renegades' — a regiment formed by the British from men of Napoleon's own birthplace — and appreciated the fact that Dr Baxter, Colonel Lyster and others of minor rank on the Governor's staff had served in the same regiment, and were now coming to St Helena to fill official positions connected with Longwood.

Napoleon regarded the appointment as a personal affront. He considered Lowe to be at best a 'desk soldier'. Lowe had some aptitude for organisation and a reputation for meticulous planning, while, through Cipriani, Napoleon was also made aware of the new Governor's efficacy as an intelligence officer. Cipriani and Lowe had already met in Capri — and the suite feared, with cause, that in consequence he came as a biased administrator.

True enough, Lowe immediately spread a network of intelligence among the simple island folk, and learned practically all there was to know about the conditions, habits, friends and even conversations of the prisoners. What information he gleaned presented a picture of an adequately guarded but unconventional prison existence; the sea guards, the soldiers of the 53rd plus the terrain combined to deter any thought of escape. He discovered also, however, seeds of acceptance and affection between the island and the newcomers, and the glimmerings of what he felt might grow into a definite attachment to the illustrious captive. Sensitive to trends and conditions, he caught the feeling immediately and feared it; with the strength of friends, what could not Napoleon achieve?

As the only British officials serving with the Emperor's household, Dr O'Meara and William Balcombe came under fire from the moment of Lowe's arrival, and his calumnies openly voiced against O'Meara are difficult to credit, and as difficult to substantiate. I may perhaps be swayed by family gossip passed on from my great-grandfather, who trusted and liked O'Meara, and as he and O'Meara were the only men of British nationality closely attached to the Emperor's person he was in a position to judge. In later years the family in Australia described O'Meara as a warm-hearted, flamboyant Irishman, well-liked generally and especially popular with the officers of the 53rd Regiment.

Forsyth, Sir Hudson Lowe's apologist and a mediocre 'Boswell', attempts in the first part of his collection of the Lowe-Bathurst letters to vindicate certain of the Governor's interpretations of British orders in respect of Napoleon's treatment. The result is unsatisfying. All through the three volumes of correspondence and reports he takes pains to highlight items of a nature favourable to Lowe and one finds him regarding complacently the harsh and obscure incidents arising from Lowe's administration. Having scrutinised the major portions of the Lowe-Bathurst letters (there are more than ninety folios), I am convinced Forsyth's choice of those included in his work confirms his bias, that overall he produces a dull collection of documents along with a revealing portrait of the Governor, a copy of which now hangs in the Castle among those of other Governors of the island. As well as Napoleon's unflattering comments on his appearance, somewhere else there is a further description of Lowe: "A man of reddish hair and pale eye-lashes, about five feet seven inches in height, spare of build, thin-lipped, a dark blemish on his face, an individual strangely out of character for the task assigned him." His portrait depicts a face of limitations and creates an impression of a man who sheltered behind the written order. Below the acquired layers of a military education, custom and discipline, an inferiority complex added impetuousness to a natural meanness. During the wars he had served on the Continent and about the Mediterranean, where it is noted he left some illegitimate children, and his rise from mediocrity dated from the time the Corsican Rangers became his command. His appointment as Napoleon's jailer appeared as a studied insult, and to Napoleon he always remained, above all else, a Colonel of a renegade Corsican regiment.

With the guns of the fleet and the army contributing their brassy welcome, Admiral Cockburn conducted the formal reception of the new Governor with full honours, and, awaiting the appropriate moment to spring from whale-boat to jetty, Lowe landed, followed by a comprehensive retinue. He was a model of correctness — cocked hat, sword and medals — but Admiral Cockburn, standing with his officers to receive him, took immediate exception to the unprepossessing manner and demeanour in which he approached the little ceremony.

His complacency and obvious satisfaction with his new command was so noticeable as to trouble the good Admiral, who felt an instinctive dislike, which William Balcombe, one of the first to meet him, shared. Indeed the latter was never on more than formal terms with Lowe all through their many dealings during the next two or three years.

On 11th May 1816, one of Sir Hudson Lowe's first orders read:

"From the Adjutant's Office ——

"In addition to the regulations hitherto enacted by Rear-Admiral Sir George Cockburn, K.C.B., and the Governor-in-Council of this island, it is further explicitly declared that no person is to receive or, to be the bearer of any letters or communications from General Bonaparte, the officers of his suite, his followers or servants of any description; or to deliver any to them (as such communications are to take place through the Governor alone). Any persons transgressing this order will be immediately arrested and otherwise dealt with accordingly.

"By Command of His Excellency, Lieut.-General Sir Hudson Lowe, K.C.B., Governor and Commander-in-Chief etc. etc. etc.

(signed) T. Reade,
"Lieut.-Colonel, Deputy-Adjutant-General."

The first act after Sir Hudson Lowe's arrival on the 5th was a curt intimation that he would visit General Bonaparte at nine a.m. on the 16th, and, accompanied by staff officers, he arrived at Longwood in a rainstorm, to be informed by a member of the suite that the Emperor was indisposed and could not be seen. It was common knowledge that Napoleon rarely rose at that hour, but that he was unwell seemed subject to doubt. Sir Hudson Lowe paced furiously up and down before the Longwood windows, in the downpour, considering the next move. The fact that Napoleon had added, "The Governor had not asked before for an audience," stung him. It was a bad start in their relations. An onlooker has left a description of the Governor's arrival the full regimentals of the accompanying officers, the nodding plumes and flash accoutrements, soaking slowly in the Longwood weather, the bleak silence outside as well as within, and the frowning bulk of the Barn.

On the next day protocol was observed and the Governor admitted to an audience. Even so, something untoward happened. Admiral Cockburn accompanied him to make the necessary presentation, and they had planned to proceed together into the room in which Napoleon was to receive them; Sir Hudson, in his anxiety, stepped forward first and Novarrez, the servant at the door, having been instructed to admit only one visitor, barred the way to the Admiral, who, in high anger, waited alone in the ante-room. Lowe, too gauche to notice his absence for some minutes, and then having no inclination to do anything about it, left him there. Cockburn walked out of Longwood almost immediately.

Napoleon took an instinctive dislike to the new Governor, saying afterwards that he was hideous and had a most ugly countenance; but, he added, he "should not judge too hastily". Between 17th May and the next visit many wordy communications passed. The correspondence between Lowe and the Secretary of State imperfectly reflects the rising tempo of anger; only the pettiness of the detail is paramount. On the thirtieth, the interview proved even more stormy. Napoleon railed at his treatment, declaring the Allies wished to kill him by a lingering death. It would be kinder to deprive him of life at once. He complained of the inadequacies of Longwood and when Lowe told him of a wooden house, equipped with every convenience, that was on its way from England, he shouted it was not a house, but a coffin and an executioner, Lowe wanted. The house was a mockery, death would be a privilege. Presently Napoleon snatched up same reports of the military campaigns of 1814, which lay on the table, and asked Lowe if he had written them; Lowe, on admitting the fact, was told they were "full of folly and falsehood".

The Governor retired, displaying more restraint than anybody had hoped, and Napoleon, in a towering rage, harangued the suite upon his 'sinister expression', abusing him in the worst terms, and called upon a servant to throw a cup of coffee out of the window because it had stood for a moment on a table beside Sir Hudson.

The portrait of Sir Hudson Lowe displays all the uncompromising stubbornness of character of a small man. Napoleon saw in him the soldier rigid from a life of discipline and knew the forced severity he presented was the mask of the psychologically unsure. That the immense fallen colossus should be placed in the charge of such a character was a tragedy and a blunder beyond comprehension. A spirit of resentment and an urge to retaliate resulted from these unfortunate interviews.

Sir Thomas Reade did nothing to soften the regime. Major Gorrequer's letters give the impression that the orders he had so often to transmit in his impeccable handwriting were distressing to him. If his notes on the closing phases of the drama were ever to be made available, a fair and unbiased picture might be expected. Unfortunately, when a move was made to print them some years ago, 'urgent considerations' prevented their publication, and they are now locked away. Perhaps it is still too early for them to be brought to the light of day. Mr Janesch, Sir Hudson Lowe's clerk, also lent valuable help in the function of amanuensis, writing a legible hand that stands out by comparison with that of other documents.

Mr Janesch's task while at Plantation House appeared to consist of writing letters from dictation and making copies for reference, and he must have spent many pleasant hours in the little office along the hall by the library. It has a lived-in feeling nowadays and the echo of many voices clings to its walls. Janesch steps in and out of the Lowe Papers, a discreet ghost content to play a minor part, leaving faithful records and a copper-plate calligraphy.

William Balcombe's methods of business and general behaviour came under review almost from the first week of the new Governor's arrival, as did the books of the Company in so far as they concerned the Emperor. Almost daily Balcombe went up the road to Plantation House in response to calls on some matter of routine or purchase of stock. The Governor probed every detail of the purveyorship, queried methods, criticised and censured, as if resentful of the regulations laid down by Sir George Cockburn. An easily roused irritation kept him moving about the room from window to desk, gesticulating and unrestful. It was usually in the little office that he and Balcombe met, though sometimes they sat in the courtyard where later the library was erected, most of their conversations faithfully recorded by Major Gorrequer. William Balcombe kept asserting strenuously that no household of the Emperor's size and calibre could be supported on the new amount of £8,000. He pointed out that provisions were expensive on the island, as indeed were most items, and the advent of a regiment did not improve the overall situation, since most commodities had to be carried by ship. Lowe brushed aside objections, however, over-ruled existing procedure and ordered the cheapest of the East India Company's stores to be sent to Longwood, saying meanly, "prisoners cannot be choosers!"

Examples of William Balcombe's letters are to be seen in the Lowe volumes; these are mainly trivial, but show a strong combatant spirit in their answers to Lowe's demands that in some cases amounted to actual accusations. In spite of these disagreements, Lowe placed in his hands large sums for negotiation on the exile's behalf. Later, by Lowe's order, the money for the Emperor's broken-up plate he alone was allowed to administer. It was the Emperor's personal influence Lowe feared, not only over William Balcombe, but on everyone else. Napoleon's uncanny charm, for men and women alike, created an intense hero-worship. Lowe saw it everywhere: among the visitors who sought a glimpse of the short, rotund figure and went away delighted if they succeeded in engaging him in a few minutes' conversation; the sailors who hung around the boundary watching for the man in white breeches, green coat and cocked hat; the children who romped with him and ran races for sugar-plums; the staff who remained voluntarily exiled, incompatible yet bound together by the same hero-worship and a devotion rarely accorded any similar character in history.

Lowe knew well enough that Napoleon did not actually entertain hopes of escape; the hazards were too great. He realised that at this stage all the good that Napoleon could do his cause would be to excite enough sympathy to influence European public opinion in his favour, so that, once the peace was signed and the troops withdrawn from Paris, he might be allowed to live privately in the English countryside or in America, for his time of active leadership had passed. All this Napoleon strove for by continuous correspondence with his family and the Bonapartist groups, and by indirect influence on travellers passing through, highlighting the primitive state of his lodging, the privations, the restraints, the rats, the climate. All the drawbacks were ventilated as well by the staff, who sent uncensored bulletins abroad with almost contemptuous ease. It showed a weakness in the administration, and so Lowe felt he must stop it or forfeit his prestige.

Nevertheless, after his arrival, letters still found their way to the British Press. He suspected everybody — O'Meara, Balcombe, the visiting sea-captains who were occasionally granted passes to call on Napoleon. The soiled linen was searched for clandestine documents, the servants were watched, yet the London papers continued to publish a wealth of uncensored information.

Officially no letter left Longwood sealed. The Governor's office read all letters and either returned or despatched them, as was thought fit, and in many instances whole portions were copied verbatim for the perusal of Lord Bathurst. Even the transcripts of Montholon's letters to his wife, after she finally returned to Europe, are still to be seen in the Lowe Papers. The French knew that there was no privacy in their correspondence and the fact created a bitterness and despair. There was little freedom now. Credit was refused in shops, no visitor came except with the Governor's pass. The household felt the pinch of reduced living expenses, no books were delivered but by the Governor's permission; newspapers were censored — the cut-out portions an insult trivial in itself, but injurious in its implication.

The boundaries within which Napoleon might ride were narrowed considerably. This was a mean and vengeful order and the Emperor rejected the idea of horseback exercise and remained within the grounds. It is possible that this deprivation hastened his end. Added to the other frustrations and curtailments, the seeds of the disease that killed him found culture in the unhealthiness of the general conditions. Both Betsy and her mother sensed some alteration in him and spoke of it. Betsy could sometimes rouse a return of the boisterous fun of their days at the Briars, but not often. With the narrowing horizon, his outlook centred on the smaller repressions the regimentation built up around him; his once immense appreciation of world affairs was replaced by a concentration upon the Governor's new strictures or on otherwise immaterial acts of petty jealousy between his fellow exiles, which he, with great gentleness, strove to resolve.

William Balcombe had a long and difficult interview with the Governor after an almost equally lengthy talk with the Controller at Longwood. By that time Napoleon's dislike for Lowe had become almost an obsession, and the petty annoyances and curtailments a constant irritant. The purveyor informed Lowe of the situation, pointing out that now fifty-one people lived in Longwood and had to be fed and that they were receiving sub-standard provisions. He was fated always to see the worst side of Lowe's character. The Governor's insecurity was made manifest in suddenly flaring outbursts of temper and stubborn refusals to consider any alteration to his orders.

He strode up and down the library biting his nails, shouting invectives against the prisoner and making such pronouncements as, "He is fortunate to have me in command." Emotion accentuated the brown disfiguring stain on his face and William Balcombe recognised the fundamental lack of balance that later clouded the Governor's actions towards Napoleon, the paroxysms of anger that made his speech unintelligible, that left him deaf to counsel and suggestion. The purveyor took his leave, filled with ill-concealed anxiety. Others beside himself had experienced similar scenes, had openly commented on them, and the tempo of the little community showed signs of being affected. The townspeople in self-defence withdrew into themselves and bore with the new Governor's moods, discussing his restless night rides to the guardhouse, his regulations and pronouncements. They watched Lady Lowe with impassive glances as she drove in her new carriage down the steep road to the little shops, missing nothing of her flamboyance, her rouge, and wondered if her cheerfulness was a front, or the outcome of a lack of sensibility. They did not know.

However, the new occupants at Plantation House settled in. Lowe treated Balcombe as a town merchant to be ordered, bullied; and at times openly mistrusted him. For a choleric ex-naval officer, with Carlton House connections, it became difficult to remain calm; but, mindful of the results, he did so, even when Lowe ordered him to buy condemned tinned provisions from the East India Company's stores, and to pay no more than a certain price for island sheep. The most trifling requisitions were required to be sent for approval. The diary of invoices, requisitions and notes from the staff make up a folio from which these few items are extracted:

"July 16, 1816: Mr Balcombe presents his compliments to Major Gorrequer and has sent herewith a request for the establishment for the calico requested by Dr O'Meara for bandages, etc., and the snuffers which are wanted, as they have now only one pair for the sitting room and require one pair each."

"Mr Balcombe presents his compliments to Major Gorrequer and requests he will give directions for claret for the establishment at Longwood as they have been without it for a day or two.

"Mr Balcombe begs to acquaint Major Gorrequer that General Montholon has requested to be supplied with a preparation of Cape butter for the purpose of making pastry as the English butter is found too soft." [Shortly afterwards, English butter was altogether discontinued]

"Mr Balcombe presents his compliments to Major Gorrequer and attention shall be paid to getting the utensils tinned as soon as possible. There being no solder in the stores, application has been made in the hospital for old pewter which will be inspected this afternoon. Mr Balcombe requests an order for the armourer to tin the utensils that are down, as they will have to be brought to the forge for that purpose."

"General Montholon intimates that the undermentioned articles will, for the future, be sufficient for daily consumption:

9 bottles of Claret
1 bottle " Madeira
1   "   " vin de Grave
1   "   " Champagne
1   "   " Constantia
6 bottles " Teneriffe
28   "   " Cape"

Answering complaints as to costs from Plantation House, William Balcombe writes, "The charges for candied oranges, dates, raisins and plums compare with the price cost of these articles and the difference of the price fixed." Ducks, goose, fowl and bread were found too expensive for the Emperor's table; complaints with regard to bread drew the answer that "the firm cannot charge the finest sort by weight as it requires much more baking".

The earlier items that were requisitioned for Napoleon at the Briars were ticked off in pencil. Later in the Lowe administration the receipts became formal.

Another communication from William Balcombe says, "There is nothing in the stores which will answer for linen and fustian but brown nankeen, or in the shop, but duck of the enclosed description at 4s. 6d. per yard." From Montholon there was an added requisition for duck 'trowsers' for soldier-servants and eight yards of duck, "which is required for bags for holding sugar, tea, candy, etc." Requisitions give an insight into the official mentality as well as the living conditions of the island. On the 4th November 1816, pork was sent to the soldier servants in lieu of beef, and on the same sheet were listed green tea, wax candles from The Honourable Company's stores, also sago, candy, flour and lard, while forty-five bushels of coal were ordered.

Montholon, incensed at the mounting petty restrictions, the refusal of requests, the scrutiny of the dirty linen, the mouldy provisions and bad bread, blamed William Balcombe and the firm, which however in no way displeased Lowe. Montholon had forgotten the first days, when, penniless, he and Bertrand had been glad enough to accept £100 each from William Balcombe to ease the situation.

CHAPTER 12

The Malcolms

Early in June the frigate *Newcastle* arrived, bringing Rear-Admiral Sir Pulteney Malcolm, his wife and two of the three Commissioners of the Allied Powers, Balmain of Russia and the Marquis de Montchenu of France. The Malcolms were to be a solace to the Emperor; kindly, fair-minded and well-born, they understood his impulses and so immediately incurred the mistrust of Lowe. The exiles had set high hopes on the Commissioners, but these faded after their attitude became known. O'Meara rode to Jamestown to gather any gossip, and Napoleon, full of questions on his return, received an unfavourable report.

Lowe came to Longwood on 20th June to introduce the newly arrived Malcolm. Cockburn had left the evening before on the *Northumberland*, his mission completed — and not unsuccessfully. He had been the instrument of transmitting unpalatable truths to the Emperor, had softened the impact of every new restriction, had quarrelled with him when it was unavoidable and now departed with a little anxiety as to the future of his erstwhile charge in the hands of Lowe, and, perhaps, with some regret. He took away with him the twelve English sailors from the *Northumberland* he had lent to Napoleon's household.

His reports to the Prince Regent must have been factual and not untinged with pity.

Sir Pulteney Malcolm's arrival was a stroke of good fortune for Napoleon. He remarked that the Admiral had an agreeable, open, intelligent and sincere face: a fine specimen of an Englishman. "Really, he is as pleasant to look at as a pretty woman. He says what he thinks frankly and courageously and is not afraid to look you in the eye." This was an oblique endorsement, by contrast, of Lowe's tendency to look away from anyone who held him in conversation.

To Lady Malcolm, Napoleon showed special favour even though he knew that, being an Elphinstone, she was a niece of Lord Keith (Lord High Admiral of the British Fleet, and Napoleon's stumbling-block at Plymouth), the first man to give him the title of General.

Napoleon admired her nevertheless. The Malcolms were of the world and as she sat beside him on the sofa at their first meeting — small, round-shouldered, frankly ugly — he reflected she was the first plain woman he had ever warmed to. She painted and powdered, had no taste in dress, and, as he said, "her colour schemes made her resemble an aged macaw." Madame Montholon derided her, but Napoleon, recognising her generous heart and sympathy, found her lively and full of good spirits, while in him she saw a strangely appealing man in a worn coat, wearing the Star of the Legion, and sensed the kindness of heart that had saved her brother at Waterloo. Later, Napoleon held intimate conversations with the Admiral, receiving him in his bedroom, without dressing. They talked out old battles, of Trafalgar and Waterloo, even the Emperor's plans for the invasion of England; they discussed the future, and what might have happened had things gone differently. Napoleon among his jailers had found a friend.

Although the Malcolms could by their code and upbringing do nothing that might run counter to their country's interests and honour, yet they were incensed at Lowe's stupidities and his unnecessary harshness. Later, they even withdrew somewhat from the Emperor's company, fearing their friendship would injure Longwood by further exciting Lowe's anger.

Lady Malcolm, plain but vivacious, was capable of easing tension and understood situations without explanation. Napoleon welcomed both herself and the Admiral and made pertinent remarks about the Longwood party. Sir Pulteney ridiculed Lowe's nightmares, his sudden springing out of bed with shouts that "he must ride to Longwood, Napoleon had escaped", but he was too loyal to say much. However, Lowe and he had some bitter passages on the exile's treatment; on the puerile bickerings concerning the boundary line; the cross-questionings that took place on a chance meeting with the suite on the road; the lack of milk (as a concession, when Napoleon lay dying, Lowe sent to know if he wanted milk) and the retention of books. The stupidity of it all angered the factual Admiral and he voiced his protest, but he found it in the Emperor's interests to be wary. Sir Pulteney had visited Paris in 1815, walked over the Waterloo battlefield and returned by Brussels, where he had danced on the eve of Waterloo and where now he found the city to be little more than a great hospital. He flinched from the immense wastage of war, still starkly displayed. Occupied Paris had left him bewildered — where travellers, by-passing the sights of Waterloo, flocked to see the concourse of kings, emperors, famous statesmen and celebrities, while the greatest of them was still under British canvas on the way to St Helena. From a theoretical standpoint, nobody in Paris was better than the next, and there were strange contrasts. From the Élysée, Wellington, with his superb evenness of mind, wrote to Sir Pulteney Malcolm:

"PARIS, APRIL 3rd, 1816.

"My dear Malcolm,
"I am very much obliged to you for Mr Simpson's book which I will read when I shall have a moment's leisure. I am glad you have taken command at St Helena, upon which I congratulate you. You must never be idle if you can avoid it.
"You may tell 'Bony' that I find his apartments at the Élysée Bourbon very convenient and that I hope he likes mine at Mr Balcombe's. It is a droll sequel enough to the affairs of Europe that we should change places of residence.

"I am yours most sincerely,

(Signed) WELLINGTON."

On the boulevards, a crowded concourse of camp followers, of broken armies and a population filled with relief and joy at the ending — any ending acceptable — of war made a kaleidoscope scene with no pattern and little reconstruction.

The Admiral had experienced it all — the parades, the crowds, Talma acting again, Wellington's formal dinners, Grassini's music (did Grassini now think of those moments with Bonaparte?), opera, with Highland pipers and reels. Sir Pulteney wrote at the time, "The joy which the people of the capital display makes me melancholy. I continue to think of what is past. They seem satisfied with the present and are no wiser ..." He discovered, however, there were people who still thought of Napoleon. One told him, "You English possess the greatest man that ever existed in the world." To see Napoleon in his threadbare coat, his moments of melancholy that lifted when he caught sight of them, hurt the Admiral and his wife miserably. The captivity was made over-drastic and ill-regulated, soul as well as body being held prisoner.

Lady Malcolm's first visit to Napoleon began adventurously. She rode from Plantation House to Hutt's Gate, where the Bertrands were still installed, to find, as was arranged, Bonaparte's carriage (Colonel Wilks's old barouche) waiting.

She described the drive, "Two of Bonaparte's former postillions [the Archambaults], slightly elevated, took the carriage at a gallop down the road where, near the guardhouse, the horses shied and nearly tipped us into the Devil's Punch Bowl."

Madame Bertrand and Lady Malcolm hung on grimly. Later she and Madame exchanged confidences — wistfully she told Lady Malcolm that hers had been the gayest house in Paris, that the months spent in St Helena were like years, and that she hoped soon she could go home.

Lady Malcolm confided she had a "sort of alarm at meeting the man whose deeds for 20 years had filled Europe". Madame bade her not to be afraid, "he was so good, so kind." They came to the ante-room where Gourgaud, Montholon and Las Cases awaited. There was a certain formality. Bertrand appeared from an adjoining room and requested them to walk in.

Napoleon asked Lady Malcolm how she felt after the voyage. Had she been sick? Did she amuse herself by embroidery? Lady Malcolm thought Napoleon spoke "thickly and quick", and as she knew little French, she lost much of his meaning. The Admiral took over, however, and they talked of Ossian, Napoleon's favourite poetry, and hers, because she was Scottish, from the Western Isles. She noted he wore an old threadbare green coat, with green velvet collar and cuffs, silver buttons and the silver Star of the Legion of Honour. She was struck by the kindness of his expression, but allowed that it changed with his mood. She noted his short upper lip and capacious forehead. His hair had rather a dirty look, he talked naval strategy with the Admiral until the end of the interview, and remarked that "many well-informed men are of the opinion that England loses more than she gains by the possession of that overgrown and remote Empire".

He spoke of escape and said he would never give his parole. He asked Malcolm, mischievously, whether he thought it possible. "I do not know what you would be tempted to do on shore, Monsieur, but keep away from the sea, for that is my province," the Admiral told him. It was then the Emperor remarked again he wished only to live in England, "a few leagues from London".

Later, when he had attained to terms of close friendship, he complained bitterly of Lowe's limitation of the boundaries; it eased his pent-up feelings.

When, at the end of the Admiral's appointment, the Malcolms came to say good-bye to Napoleon on their return to England, the Admiral told him he was hoping to come back. Napoleon gave Lady Malcolm a Sèvres cup and saucer, one of his depleted set (for he gave portions of it away on one special occasion after another). He told Malcolm he would not make any present to him because he was "not a man to listen to reason". He went on, more seriously, "The ladies have a softer heart for us unfortunates."

O'Meara, Balcombe and the Admiral, in their several ways, watched Napoleon with anxiety and some pity. They could only give alleviation in some minor instances but they did what was possible.

Lowe, ever suspicious, could not at first interfere with the visits but later had some brushes with the Admiral. Perhaps he felt that Sir Pulteney might supersede him in the position of Governor. It was rumoured. By now his hatred of the exile was almost psychopathic; and badly advised by rough-spoken Reade, with nobody close enough in rank to exercise influence, Lowe persisted with the silly regulations and restrictions. Daily incidents occurred on the main roads between exiles and guards. Blatant spying by the two gardeners working under the Emperor's windows became a constant irritation to him, and although the house was now a little more habitable it still bore the atmosphere of a jail. Napoleon clung to his 'inner rooms' and none could enter them unbidden. The pistols lay ready for use and the orderly officer knew if he entered he would face death. In later days a tense interlude occurred when Lowe, goaded by long intervals of withdrawal on the part of the Emperor, endeavoured to force the situation. Unless Bonaparte was 'sighted', no ships could sail. Indeed some were held for days awaiting the signal that told of his reappearance.

One morning William Balcombe told the girls to be ready to ride with him, as they had been specially invited to visit Longwood. Napoleon, declaring he was ill, had not been seen for several days and had kept closely indoors, causing Captain Nicholls to send despairing despatches to the Governor, announcing that he had caught no glimpses of Napoleon nor had 'the gardener'. It was misty weather, with intermittent rain squalls. A kind of *crise-de-nerfs* invaded Longwood, creating bickering and more than usual discontent among the suite, and, in the case of Gourgaud, an outbreak of jealousy over the Emperor's favour that caused him to weep and declare he would return to France.

After greeting the girls, Napoleon demanded to know why they had stayed away so long; they were neglecting him, he declared. Had the Governor instilled fear in their hearts? Betsy answered, for her part, that she had been suffering from a sunstroke contracted when climbing earlier in the week. She, Jane and the latter's new beau, Captain Mackie, had decided to walk to the Wilkses' — then on the eve of departure to England — by way of Peak Hill, a mountain just at the back of the Briars. The going was too steep for horse to climb, so they went on foot, toiling up the 2,000 feet of volcanic rock to cross Francis Plain and scramble over two other ridges before gaining Plantation House. After lunch they had set off for Sir William Doveton's and finally returned home exhausted, with Betsy dizzy and inclined to vomit. "A senseless day," Napoleon commented; "I think the climb must have been the idea of Betsy." He had invited them to Longwood to show them a new and wonderful invention, that of turning water into ice by "one of Leslie's machines", and to explain the process. On Betsy becoming inattentive, he advised her tartly to get a book on elementary chemistry and finished, as usual, by turning to William Balcombe and recommending him to enforce a lesson every day. "The good O'Meara will act as examiner." He then made a cup of ice in the machine and put a large piece in Betsy's mouth, greatly enjoying her contortions. It was the first ice ever to have been seen at St Helena and few would credit it until, when lumps were given them, they watched them melt in their hands and water stream down their fingers. Betsy retaliated by cutting an embroidered bugle from the Emperor's coat and running away with it as a trophy, at which Marchand became seriously put out, as the coat was the one the Emperor had worn at Waterloo. The family and the suite, accustomed to these scenes, paid little attention, glad indeed to observe the animation in Napoleon's manner — a change from the days of listlessness and despair, of repressions and ill-humour. He took Betsy to play billiards and questioned her closely on the activities of the past week. How did the Wilkses feel at their projected departure? Was the Dovetons' garden as good as reported? (He later paid a visit to Sir William). Had Betsy seen Captain Wallis? As most of the commanders came to the Briars at one time or another, Captain Wallis among them, Betsy told him she had. "What does he think of me?" demanded the Emperor earnestly. It so happened that in the case of this officer the prejudice against Napoleon, and indeed all the French, was marked, bred by bitter experiences as a prisoner-of-war. Captain Wallis's mind was filled with rancour and hate, and Betsy told the unvarnished truth when she said, "Oh, he has the most abominable opinion of you in the world." The Emperor grunted, as he did when disturbed, and rolled the billiard balls about the table with his hand. "He says you shut him up for ten years in The Temple and there is no end to the barbarities he says took place. He told us that he was taken from one cell to another, where a man had shot himself through the head, and he saw the body being carried out. The jailers had not the decency to wash away the dead man's brains scattered on the wall, and left them there to distress the next occupant. He accused you of almost starving the prisoners, so that he and Captain Shaw tore a live duck to pieces and ate it like cannibals." Napoleon observed that it certainly was not to be wondered at that Captain Wallis was so bitter.

CHAPTER 13

Nostalgia

In 1816 Madame Montholon gave birth to a girl, Napoleone. In writing of the event to Gorrequer, O'Meara remarked, "I don't imagine that there was half so much anxiety over the birth of the King of Rome. You would have thought it the case of a girl of 15, newly married, instead of the wrinkled, middle-aged woman who has three husbands, all living, and eight or nine children." The Emperor paid the mother protracted visits every day. Some say it was his child, though common sense dismisses the notion.

If any intimacy had taken place, it must have been on the *Northumberland*, a crowded vessel in which Madame, her husband, her child and a nurse all lived in one cabin. Moreover, at that time Napoleon, oppressed and distraught by his falling world, was not thinking of women and was very distant — almost hostile — towards the lady.

Later his tone changed. However, Gourgaud noted that "between them the talk was often very free". He also commented that Madame Montholon had a way with men, but as her husband was in love with her and jealous, it was probably only an observation. With three husbands living, anyone is suspect.

On the other hand, Jane Balcombe liked her, and her mother, who was inclined to be strait-laced, said she was quiet and unassuming. It was said she had a love of admiration and made eyes at the Emperor and by any means tried to intrigue him, which was difficult in clothes always limp from the prevailing dampness and shabby from long wear. Madame later gained more confidence in herself and the temperamental Parisienne came uppermost when she declared to Gourgaud that it was foretold that some day she would be a queen in fact, if not in name. The observation left Gourgaud cold.

Napoleon failed to show her any attention when they first re-assembled at Longwood. Once, before dinner, she found him in the drawing-room with Gourgaud. The Emperor asked her to go into the billiard room and play something on the piano. He continued talking grammar with his aide-de-camp while a tuneless jumble of notes emerged from the distance. Madame played 'Marlborough', 'Vivre Henri Quatre', even practised scales and reversed the pedals to catch his attention, but he only shouted for her to go on and continued with his conversation. They gossiped openly about her among themselves. "Madame de Montholon is not in good form," said Gourgaud. "She thinks she has a throat and a pretty foot." The Emperor, wanting peace, enquired, "Cannot you say something nice to her." But Gourgaud went on, warming to his subject, "She is always scratching her neck and spitting her food into her plate. I never thought Your Majesty would like her for — that, but she does her best to make people think you do." Napoleon spoke plainly, if one can believe Gourgaud, who was biased. "Do you think," he said, "that I don't realise all that they [the Montholons] are up to? They are thinking of themselves more than of me. They have taken the rivalries of my former court to themselves. Well, I pretend not to notice. You ought to be able to get along with them. Don't imagine that I like her. I have been accustomed to living with too many charming women not to be aware of Madame de Montholon's ridiculous aspects and bad manners. But after all, here one would have to make one's society out of a green parrot if there were nothing else. We have no choice." Later, he surmised Madame Montholon was there only "because she was in bad odour in Paris. Her stay here will give her a coat of whitewash, and a certain amount of esteem, but what do I care about her reasons? They all make company for me, and if the woman were prettier, I would take advantage of her for that, too."

Which fairly sums up Bonaparte's feelings.

It was later remarked that he still paid no more attention to her than if she had been one of the men, and was heard to say when she was about to have another child, "Are you trying to be like Madame Tallien, always with a peaked belly." At this Madame was extremely offended and shocked.

When the child was born, Madame Bertrand urged Gourgaud to go and look at it. "She resembles neither Montholon nor Madame. She has a broad and heavy chin," she told him with an air of significance. "Does she look like the Emperor?" Gourgaud enquired, scenting more gossip. Madame answered with another question, "Did you see how worried His Majesty was while the Montholon was in labour?" They peeked and pried, their empty little world stirred by trivialities, jealousies and discontent. There was no love lost between the two Frenchwomen, so vastly dissimilar in temperament. They were jealous of Napoleon's regard, quarrelled about servants, about children and gowns. They met, outside the Emperor's presence, only as a matter of form. Madame Bertrand accused Madame Montholon of being an arrant flirt; declared that Montholon was unhappy because of her neglect of her children — which may in some respects have been true. Madame Montholon seemed to suffer from bad health. She rarely made an effort and the records constantly state that she was "confined to the house by illness". She bewailed the fact that "one aged rapidly in St Helena". Napoleon, eyeing her dispassionately, agreed, adding he could no longer think of paying court to the lady. "At 48," she persisted, "many men are still young." "They haven't been through what I've been through. At 50 a man cannot love again." "Berthier managed to keep on." "As for me, my heart has hardened [*j'ai le coeur bronzé*]."

Gourgaud preferred however, to think that the Emperor had slipped into a relationship with Madame. Gourgaud hated her — was ready to believe any *canard* — and did not hesitate to record his feelings. He wrote in November, 1817, "Madame de Montholon went in full court dress to call on His Majesty. He was in the bath. Montholon came out and I said to him, 'That's fine: they put you out when Madame goes in.' I stood outside the door chatting with him for nearly an hour. Then His Majesty asked for Montholon. 'General, the candles!' I nearly said."

For all this, Madame Montholon became necessary to the Emperor. She surrounded him with little attentions that appeared greater than they were by contrast with the barren life he led. She was close by — "His windows," as Montchenu wrote, "overlooked her bedroom." He came to her fireside, listened while she chattered, poked at the logs at — the Emperor's behest, no coal was burnt — and she became his favourite companion on his walks around the grounds.

Physically she presented no appeal to him, and he told Gourgaud so plainly — asking him to stop any gossip there might be. "Such talk might get into the newspapers and do harm." His senses, on his own admission, had lost their edge even before his departure to Elba, a fact which appears to be substantiated by a later medical note. One of the doctors who attended the autopsy wrote an addendum to a report he sent to Lowe some years later, in connection with the O'Meara libel action. "The whole genital system of the deceased seemed to show a physical basis for the absence of sexual desire, the continence which was known to have been characteristic of him." As he was the surgeon of the 66th, and well placed to hear gossip from the officers in the camp, one can take it the comment was a fair one.

On the 21st September, about ten o'clock, three distinct earthquake shocks were felt. The Balcombes, guests of the Emperor, were sitting after dinner outside on the grass, with the Montholons and Bertrands. Napoleon, feeling unwell, had gone to bed. Dr O'Meara and the orderly officer (Captain Blakeney now) were in the mess and Betsy wrote, "It was calm and windless, with crickets making the ears vibrate ..." a night for desultory conversation and long silences; following lively discussions at dinner, on varying subjects, Napoleon's lack of precaution in the past against assassination was voiced. "Never was a woman more astonished than Marie-Louise," he said, "when she saw no sentinels except at the out-gate of the palace. She remarked there were no lords sleeping before the doors of my apartments, no locked doors, no guns or pistols in the rooms where I slept." Napoleon shrugged, "I am *trop fataliste*." He went on to say his life was in greatest danger at Arcola. His horse was shot under him and, maddened, galloped towards the enemy's lines. In agony, he plunged into a deep swamp and died, leaving Napoleon up to his neck in the mud and unable to move. He knew if the Austrians sighted him they would cut off his head — which was just visible — but fortunately for him the approaching soldiers were French. He added he had had eighteen or nineteen horses shot under him during his life. He said he had been wounded several times but more often than not did not disclose the fact, using salt and water to bathe the part.

Longwood, never at any time a very securely built house, was badly shaken by the earth tremors and the party on the lawn heard a rumbling and clattering like a loaded wagon being dragged along the roof. It lasted twenty seconds. O'Meara and Captain Blakeney rushed out to see if any damage was done and Montholon's young son cried that someone was throwing him out of bed. Servants went to the Emperor's room and found that he was undisturbed, having grasped immediately what was the cause. "*Tremblement de terre*," he announced, adding, rather regretfully, "At first I thought the *Conqueror* had caught on fire and blown up."

All of them at Longwood dwelt in the past, re-creating it in discussions of scenes and situations — the Emperor, servants and suite alike, although the servants, with more opportunity for close contact with the natives, interspersed their nostalgic memories with local gossip. A few had established connection with the island girls. Marchand, indeed was going to be a father! It was a more interesting life below stairs.

The gossipy St Denis watched the growth of the young Bertrands and deplored the deterioration of their manners and speech, now coloured with oaths from contact with the soldiers in the guardhouse — half of which, happily, they did not understand. The young ones reminded him of the Emperor's son. As one of his duties had been to serve breakfast, he frequently saw the child, little more than a chubby babe, who 'at dessert' was carried in by Madame Montesquiou, the governess, to see his father, while the Empress sat watching, an impassive mother — and one would imagine an unresponsive wife. It was Napoleon's delight to kiss and caress the baby and carry him to the

Tuileries windows, under which people lingered during breakfast in the hope of catching a glimpse of the Emperor. The baby aroused great interest, the chubby face curiously innocent in the surroundings of magnificence, of grand uniforms, plumes and extravagantly gowned women. Napoleon hugged him close, pulled his button nose, his ears, felt the down which was soon to grow into golden curls, and once, turning to the Empress, said, "Here, kiss your son." She drew away hastily and, St Denis remarked, "replied in a tone almost of repugnance and disgust, 'I do not see how anyone can kiss a child.'"

Ali commented, "What do mothers of families think of it?" — those homely women who peered up to the bay-window where Napoleon held the baby in his arms, the maternal instinct manifest in their smiles.

Napoleon liked being at the Élysée better than at the Tuileries. Once they heard him say the latter made him feel a prisoner. He found it lacked privacy, the building not being conducive to individual comfort, and he caused a wooden fence to be built on the stonewall on the side of the Hôtel Sebastiani, liking that part of the grounds best for a walk. There the Empress came with her women to pick violets.

The valets considered St Cloud very inconvenient, having long corridors, and St Denis added that his bedroom had to be crossed before the Empress could reach the staircase leading to the Emperor's rooms.

They drifted to a discussion of Count Neipperg. Ali had seen him when he came at breakfast at Dresden to enquire after the Emperor's health. The Empress was present and met him. As St Denis put it, "He was a man in full manhood, rather tall, very distinguished, a bandage over one eye. He wore the uniform of a Colonel of Hussars." They knew Neipperg was later attached to Marie-Louise's service by her father after Napoleon went to Elba "to wean her from the remaining sentiment of connubiality which still held her to the Emperor". Neipperg, having full confidence in his powers, remarked, "in six months I shall be her lover, and later I shall be her husband." The valets, with Gallic candour, discussed his romantic prowess. Did their master know of the affair? They felt that he did. Anyhow, what matter? She was now one of the drifting memories they recalled and talked over on the hot evenings when the trade wind had died and only the crickets challenged their voices in the darkness.

They aired little unrelated facts: that the Empress of Austria did not take off her gloves when eating — had she a skin disease? that the Emperor Francis wore a very long *queue* reaching below his waist — surely Commissioner Montchenu must have imitated it. Marchand sighed for better conditions for his master, and Ali reminded him the Emperor had once slept in a coal-shed during a battle. "And this, after all, is a kind of campaign," he added. "A long one," Marchand commented; and the boredom of their lot kept them pensive.

They talked of the Empress Josephine with all the familiarity of old servants — of her kindliness, her unpunctuality, her bad breath (a family complaint), her roses at Malmaison, the grace of her figure. They whispered of her *amants* — Barras, Tallien, Rappe, Caferelle, Talma, Julien, even Rostan — Rostan, the mameluke? Not possible! Their eyebrows raised. They knew for certain of some …

They became speculative at the memory of the old *canard* that Madame Mère, an old, very religious lady, now in Rome, had once kept a brothel in Corsica. What had really happened at Marseilles? How far-off these days had become. All the triumphs, the glamour and the heat of life had passed. Memories were grey embers of the Imperial fire. St Denis's mind dwelt on the swift-moving incidents of campaigns. He once saw a woman kiss Napoleon's feet, after he had given her one thousand two hundred francs for a dish of eggs, all she had in an impoverished larder. Marchand talked of vermin-ridden lodgings. Even the Emperor collected lice on their journeys. Once their clothing and a carriage had to be burnt as they had become so infested. In tacit agreement they did not dwell on the retreat. Those memories were beyond discussion.

Napoleon's impulsiveness they smiled over. His sudden decision to go to Fontainebleau and the Grand Marshal's dismay — no carpets laid, no fires, no bed linen aired. They recalled the details and the censure of Bertrand on the Emperor's arrival — his rage at finding workmen hammering carpet tacks in a half-laid carpet when he came to breakfast. They gossiped of Elba and Madame Walewska's visit there; of the first dinner in Napoleon's tent when she came to see him at the Rectory of the Madonna of Marciane — herself, his sister and her son — the fair boy older than the King of Rome, with the same curling hair. Not unlike, these two boys. There was no ceremony. Napoleon carved, Marchand and St Denis waited. Laughter and light conversation delighted their French love of a situation. They dwelt upon the child — about ten years old — and the likeness of the boy to their master. Madame Walewska they considered handsome except that "there were red spots on her face, and she was a little stout". How all Elba had gossiped and the valets shook their heads. "It was unwise to be so careless. He made no bones about visiting the lady's apartment in his dressing-gown, nor did he leave until daybreak." They considered that in love affairs "the simplest man is more adroit than the Emperor was." Madame remained some twelve days. Marchand reminded St Denis of the Emperor's request for money; he had none, and in confidence he went to St Denis for two thousand or three thousand francs for Madame — and St Denis's money belt was the lighter.

They laughed and sighed and the crickets continued their noise. The past was not quite dead while they could talk and sometimes smile. St Denis prepared to go to bed. He would be awakened at dawn by clods of earth on his window (Napoleon had commenced to plan a garden) and his master's voice calling, "Ali, Ali, it is day; get up! Come, lazybones — don't you see the sun?" Marchand would also be roused and later the suite, rather unwillingly, for manual labour irked them.

Yes, there was still fun to be had and situations to enjoy, the valets decided. The sight of the Governor's unopened letters flying out of their master's window, for instance, and the orderly officer's efforts at 'sightings'.

CHAPTER 14

The Elusive Prisoner

Napoleon's bedroom, in which he received the Governor on his second visit, is worthy of more detailed description than is afforded by Betsy's brief notes. To the man who, without reflection, stepped into the magnificence of Versailles, the Tuileries and even the small, luxurious Malmaison, who stayed a welcome guest, as well as brother, with the crowned heads of Europe, it must have come as a shock to find a rat-ridden apartment his final, and to all intents his permanent, abode. The implication was unmistakable. The lack of common necessities, the make-shift structure, the impersonal, almost jail-like furniture, the walls covered to hide blemishes and rat-holes, the second-hand carpet, betrayed such disregard as might be meted out to one of ordinary, even mean, calibre; not to a man who, until a few months before, had been the virtual ruler of Europe. His room measured about fourteen feet by twelve feet and was eleven feet high. The windows were small apertures (the sash of one supported by a wedge of notched wood), opened towards the camp of the 53rd Regiment at Deadwood Plain, from where bugle calls came in a crescendo, marking the hours. The window curtains were of white longcloth. (A note remains that they had one width of material.) There was a small fireplace with a shabby grate and fire-irons to match, and a narrow mantelpiece of wood, painted white, on which he placed the marble bust of his son. Above hung the portrait of Marie-Louise and four or five pictures of the young Napoleon, one of which had been embroidered by the hands of his mother, possibly a 'silk' picture of the day when the clothing was contrived out of real pieces of silk and damask and only the face and hands were painted. A little to the right hung the miniature of Josephine and to the left Frederick the Great's alarm watch, obtained by Napoleon at Potsdam. There also was the Consular watch decorated with the diamond 'B' known to Betsy in the Pavilion, and hung by a chain of Marie-Louise's plaited hair from a pin in the Nankin wall-lining.

The setting suited the plain iron bed designed to open and fold in the briefest space of time and constructed for use on a battlefield, green silk curtains to keep away the draught. Between the windows stood a chest of drawers, strictly utilitarian, and an equally plain bookcase was at the left of the door. There were four or five green-painted cane-bottomed chairs. The Emperor ordered a screen of Nankin to obviate draught from the door and an old-fashioned sofa by the fire, covered in the white longcloth of the curtains, gave him a small measure of comfort. Later he was to spend much time here, bugle calls marking the passing of day to darkness while intermittent squalls, caught by the mountain, would give way to the peculiarly blinding sunshine of high places to which he was unduly sensitive. Always the south-east trade beat on the doors, blowing, blowing.

Napoleon, incensed, told Las Cases of a further gratuitous insult at the hands of Lowe. "The Governor," he said, "has just sent an invitation by Bertrand for 'General' Bonaparte to come to Plantation House to meet Lady Loudon.[3] I have told Bertrand to return no answer. If he really wanted me to see her he should have put Plantation House within bounds, but to send such an invitation, knowing I must go under the charge of a guard, if I wanted to avail myself of it, was an insult." Whether Sir Hudson Lowe had not paused to consider the situation or whether he wished to discipline his captive is uncertain.

To Sir Hudson Lowe's unfortunate manner, Sir Thomas Reade added the final touch of insensitive conduct by inserting a malicious twist to the communications sent forth, his phraseology incomprehensible except as a result of the natural churlishness of a man incapable of finer feelings. Major Gorrequer had insufficient rank and personality to combat such a massive front of social gaucherie. Napoleon and the Governor met five times in all; five stormy interviews showing neither in their best light and it was better for the Emperor's health not to see the Governor again. Napoleon called Lowe a shark and precipitately retired to the house when he sighted him coming to Longwood, watching from behind curtains as the new Governor rode around the grounds and dismounted to prowl by the windows. Nowadays the intrigues, discourtesies and suspicions read like a fantasia, but they were real enough to wound deeply, and in some cases to ruin the actors.

Longwood's treeless grounds were freely ridden over by the Austrian, French and Russian Commissioners after they arrived. They had, however, no entrée to the house. This did not deter them from riding around the windows and visiting the Bertrands at Hutt's Gate. Their lack of courtesy, added to the needless privations arising from the Governor's petty spite, caused the suite to complain bitterly to William Balcombe. Fresh milk and cream were cut off,

Lowe requiring them for his own table. The detention at Plantation House of articles of clothing ordered for the Emperor and his suite likewise caused delay. These garments were not of their own selection but collected as if for displaced persons and this insult aroused the Emperor as perhaps nothing else. A dozen shirts ordered for his personal wear were seen, in 1816, in the possession of an individual, generally supposed to be a relative of Sir Hudson Lowe.

Captain Cook, master of the store-ship *Tortoise*, arriving early in 1817 when the food position was tight, sent a present of three English hams and a keg of American biscuits to Longwood. A few days subsequent to this act of politeness he dined with William Balcombe. Sir Thomas Reade happened to be present and the Captain requested Sir Thomas to furnish him with the counter-sign, so that he might visit Longwood, since nobody in St Helena could move without it. The adjutant-general, who prepared all paroles and watchwords, purposely gave Captain Cook a false counter-sign with the object, so he boasted the following day, of getting "the damned fellow who had given the biscuits to Mme Bertrand seized by sentries and lodged in the guard-house with the soldiers for the night".

When first he heard of the French Commissioner's arrival, Napoleon had been filled with curiosity to ascertain his attitude. Although admittedly a follower of the Bourbons, Napoleon entertained a lingering hope that some kindred spark might cause the newcomer to be 'compatible'. He sent O'Meara to Jamestown on the day of the ship's arrival, in quest of information.

On his return to Longwood, O'Meara told him he was not prepossessed by the French representative, "An old *émigré*, he came to me and said, 'For the love of heaven, if any of you speak French, tell me! I have come to the end of my days in the midst of these rocks and I don't know a word of the language.'"

Into the drama of the island, the three continental commissioners brought a kind of light relief. Castlereagh, England's Prime Minister, had made it possible, through the Treaty of 2nd August 1815, for them to come "without being responsible for the custody", but to "assure themselves of Napoleon's presence". Later Castlereagh regretted it. Russia, Austria and France were represented, but none of their delegates actually saw the Emperor face to face except one, who passed by his corpse. Napoleon refused to receive them in their official capacity, but later he invited them to lunch as purely private individuals, with disastrous results.

There was much preparation in Longwood kitchen, and the chef's ingenuity stretched to produce something close to old-time standards in the Napoleonic cuisine. With sufficient plate to make an imposing table array, the Emperor kept himself busy overseeing arrangements and composing an impassioned appeal for the visitors to send to their respective countries.

He waited until five o'clock, when an orderly rode to Longwood bearing a brusque refusal from Sturmer and Balmain, the Austrian and Russian representatives respectively. Lowe had evidently been at work, for they wrote of 'les convenances'. Montchenu sent no word whatever. Afterwards, realising their mistake, and infuriated with Lowe and his strictures, they prowled and hunted in vain for a glimpse of the prisoner. From Deadwood Camp, Balmain thought he saw him on the steps of the Bertrand home. It might have been so, for from the little terrace there is a view of Deadwood and the lowering bulk of the Barn beyond. Sturmer, passing up a trench in an effort to get near, saw him, or someone like him, in a tricorn hat. Montchenu wrote demanding a sight of him in the name of France, and it was he who passed by Napoleon in the procession that came to pay a last tribute.

Napoleon, with malice, watched the commissioners from behind the venetian blinds when they appeared near his garden. He knew when they spoke to the suite and questioned them about him, and he guessed how uneasily they lived on the fringe of the official regulations with which Lowe encompassed Longwood. Napoleon called Montchenu "an old fool", "a chatterbox", "a carriage-general who never saw powder". Later Montchenu, throwing off Lowe's restrictive orders, came to the guard-house to demand, unsuccessfully, access to the Emperor and threatened to break in with a company of Grenadiers — presumably British — to be reminded by the orderly officer that Napoleon had sworn to shoot any man who entered his rooms without his permission. Notwithstanding, Montchenu tried to by-pass officialdom and walk up the Longwood drive, and was repulsed by a sentinel and returned to the main road. Eventually he became friendly with Gourgaud and they talked of women together, the lack of them mainly. They sighed from boredom.

Montchenu's journal is a series of incidents, some scandalous, a trumpery collection in the main, that makes amusing reading in French, but becomes laboured in another language. Time has now relegated the politics of the day to their proper perspective, the figures strut bravely enough but are diminutive, dwarfed by the tremendous era which they had just survived.

As well as Austria, Sturmer represented the Emperor's father-in-law. One wonders at the lack of sympathy extended to the fallen monarch and son-in-law, and at the monarch's lack of censure over Marie-Louise's liaison with Neipperg — policy remained paramount over morals.

Of Lowe, Baron Sturmer wrote, "it would have been impossible to make a worse choice. It would be difficult to find a man more awkward, extravagant or despicable."

On many occasions, after the first débâcle, they endeavoured, without avail, to approach Napoleon formally, as representatives of their several countries. Lowe was not desirous of this, so the inner boundaries of Longwood marked their limit of passage and they continued to ride around the outer garden in the hope of seeing the Emperor. They visited the Bertrands and met the Montholons in Jamestown. Lowe was acting under orders in this case, for on 1st January 1818 from Downing Street went a confidential note from Bathurst, voicing "caution against admitting the commissioners of the Allied Powers or the persons composing their families or suites — you will abstain from assigning any reason".

Montholon once offered Montchenu a few beans from Longwood garden to plant — both white and green. In this the Governor scented a plot. He suspected some association in the white bean with the Bourbon flag and the green with Napoleon's coat and the Longwood livery, and twice mentioned this in letters to Bathurst.

Not content with the calumnies that caused Betsy's father to call him out to a duel, Montchenu gathered still further gossip and noted it in his book. Reading his words and finding a strange silence in Betsy's diary about that period, it would appear that something had occurred to disrupt, temporarily, her friendship with Napoleon. Was it the 'Nymph' who had taken his fancy — the lovely Miss Robinson? The Emperor categorically denied any romance; said he had never dismounted at her door, but hinted that she had made suggestions to him.

"I have already had occasion to mention Betzi Balcombe," writes Montchenu in his diary. "Last Sunday a few people were invited to Madame de Montholon's first public appearance since her illness (you had to be invited by writing). When everyone was gathered in Madame de Montholon's apartments, Napoleon, who knew that the visitors were there, and whose window looked directly down into Madame de Montholon's bed-chamber, showed himself, and greeted everyone. He talked a few minutes and then went down into the garden [the little rose garden] where he was followed by the visitors. Napoleon asked young Betzi, whom he had not seen for some time (and to whom he was not attracted any more because she was too familiar), whether she was as naughty as ever. He remarked she had grown a lot and added [Montchenu's words], 'because weeds grow easily.' Young Betzi, piqued, retorted that she could see he had not shaved and added, 'One must be very rude to receive ladies with such a growth.'"

The commissioner continued that "from reports, since Napoleon left the Briars for Longwood he had met Miss Robinson, with whom he had been quite 'gallant'. He talked regularly of her in the presence of Betzi and his hearers were asked whether they did not think the Nymph pretty. The answer being in the affirmative, young Betzi burst out in a rage, 'Oh, that is not true — she is very ugly indeed.'"

Montchenu's journal contains a long collection of anecdotes, half-truths and scandals. He records what at the moment took his interest and from his story one can gather any amount of local colour. It coincides with the period in Betsy's recollections during which she said she did not see the Emperor much — although her father went almost daily to Longwood. Something had apparently arisen to interfere with her visits, whether from her family's ban, or Napoleon's disregard, or her own decision, is not known. She makes mention of Major Fehrzen and Carstairs — and the young officers of the 53rd, also George Heathcote from the *Conqueror*, so it would appear that the first part of her adolescent infatuation for Napoleon had passed. She was growing up quickly and with her more mature development came the full implication of the Emperor's attentions. It was shortly after Sir Hudson Lowe's arrival, when the loose-knit conditions between the island and Napoleon were summarily tightened. Plantation House records kept by Gorrequer note that Betsy and the family were repeatedly invited to dine or take lunch and spend the afternoon at Longwood and that Madame Bertrand invited Betsy to stay at Hutt's Gate on several occasions and that Napoleon went there when he knew she was coming, evidently anxious to see her. But there is a subtle change in her own journal. The shadow of maturity influences hitherto forthright statements. She rides with Fehrzen, sees Carstairs at dances, the Ensigns of the Fleet go to dinner at the Briars. George Heathcote is mentioned as being ill; Dr Stokoe, surgeon to the *Conqueror*, comes into the picture as paying court to Jane. Later the doctor attended the Emperor, and ended by being dismissed the Navy on half-pay on Lowe's demand — another casualty in the cause of Bonaparte's treatment.

For a little while Ensign Heathcote became a passing fancy in Betsy's fickle heart, possibly from propinquity. He had been forced to remain at Arnos Vale, a convalescent depot, suffering from hepatitis, the while his ship beat around the island on guard duty. Arnos Vale, a hollow between steep cliffs, lay three miles from the Briars — the Balcombe children counted the distance less, owing to the short cuts they took when they descended the precipitous mountain-side to visit him.

They brought fruit from the garden and Jane came to read to him — it was an accepted diversion, by means of which to amuse a convalescent; and when he had recovered sufficiently to stand, Betsy and her brothers organised games on the green stretch of grass. From his letters it would appear that George Heathcote viewed both girls objectively. He could not separate their attractions. In his eyes, sometimes Jane held superior qualities, at others Betsy captivated him. He suspected that Dr Stokoe, who attended him, was Jane's suitor, which suspicion appeared to lend an added value to the charms of the older girl.

1. Napoleon on board HMS *Bellerophon*; detail from a painting by Sir William Quiller Orchardson. From left to right: Colonel Planat, (a member of Napoleon's suite); Charles Tristan, Comte de Montholon, (secretary, ambassador and long-serving confidante to Napoleon); Pierre Maingaut, (Napoleon's surgeon); Emanuel Auguste Dieudonné Marius Joseph, Marquis Las Cases, (secretary); General Anne Jean Marie René Savary, 1st Duc de Rovigo, (a member of Napoleon's suite); General Charles François Antoine Lallemand, (a member of Napoleon's suite); General Henri Gratien Comte de Bertrand, (Grand Marshal of the Chamber); Emanuel Pons Dieudonné, (later Comte de) Las Cases, (son of the marquis) and Napoleon Bonaparte. Of these, Planat, Maingaut, Savary and Lallemand did <u>not</u> trans-ship to HMS *Northumberland* for the onward journey to St Helena.

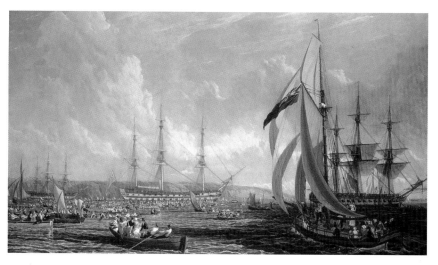

2. The scene in Plymouth Sound, August 1815 by John James Chalon. Curious sightseers try to catch a glimpse of Napoleon on HMS *Bellerophon*.

3. The approach to St Helena — a first view that is reported to have made Napoleon's heart sink.

4. One of a series of six aquatints by George Hutchins Bellasis; 'The Roads, St Helena' published November 1815.

5. Another of the Bellasis aquatints; 'Scene Taken from the Castle Terrace, St Helena'.

6. The shore front of James Town looking towards the west. James Town is on the north of the island.

7. A view of James Town from the road leading to the Briars. The church of St James, built in 1774, gained a spire in 1843, but this was demolished in 1980 on the grounds of safety. This view would have been similar to that seen by Napoleon. This is one of a series of views published in 1857 by G. W. Melliss.

8. An older engraving showing the road leading to the Briars, demonstrating the precipitous nature of the island geography.

9. This view from T. E. Fowler's 1863 book on St Helena shows that new buildings had sprung up between the battery and St James's Church. The castelletated front has changed with the insertion of a new battery. This view shows more clearly the second line of defence, with a high wall behind the trees.

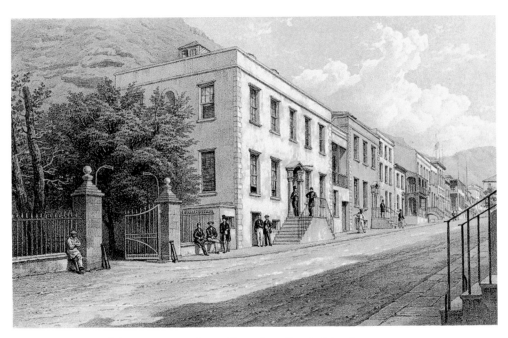

10. A view of the Main Street James Town from Fowler's book.

11. Melliss's Views: A view of the upper part of the Main Street of James Town. Note the tricolour on the left-hand side.

12. Admiral Sir George Cockburn, (1772-1853).

13. Governor Mark Wilks, (1760-1831).

Right: 14. Fowler's Views: Plantation House.

Below: 15. An old engraving of Plantation House.

Bottom: 16. Plantation House from the Bellasis aquatints.

Left: 17. Fowler's Views: The Briars.

Centre: 18. Melliss's Views: The Briars.

Below: 19. The Briars from an old engraving.

20. Napoleon meets Jane and Betsy Balcombe. Behind Napoleon stands Las Cases and to the right on the picture, Toby, the Malay slave.

21. William Balcombe, (1779-1829).

22. Jane Balcombe senior.

23. The races on Deadwood Plain, a watercolour by Denzil Ibbetson, (1788-1857), the Commissary in St Helena. Ibbetson sailed on board HMS *Northumberland* and remained on the island throughout Napoelon's captivity.

24. An invented scene by a French artist, with Napoleon dictating to the young Las Cases.

25. A painting of General Henri Gratien Comte de Bertrand, (1773-1844). Count Bertrand remained with Napoleon throughout the captivity. In 1840 he was chosen by the French government, following agreement with the British government to bring Napoleon's remains to France — *le retour des cendres*.

26. An engraving of Emanuel Auguste Dieudonné Marius Joseph Marquis Las Cases, (1776-1842. Las Cases was arrested on 25 November 1816 by Sir Hudson Lowe and deported on 30 December 1816 together with his son.

27. Charles Tristan Comte de Montholon, (1783-1853). Count Montholon remained with Napoleon throughout the captivity.

28. Louis Marchand, (1792-1876). Marchand was First Valet to Napoleon at Longwood and executor to his will. His mother was nurse to Napleon's son, the King of Rome. He remained throughout the captivity and returned in 1840 for the exhumation and *le retour des cendres*.

29. The upper James Town valley.

30. The modern road at the upper James Town valley.

31. A current view of the site of the Briars. The original bungalow was destroyed by termites and demolished. In the later nineteenth century the site was the property of Solomon and Cole, the main island traders. It became a French domain following the purchase and donation by Dame Mabel Brooke, the grand-niece of Betsy, in 1957.

32. The mountainous track close to the Briars.

33. A continuation of a track close to the Briars.

34. An island view close to High Ridge.

35. A general view from High Ridge.

36. A view towards Sandy Bay.

37. Diana's Peak.

38. Another view from High Ridge.

39. Pastoral St Helena.

40. The current view from Longwood. The garden would have looked very different in 1820.

41. A view from General Bertrand's cottage, close to Longwood.

42. Melliss's Views: General Bertrand's cottage. Bertrand lived here with his Irish-born wife, Frances, née Dillon, the daughter of General Arthur Dillon, an Irish refugee. Their children (of whom Napoleon was very fond) were Napoleon, Henri, Hortense and Arthur. The latter was born on the island.

43. An engraving of Longwood, date unknown. The illustration is something of a mystery as it shows a wooden outbuilding and a masonry wall not shown on other illustrations. It appears in Jacques Bainville's *Napoleon*, 1932. A building looking like a watchtower is to the left, apparently with a flag flying. Longwood appears in a dilapidated state and it may be mid-nineteenth century when the building was used as a granary.

44. A wash illustration of Longwood from Julian Park's *Count Balmain*, 1928. This is presumably an early twentieth-century illustration with the building now under French protection. The wooden building has been removed and the property looks in much better condition.

45. Napoleon and Betsy, an imaginary French illustration — *composition de fantaisie*. It appears as if Napoleon is about to give Betsy his gift of a snuff box.

46. Napoleon in his garden. Towards the end when he threw his enthusiasm into his garden, he abandoned his bicorn cocked hat with cockade, and adopted a straw hat and a flannel suit.

47. An illustration, apparently drawn from life and dated 1820 from Philippe Gonnard, *The Exile of St Helena*, 1909.

48. Napoleon gardening at Longwood, another imaginary French illustration.

49. Napoleon in 1818, a watercolour painted from life and said to be a very good likeness. It was painted by Lt.-Colonel Basil Jackson of the Staff Corps in St Helena. This was given by the artist to the Countess of Bertrand.

50. Napoleon in 1820 from a drawing made by Captain Henry Duncan Dodgin of the 66th Regiment.

51. The Friar Rock in Friars Valley, from the G. H. Bellasis 'Views'.

52. Lot's Column, Friar Land and Sandy Bay, from the G. H. Bellasis 'Views'.

53. Lieutenant-General Sir
Hudson Lowe, (1769-1844).

54. Napoleon arguing at Longwood, with Sir Hudson Lowe; another imaginary French
illustration.

55. Major Charles Robert George Hodson, (1779-1858); of the St Helena Regiment, and Judge Advocate.

56. Major Gideon Gorrequer, (1781-1841); Aide-de-Camp and Acting Military Secretary to Sir Hudson Lowe.

57. John Stokoe, (1775-1852); Surgeon to the *Conqueror*. Stokoe was summoned to attend Napoleon 17 January 1819 and over the next four days paid five visits incurring the displeasure of Lowe.

58. Barry Edward O'Meara, (1782-1836); Medical Attendant to Napoleon until 25 July 1818 when Lowe caused him to be removed.

59. A portrait of Napoleon in the last phase of his life.

60. Archibald Arnott M.D., (1771-1855); Surgeon to the 20th Foot Regiment. Arnott had excellent relations with Napoleon who gave him a gold snuff box. He attended Napoleon in his last days and attended the post-mortem.

61. Thomas Shortt, (1788-1843); Principal Medical Officer in St Helena. He arrived at the island in December 1820 and was consulted on Napoleon's illness, He attended the post-mortem.

62. Laura Wilks, (1797-1888); daughter of the Governor, Mark Wilks. Laura was a friend to Betsy and Jane; she was received by Napoleon on several occasions and he remarked on her beauty. She left the island with her father and mother on 20 April 1816.

Above: 63. A watercolour painting presumably by Louis Marchand, Napoleon's valet. This painting was offered to Napoleon 1 January 1820 and appears to be reasonably faithful depiction of the garden Napoleon created. At the far back of the garden is the tall turf wall Napoleon had built. Given Sir Hudson Lowe's antagonism, it is somewhat surprising that he was allowed to get away with it.

Below: 64. A watercolour by Denzil Ibbetson. He remained on the island until June 1823, so presumably this painting was executed between May 1821 and June 1823. It attributes the various chambers of the house and adds: 'the House in which Napoleon died . . . which is now a granary'. In the turf wall is the spy hole cut for Napoleon to use for his telescope.

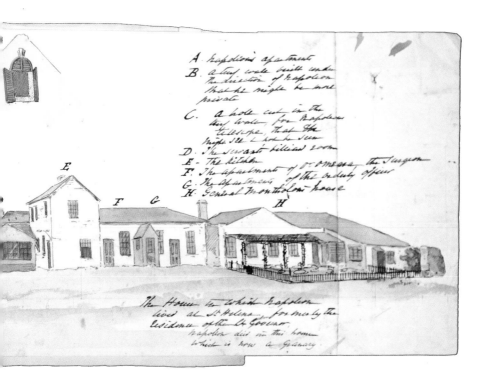

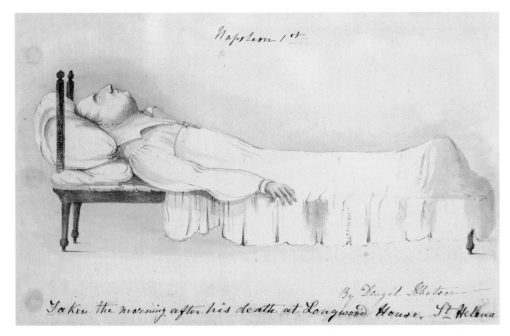

65. Napoleon on his death bed by Denzil Ibbetson. Napoleon died of a stomach ulcer with cancerous complications.

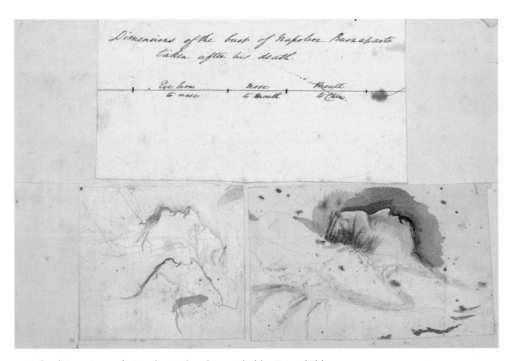

66. The dimensions of Napoleon's head recorded by Denzil Ibbetson.

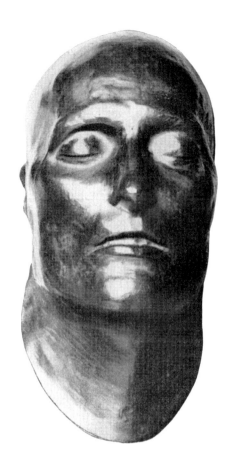

Right: 67. Napoleon's death mask. Great problems were encountered by this; a first mask was only partly successful due to faulty plaster. A second mask was successful when quality plaster was sourced, but by that time bodily decomposition had set it in.

68. The death chamber at Longwood.

Above: 69. Napoleon's funeral, 21 May 1821.

Centre top: 70. Melliss's Views: The tomb of Napoleon.

Centre bottom: 71. Fowler's Views: The tomb valley and the road to Longwood.

Below: 72. *Le retour des cendres* from the St Helena to France and their burial in the Hôtel des Invalides in Paris in 1840, on the initiative of Adolphe Thiers and King Louis-Philippe. On 10 May 1840 François Guizot, then French ambassador in London, submitted an official request to the British government, which was immediately approved according to the promise made in 1822. By the light of torches, British soldiers exhumed the body on 14 October 1840.

73. A sketch of Betsy in early adult life.

74. A painting of Betsy *c.* 1822.

75. An engraving of Betsy —
Mrs Abell, in 1844.

76. A miniature of Betsy's daughter, Jane
Elizabeth Balcombe Abell, (1827-1892).

Above 77. A gold and tortoise-shell box: the Montholons' wedding gift to Betsy, 1822.

Left 78. Dame Mabel Brookes, (1890-1975), Betsy's grand-niece, at the gates of the Briars, 1957.

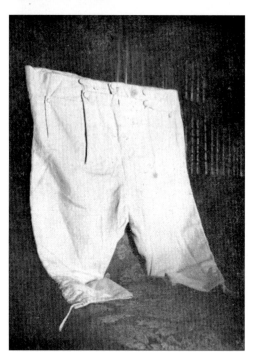

79. Napoleon's 40-inch waist breeches.

80. A lock of Napoleon's hair that had been in the possession of Denzil Ibbetson.

CHAPTER 15

Deadwood Races

Somewhat of a dandy, the French commissioner habitually wore a long wig to which was attached a *queue*. After his outspoken comments on the Balcombe girls, and Betsy in particular, Napoleon entreated Betsy to burn it off with caustic, and demonstrated how easily it could be done, especially by a girl of her quickness and resource, and if she succeeded he promised he would buy her the best fan in Mr Solomon's shop. Her mother, overhearing the conversation, took immediate measures to circumvent any attempt at such sabotage, which if successfully accomplished would have caused considerable comment. Not that she admired the gross Commissioner but she had experienced trouble already in restraining her husband from "calling him out", notwithstanding the ample apology demanded and "given with every mark of sincerity". The next time they met, Napoleon immediately asked Betsy, "*Eh, Betsee, as tu obéi mes ordres et gagné l'éventail?*" Betsy made great play that she dared not disobey her mother, at which he remarked, "*Eh, Betsee, tu commences à être sage,*" and, instead of the promised fan, presented her with a ring of diamonds fringeing the letter 'N', surmounted by a small eagle.

However, Betsy found an opportunity for revenge. She circulated a story of the Marquis, whose greed at table was proverbial. When dining at the Briars, the servants overlooked him when serving his favourite dish, cauliflower, and as Captain Gors, his aide-de-camp, failed to remark on it until the dish had been removed, the commissioner shouted with rage and much gesticulation, "*Bête — pourquoi ne m'as tu pas dit qu'il y avait des choux-fleurs?*" By then it was too late.[4]

Montchenu's manners, appearance and conversation both intrigued and shocked the community, but he produced an amusing chronicle of the years he spent at St Helena.

Count Balmain, the Russian representative, one of the Scottish family of Ramsay settled a century before in Russia, had hoped to bring a Parisian seamstress to St Helena with him but the other commissioners vetoed the idea and he reluctantly set out unattended.

He repeated a conversation of Lowe's to demonstrate the Governor's exaggeration of matters pertaining to Longwood: "Dr O'Meara had committed unpardonable faults. He informed the people at Longwood of what is going on in the town, in the country and on board the ships — he went in search of news for them — he gave an Englishman, on behalf of Napoleon, a snuff-box —— what infamy——!"

Balmain considered Lowe half-crazy and noted, not without satisfaction, that much of what went on at Plantation House was known at Longwood.

The commissioners resented the fact that though Lowe spoke fluent French, in all their meetings he insisted on addressing them in English. Montchenu did not understand a word and complained, whereupon Lowe offered to correspond in Latin. Montchenu wrote, "what a man! I am convinced that with every possible search one could not discover the like of him. He makes himself odious, the English dread him and fly from him. Everyone agrees that he is half-crazy."

Later Balmain became a favoured guest of Lowe's and ended by marrying his step-daughter, but Montchenu continued to write, "Lowe can get on with nobody and sees everywhere nothing but treason and traitors. He is not a tyrant but he is troublesome and unreasonable beyond endurance."[5]

The commissioners agreed on three points: their contempt for Lowe, the inadequacies of their salaries and the dreariness of St Helena. Balmain wrote vindictively of the 'horrible rock', and the effect it had on his nerves — which must have contained truth, for he developed a type of hysteria that caused him to laugh and weep until his violence necessitated his being held down until it passed.

Madame Sturmer, French by birth, by the necessity of her position had no contact with Longwood, but made the best of her life with the limited society of her choice, which included the British officers. She shared a secret with Betsy, a well kept one, for even in her memoirs and notes of the time the girl referred to her as Madame 'St', and only from another source does this prove to represent the beautiful wife of the Austrian representative.[6]

Soon after Madame Sturmer's arrival on St Helena, when Napoleon had departed from the Pavilion to Longwood, she rode to the Briars. Betsy happened to be on the lawn and ran to meet her — the loveliest woman, it was popularly supposed, ever to have come to the island; famous in the world of fashion and very approachable. She asked the girl to be allowed to see the part of the Pavilion where Napoleon had lived. Betsy and she climbed the little winding path to the building before which the tent still remained, not yet having been pulled down by the Army.

She showed her visitor the crown deep cut in the turf by Toby and, to use Betsy's words, "At that she lost all control of her feelings, burst into a fit of passionate weeping and sank on her knees upon the ground, sobbing hysterically." Betsy saw her fall forward across the crown, and, feeling the situation beyond her, commenced to call for help, but the Countess, in a broken voice, implored her to bring no one, that she would presently recover. Later she rose and dried her eyes, oblivious of appearance and the wreck of her complexion and proceeded to beg Betsy to keep the incident a secret. She told her the memory of Napoleon was treasured in the hearts of the French people as it was in hers and they would all willingly die for him. She asked a multitude of questions: how he had fared while with the family; his habits of life; his tastes; his conversations — her eyes searching the young face, her practised ear gaining almost more from inflections than from actual words. Sitting on the grass beside the crown, she reconstructed the past months and, nodding, said several times, "How happy it must have made you to be with the Emperor." She gazed at the garden below, the roofs of Jamestown in the distance and the sea beyond, as if to memorise the scene, for it had been a picture looked upon daily by the Emperor and for that reason of precious value. Nearby, her horse stood in the shade of the drive. There were chairs and the marble-topped table on the lawn. Betsy told her Napoleon had often used that table to write upon, in the shade by the pond, had seated himself upon those chairs, had slept there during the heat of the day. Madame Sturmer took it all in, gathering impressions that she was later to recount in Europe. After a long interval, she rose as if unwilling to leave, pulling down a thick veil, mounted her horse, and rode away. Betsy respected her wishes for silence, although questioned on the subject of the visit by others than the family, for the whole island was rife with suspicion and the unusual visit had been noted.

Deadwood races, a jubilee fixture, the jubilee of which occasion Betsy does not recall in her diary, commenced on 15th November, and equally opened a period of tribulation for the whole family. For some reason she had been unable to ride in the ladies events, her pony Tom going to a friend.

Dr O'Meara called on his way to the racecourse, to find most of the family preparing to leave and Betsy registering rebellion and anger at the ban placed on her riding. O'Meara stayed on after the family had become lost in the curves of the track leading to Deadwood. Half idly he remarked that Napoleon would be watching the races unobserved — he had holes bored in the shutters of the Bertrands' cottage to fit his spyglass. Deadwood Course was plainly visible from the Bertrands' cottage. "It will amuse him," remarked the doctor to Betsy, "he sadly needs it." "You have not been near us for a while," he added slyly. Betsy assured him she would come the next day, indeed had arranged to help Madame Montholon with the new baby. Jane had been shopping for her in Jamestown and they would bring the things up. After a while, Dr O'Meara rode off towards Longwood, but later Betsy saw him returning down the winding mountain path, followed by a groom leading Mameluke, a superb grey, one of the Emperor's best, with Madame Bertrand's saddle on the saddle cloth of crimson velvet and heavy gold embroidery which belonged to the Emperor.

Betsy had ridden Mameluke before and knew him for a tractable mount with a good mouth. Dr O'Meara told her that the Emperor, hearing of her distress had ordered his quietest and best horse to be sent for her at once, so with joy Betsy rode, chattering and excited, beside the doctor, to Deadwood, where all the official world of St Helena had gathered. The picnic races which had been organised by the Hon. Henry John Rous, later MP for Westminster, was a popular fixture. The army, the visiting naval men, the French suite, the foreign commissioners and their officers, with a diversity in uniforms and a range of colour, lent a spurious kind of importance to the scene, with the Hon. Henry John Rous as Master of Ceremonies.

Betsy's horse and royal trappings went unnoted, and she became part of the gathering, most of the members of which she and her family knew very well. She curtsied to Lady Lowe, a fashionable, flamboyant lady with nothing of Mrs Wilks's gay charm; and later met the Governor, who made an appearance and departed, accompanied by Sir Thomas Reade, at as early an hour as he conveniently could. The little world of the island was all there, navy ensigns, young army officers, Lieutenant Carstairs, the Younghusbands, little Major Gorrequer, General Gourgaud, also showing an imperial saddle cloth, and Major Fehrzen, temporarily in command of the 53rd. The riding-habits of the women — it was still the era of side-saddles — trailed over the horses' flanks in dark folds. The French commissioner made a play for Jane, notwithstanding William Balcombe's recent threat to call him out in respect of his calumnies about Betsy and that Dr Stokoe was in attendance and on the verge of becoming engaged to her. Lovely Baroness Sturmer was the centre of an admiring group. Napoleon spoke of her as "lovely in the true sense of the word", and she was a noted beauty in Paris, now dazzling the simple island women by her foreign appearance of dainty divinity. Later Napoleon told Count Montholon privately that after all she was "not so handsome as Betsee" and had "*la tournure d'une grisette*", a favourite description of his.

The Ladies' Race was won by Mameluke, a victory that made the public aware of the Imperial saddle cloth and the real ownership of Betsy's grey. It did not immediately arouse comment since it was usual to see the Balcombe girls with members of the Emperor's suite and, indeed, when he lived in the Pavilion they rode with the Emperor himself; retribution was to follow once Sir Hudson Lowe learned of the incident. William Balcombe, calling at Plantation House, received a severe reprimand and all but lost his post as purveyor for having committed what was termed a breach of discipline by permitting one of his family to ride a horse belonging to the Emperor's establishment. Lowe had strict ideas on fraternisation.

That evening, dining at Longwood, Betsy described the race, placing the little silver trophy on the table before the Emperor, protocol forgotten as she chattered happily about the exciting day, the crowds, the betting ring, and the mixed company of people. She told of regimental horses, of those sent from the Cape and the few acclimatised on the island. Driven home later in Napoleon's carriage, she found that her father was already on his way to Plantation House in response to a call from the Governor.

The family observed his gravity and preoccupation on his return but there were no recriminations for Betsy although it was manifest that some important and disturbing incident occupied him. When Betsy discovered he had been censured, and indeed almost dismissed from the purveyorship, on account of a thoughtless action on her part, she was appalled. It seemed to her unthinkable that Sir Hudson Lowe should have acted in such a manner. She went over the incidents of the day; the winning of the race was in itself a matter for laudation. Mameluke and the trophy were at Longwood; herself home; the question of protocol, expediency and appearance did not enter her head. That her father should be made to suffer was just confirmation of what they all believed — the Governor was 'touched'. The next day she slipped out of the house, mounted Tom and rode over the few miles that separated the Briars from Plantation House, received the sentries' salute with gravity, and a small figure in a voluminous habit asked to see His Excellency. Major Gorrequer came to her in the square hall, but she gave no hint of her business and pleaded to speak to the Governor in person.

The precise and polite Gorrequer left her to see what he could do, and she had time to look about, missing the Wilkses' flower arrangement, their personal treasures that once littered the tables, their gay voices and the air of luxury they imparted, for Governor Wilks and his family had contrived to make the official house a focal point in the lives of the island people. The servants, who knew Betsy well from earlier days, were withdrawn in manner as they went by.

The sound of dictation given in a harsh voice issued from the office down the passage and the words stopped abruptly when Major Gorrequer entered.

Presently the door of the library opened, and she was ushered in to an unsmiling Lowe seated behind the desk, surprise and suspicion in his foxy stare. "Miss Elizabeth Balcombe, Your Excellency," Gorrequer formally announced behind her. The time had come! She burst out, "Sir, my father knew nothing about my ride on Mameluke," a beating heart and ebbing courage causing her to make her point with all despatch before she dissolved into unaccustomed tears. "He does not know I am here, but I came to tell you it was not his fault and if you are displeased with anyone it must be with me. I am indeed sorry if I have done wrong. Dr O'Meara ..." "Ah, so it was his suggestion," interrupted the Governor in a flat voice. "The doctor found I had no mount and told the Emperor — so he sent me Mameluke," she answered quickly. Lowe eyed her, making no comment, letting silence do its work, while Sir Thomas Reade, lounging at the open door leading to the courtyard watched the scene, seeing more than Lowe, whose appraisement failed to find the true motive behind her visit, the loyalty of a distressed girl whose honesty of purpose had driven her to bring him the truthful rendering of the incident. Lowe saw only the "smile of St Helena", the irrepressible playmate of the exile, the hoyden and tomboy, the extrovert that made island gossip, and the untidy curls and bunched habit helped him in that picture. He noticed also her undisputed good looks, soon to turn to beauty, but as yet unemphasised and unregarded by her — a strange, unsettling girl, strong, with a direct challenging glance. He noted with satisfaction that his reprimand had evidently shaken both father and daughter. Longwood would know of it and take notice. After a moment the Governor rose and went across to Reade, leaving Betsy to stand by the desk, her skirt gathered in one hand, her courage rapidly returning; after all, they could do her no injury, and she had apologised, for what offence she did not appreciate since a ride on a Longwood horse was a normal occurrence. She registered the office-like appearance of the new and handsome room, and the two figures talking in low tones by the doorway. She heard O'Meara's name mentioned, and something about "too much relaxation" and "inadequate regulations". Then with a shrug and no further glance in her direction the Governor passed out to the courtyard.

Without comment, Reade ushered her to the front door, where Gorrequer mounted her on Tom and gave her hand a little squeeze. Riding home she realised that they had shown her no indication of their feelings. Non-committal to the degree of rudeness, they had ignored her supplication. She realised that anybody close to the Emperor shared in official disfavour and suspicion.

However, nothing further was heard of the incident, nor did she ever inform her father of the visit.

CHAPTER 16

Regimented Social Life

Although the smaller rooms of Longwood held most of Napoleon's personal possessions, it was to the billiard room, the common-room of the house, where most of the movement and life gravitated. Being newly erected it did not smell of mould as did the rest of the building — mainly because of properly constructed foundations. Large-scale maps of the places of campaign served as a guide to memory; sometimes Bertrand, tracing a highway, talked of engineering feats and fired the interests of the others and they gesticulated, argued and exchanged reminiscences. It was only when Napoleon entered that they reverted to silence. To him the coloured divisions meant triumph and disaster; which took precedence they could not tell: he displayed no emotion and under the deepest hurt habitually remained immobile. Leaning against the billiard table or, as was his custom, knocking his heels on the fender of the fireplace while he warmed himself, he recalled pieces of strategy to Gourgaud. Temperament was always there although he held it under restraint. Sometimes he considered a little expression of warmth assisted the point of an argument, but with the plans of his campaign laid out before him, his voice became strong and he lectured with a swift, cold lucidity on the moves, on the battles that had been fought, the motives, the politics that made the situation, and the human element that brought into play courage, avarice and expediency.

The anti-climax sometimes was too much to bear. More often than not it was news of yet another restriction; Montholon for instance brought an order that "after 6 o'clock nobody will be allowed to cross the line of sentries except by special permission and accompanied by two soldiers, who are ordered to point their bayonets at the visitor's heart." That roused sardonic laughter. At times Napoleon gave lectures on the battles of the Old Testament, moving the coloured pins on biblical maps, reviewing ancient strategy, discussing with General Gourgaud the possibility of a better result from other positions. In his own campaigns the red pins represented the English, the black stood for the French.

Those days lent him a measure of forgetfulness, and something of the original easiness experienced in the period of informal residence at the Briars. Napoleon was frankly curious about the Hudson Lowes' *ménage* at Plantation House, and examined Betsy about the family. She told him that, just as he was questioning her about Lowe, so also was Lowe interrogating others about him. She gave a full description of the whispered debate which had taken place on her visit to Plantation House, between Sir Hudson and Sir Thomas Reade. She also told him of an incident at the regimental dance held a day or so after the race meeting in which she had ridden the royal horse. The ensigns and young sailors showed sympathy and indignation on hearing of her father's reprimand but certain of the English officials registered sycophantic coolness, while the resplendent Carstairs went so far as to ignore both the Balcombe girls altogether. To Betsy this was less supportable than the chilly disapproval of Sir Hudson Lowe, for, to her, the Governor's anger ranked on a level with paternal wrath — she was still child enough to be accustomed to domestic censure. Disapproval from one of approximately her own age presented a different aspect. At length as the night wore on and she danced with a succession of uniformed young men of the fleet and found outlet for her high spirits and expressions of health and youth, her sense of injustice grew. If he were so spineless as to ally himself with the Lowe faction it was the end of their friendship. This she told the Emperor, but, for once, he did not show any interest in her affairs.

Mrs Balcombe, quick to register public opinion, cautioned both of the girls on their behaviour, but nothing she might do could withstand the flood of gossip. The peculiar circumstances, Baron Montchenu's calumnies, and now Sir Hudson Lowe's censure and Sir Thomas Reade's coarse expressions, were all very distressing to a woman of a rather puritanical turn of mind. She knew William Balcombe and his purveyorship had sheltered Napoleon in many material ways, and that he would ignore the local gossip, but she realised it would be at the expense of Betsy, who, half-comprehending all the implications, cared only that her beau had slighted her and was, in consequence, furious.

When she harped on Carstairs's disaffection, it was Napoleon who brought the situation home, and put the Ensign in his right perspective. "I told you he was too aristocratic for you, Betsee," he remarked impatiently; "forget him." He waved an imperial hand and dismissed the subject. Incidents in the lives of the island's inhabitants now ranked as small beer beside a further verbal encounter with Sir Hudson Lowe. Napoleon described it at length to Dr O'Meara, but from other sources Betsy and her father learned more of the scene.

Unannounced, the Governor, accompanied by Sir Pulteney Malcolm and several staff officers, Major Gorrequer and Sir Thomas Reade, entered the grounds of Longwood and, discovering the Emperor walking with Las Cases, Bertrand, Montholon and the page, sent a request for an interview. The cavalcade of officers halted at some short distance, making an impressive grouping of colour and movement, of well-groomed men and horses, upon which Napoleon cast an unforgiving glance. "I never see that Governor without thinking I view the man heating the poker for your Edward II in Berkeley Castle," he said to O'Meara later. "If I were in London and Sir Hudson Lowe were presented to me *en bourgeois* and I were asked, 'Whom do you conceive that man to be? I should reply '*C'est le bourreau de la municipalité.*'" The fact that Sir Hudson Lowe had at one stage commanded, if only briefly, what the Emperor termed "the traitors from Corsica" had never been forgotten. Early in their acquaintance he had once questioned the Governor on his military history, extracting the admission that he had seen little other active service than with the Corsican Rangers, having spent most of his military life at a desk behind the battle lines. Stung to sudden self-defence, Lowe had ended by saying he had obeyed orders and had done all that was required of him, a remark Napoleon dismissed with a significant shrug.

On the occasion of the present visit to Longwood, the Emperor, waylaid in the garden, had no means of escape and so waited unwillingly for the Governor and Admiral Malcolm to come forward on foot. Captain Poppleton and Dr O'Meara appeared from the house and stood to one side, near enough to hear some of the conversation, for the doctor afterwards recorded a detailed description in his diary, not all of which could have come from the lips of Napoleon himself.

The three principal personages, Napoleon, Sir Hudson Lowe and the Admiral, formed a group on the path. The Emperor spoke freely, in fact dominated the scene with animation of voice and descriptive gestures. He paced to and fro, stopping now and then to emphasise his theme, then continuing his impatient striding. Sir Hudson's manner similarly betrayed marked agitation, only the Admiral remaining calm. It took half an hour of argument and mounting tension to reach a climax, then the Governor abruptly turned about and walked off, omitting to salute the Emperor. The Admiral, however, with courtesy and deliberation took off his hat, made his bow and walked away with accustomed dignity, his manner being that of an onlooker departing at the end of a play.

Sir Hudson crossed to Poppleton and O'Meara. They observed that he was in a towering passion and paced the lawn waiting for his horse. "General Bonaparte has been very abusive to me," he told them in his rasping voice.

"I parted with him rather abruptly and said to him, 'You are uncivil, sir.'" From what they had just perceived, this was a masterly understatement. He then snatched at the reins, mounted and galloped away, the Admiral joining the group of officers, who lingered uncertainly. The Emperor and his suite withdrew to the house. It had been a critical and highly unpleasant interlude, an inconclusive and undignified argument conducted under the curious eyes of orderlies, sentinels and gardeners; finesse of approach and timing had never been Sir Hudson Lowe's strong point.

The following day Napoleon repeated some of the conversation to O'Meara. He had recovered his temper by then and was viewing the occasion objectively. "He came to annoy me," he declared. "He saw me walking in the garden and in consequence I could not refuse to admit him. He wanted to enter into some details about reducing the expense of the establishment to eight thousand pounds. He had the audacity to tell me he wanted to justify himself, that he had come up two or three times but that I was in the bath … I said 'No sir, I was not in the bath but I ordered one in order not to see you.' He then said I did not know him … 'Know you, sir? How could I know you? People make themselves known by their actions, by commanding in the field. You have never commanded in battle, you have never ruled any but vagabond Corsican deserters! I know the name of every English General who has distinguished himself but I never heard of you except as a *scrivano* [clerk] to Blücher, the chief of brigands. You have never commanded or been accustomed to men of honour.'"

Lowe retorted that he only did his duty, to which Napoleon responded, "So does the hangman." Napoleon went on to say he could not believe that the Government would issue such orders as Lowe promulgated, that if he pleased he need not send up any provisions for him and he would dine with the 53rd, who were officers and gentlemen and who would set a plate at their mess for an old soldier. He then became even more enraged, accusing the Governor of according him treatment worse than a condemned criminal or galley-slave might expect, since these at least were permitted newspapers and books. (Evidently the supply had again been delayed at Plantation House.) Napoleon declared, "I said you have power over my body but none over my soul, that soul is as proud, fierce and determined at the present moment as when it commands Europe. I told him finally he was a Sicilian thief-catcher," he ended, not without satisfaction.

The Emperor's gibes about his commands evidently struck Lowe in a tender spot, for later in the week he told O'Meara that, though never commanding an army against Napoleon, he had probably contributed more to his downfall than most, by advice and influence; that what he had pointed out at the

Châtillon Conference had been subsequently acted upon. "I should like to let him know this in order to give him some cause for hatred," he exclaimed in tones of excitement. Then he suddenly enquired if Madame Bertrand had repeated any of the conversations between Bonaparte and himself. O'Meara replied that as far as he was aware Madame Bertrand knew nothing of the occurrence. "She had better not," Lowe exclaimed, "lest it tender their situation more disagreeable than it is at present." His uncertain temper getting the better of him, he continued violently, "Did General Bonaparte inform you that I told him his language was impolite and indecent? He had better reflect on his position.... If he continues his abuse I shall make him feel his situation. He is a prisoner-of-war and I have the right to treat him according to his conduct." By then Sir Hudson had commenced to tramp around the library, biting his nails, his face a mask of hate. "Tell General Bonaparte that he had better take care what he does ... I consider Ali Pasha to be a much more respectable scoundrel than Bonaparte ..."[7]

Later on there occurred an even more violent passage, the sixth and last interview. After that Napoleon never spoke to him again.[8] Following his altercation with the Governor in the Longwood garden, Napoleon showed signs of serious indisposition. They all noticed his lassitude, remarked on his changed colour and put it down to the nervous tension arising from the quarrel. He spent more time in his bath — on occasions ate his breakfast there from a board placed across the sides. He rose late, and by now had given up his habitual daily exercise, the combination of sentries, officers and surveillance becoming irritating. Instead he busied himself re-planning and enlarging the garden, an almost impossible task in barren ground where gum trees, coarse grass and small native shrubs struggled against the wind. He even pressed Gourgaud into service. Spades and rakes were foreign implements to a hand that had once saved the Emperor's life — he made a feeble joke about it, but Napoleon was not interested. Presently he would leave the garden and sit, listless and brooding. The curtailment of luxuries irked him, the implication in their refusal rated more than the actual loss. His meals were simple, but he had begun to eat more heartily and was growing fatter. He had taken to wearing loose clothing while working in the grounds, and had obtained a large straw hat. The symbolic figure of power was no more. Dr O'Meara watched his symptoms. Perhaps no case has ever had the same scrutiny, and such faulty diagnosis — although the doctor was probably correct in the beginning when he pronounced it hepatitis, the current scourge of the island.

Later, when further progress of the disease that killed him manifested itself and was superimposed on the original complaint, confusion resulted. Possibly Napoleon's repugnance to medicine helped him to survive, for judging by the drugs known to have been prescribed, their effects must have proved drastic to a man suffering from an ulcerous condition. He habitually starved himself when ill, his own cure; that and many hot baths gave relief when stomach upsets assailed him. Given a more equable climate to live in, and a routine of life that did not prove a constant irritant, Napoleon might conceivably have survived several years longer, but the combined effect of a prevailing ailment and the mental repressions and privations of a prisoner's lot proved too powerful, and so became a fruitful medium for his subsequent illness and death. When he arrived on the island he was not a sick man. During his time at the Briars he showed, except for a simple cold, no outward symptoms of ill-health. He took exercise, rode and displayed the fluctuation of mood that was already one of his characteristics. The subsequent regimentation and tyrannic behaviour of Lowe, however, bore on his spirit as did the symbols of detention, the guard-house, the sentinels and the guns in the hills. Once he had ridden "followed by Kings", once the civilised world had moved to his command, and the memory of that immense past and its loss added to the frustrations of Lowe's making. That he could remain sane, have the power to play, to dictate, to behave normally, was in itself a feat worthy of notice and admiration. Other wars more gigantic and terrible have yet not dimmed the lustre of his military prowess, nor his personality.

The English way of life, the role of a retired squire, were not for him; the shadow of the Barn, the fleeting clouds on the peak and the pounding rollers at the mountain's base made a fitting stage from which to take a final curtain. It was a gigantic, wild and lonely background matching the unflinching spirit that came from his own essence. Religion did not motivate his actions, logic rather than fate directed him.

Lowe had now promoted the instrument of his regimentation, Sir Thomas Reade, to be Chief of Police at a salary of £565 a year, and Reade pursued his course of petty persecutions until both the Austrian and French commissioners registered formal objections.

Betsy, perhaps more generous-minded than her hard-pressed father, stated in her recollections that "nobody could have adequately dealt with the French staff in their frame of mind". Lowe had been assigned an impossible task and he performed it remarkably badly. He demanded always of Balcombe a full recapitulation of conversations held with the Emperor, as he later did from Betsy and the other members of the family. Some of the transcriptions are extant — innocuous remarks, so trivial and immaterial as to be waste of time to record. He was intensely curious about the Emperor's reaction to himself but obtained little satisfaction. He refused three requests at different times from the Emperor to remove to the Briars that he might obtain shelter from the strong winds of the plateau, about which he constantly complained with emphatic irritation and distaste.

After a study of the folios of letters and depositions, so often in the cramped writing and meticulous transcriptions of Major Gorrequer, it becomes an accent on human fallibility. How trivial it all appears! The complaints and accusations are academic and a little pathetic, the authors, puppets in the hands of some unseen manipulator. Only rarely does any spirit stir in the written word. Lowe's mentality is demonstrated; the rough drafts, the jerky phraseology, the handwriting — a quill was used and the workings of his mind are displayed in his erasures and marginal additions and in some cases the deletions from documents sent to the Minister. He advised Bathurst to let O'Meara "have plenty of rope" and in another he struck out mention of certain symptoms in Napoleon's last illness and altered the surgeon's medical report. In another he changed his mind twice and appended 'stet' to the side of the column — his usual draft was written on thick foolscap in two columns.

Ross Cottage, belonging to William Balcombe, and within the boundary set for the Emperor's rides, had been made available for the Montholons while their apartments in Longwood House underwent enlargement and renovation. Napoleon was sentimentally attached to the place, named after the *Northumberland*'s Flag Captain, Charles Ross, whom he designated "*un bravissimo uomo*". The family made an opportunity of a birthday celebration the excuse to allow the exiles some companionship with the people they had come to know and like, and Napoleon promised to attend the party.

He was seen riding along the hillside, evidently on his way to join the little gathering, a British officer tagging behind; but presently he reined in his horse and remained watching from the heights above. Some feeling had prompted him not to take part, mainly distaste for the curious though friendly stares. He had not seen any of them since the Lowe regime, and he disdained their pity. Betsy ran panting up the hill and, notwithstanding all her entreaties, he still refused to ride down. She took him a piece of birthday cake, recently sent from England surmounted by a large eagle, and told him of the strictures from the governing powers when they had heard of its arrival. Eagles were unpopular at Plantation House, even surmounting an English-baked cake. "Eat some: it is the least you can do after getting us into such disgrace," she told him. And as he did so, she stood by Hope's head and watched the scene below, while the uncomfortable British officer remained discreetly behind. No cake for him, no attractive girl at his horse's head, no *entrée* to the party of island people mingling with his brother officers of the 53rd, whose voices floated up to them on the little path above. He had been relegated to the post of jailer, ignored, distrusted; an honourable and simple man, he deplored the situation.

Having obediently disposed of the cake, the Emperor pinched Betsy's ear, called her "a saucy simpleton" [one of his new English phrases], and galloped away singing, or attempting to sing, his most unmusical rendering of 'Vive Henri Quatre', Captain Nicholls following at a short distance.

Earlier it had been Napoleon's special desire to learn English. So far a few words sufficed to convey to him the meaning of conversations around him, and he was quick to understand from the inflection of the voices, but idioms were beyond him. Now Betsy and Jane were pressed into service, long morning lessons in the billiard room resulting. They set Napoleon a lesson like any schoolboy. Betsy's notes say that, attracted by something, she would stray out, to return presently and be saluted by a tap on the cheek and an exclamation, "*Ah, Betsee, petite étourdie que vous êtes, vous ne deviendrez jamais sage.*"

She recorded his regard for sailors. Napoleon said, "The English are kings upon the sea — I wonder what they think of our beautiful island? They cannot be much elated by the sight of my gigantic prison walls." He stood by his horse on the Longwood boundary eyeing a convoy of store-ships edging their way into a rather rough James Roads anchorage.

Betsy, aware of the privations experienced by men of sailing-ships, told him they often viewed the rock with relief, and had dropped anchor off Jamestown, hungry and, what was worse, with little water remaining in their casks. Sometimes they brought sick men to the hospital. Slave ships habitually called.[9]

The traffic of the ships passed through her father's hands, and she heard the gossip — how slaves transported from Africa lay manacled in the holds, how undesirable island residents were deported to the mainland, how the Company store-ships made the island a revictualling depot in their constant traffic to India. She had watched unsuitably clad red-coats swarm around the dives, bemused with rum and heat. The indeterminate dusky colour of the inhabitants of the island spoke of the passage of many nationalities, and the curiously pure English diction marked the island as having belonged to Britain for some centuries.

Napoleon's viewpoint, from a personal angle, rendered him blind to its natural beauties. He complained often at his confinement to such a barren spot, which indeed it was not, and so created a wordy argument with Betsy, who weighed against his strictures the luxuries of the Briars garden, the rides and freedom which she experienced at all times and the shelter and the comfort of a happy home. She told the Emperor she knew the naval officers considered St Helena a very important part of the Empire. She wrote later that sometimes he laughed at her impertinence in combating his assertions, at others he pinched her ear rather hard and demanded how she could possibly dare to have an opinion on the subject.

The new Longwood home in course of erection annoyed the Emperor. He had not been consulted about the site or architecture. The cost, with the iron railing, suggestive of internment, was commonly supposed to have been £50,000. No trees grew on the bare slopes and the Barn became the dominant feature in the landscape. Napoleon only once entered the house, immediately criticised the servants' quarters and the indifferent accommodation for his own valets, whom he liked to have near him, and refused to move from the original Longwood — rats, damp and discomfort notwithstanding.

Occasionally Sir Hudson Lowe held meetings in the empty rooms with his officers; frequently he called uninvited on the Bertrands, and entered the Montholons' quarters, or spent long periods in the orderly officers' rooms on some trivial excuse, as if unable to keep away. On these occasions Napoleon remained out of sight. Short of opening the doors of the Emperor's private apartments, Lowe intruded everywhere — in the stables, the kitchen and domestic quarters — like a prying landlord. On one occasion, without the knowledge of the suite, he issued orders to the English servants employed in the establishment. On hearing this, Napoleon dismissed them immediately.

At times Lowe arrived early, surrounded by an imposing guard of officers, ostensibly to see Captain Nicholls, the orderly officer. At others he would gallop alone to the guard-house and interrogate the sentries: Who had passed? — Who had entered?

His obsession was Napoleon's escape; his daily fear, a sight of the blue flag hoisted to announce the Emperor's absence. He would rise from his bed and ride at midnight up the road from Plantation House. He interviewed Bertrand and Montholon frequently on trivialities, but the closed doors of the Emperor's little suite marked his limit of investigations just as it blocked the orderly officer in his endeavour for a daily 'sighting'.

Colonel Nicholls, aware of the captive's loaded pistols and of his unequivocal remark that he would shoot anyone who forced entry into his bedroom, made a point of keeping well away. Lowe, marching about outside, was often near enough to hear voices in the billiard room and behind the venetian shutters knew that Napoleon sat dictating or perhaps talking to some visitor (the last becoming increasingly scarce by Lowe's own orders), and his jealous anxiety knew no bounds. Sometimes Betsy's clear voice was easily recognisable; it had a carrying quality, and bore the inflections of "a young ladies' seminary", noticeable even among the low-toned voices of the 'Yamstocks'. Once he heard her translating a portion of Warden's letters from the *Northumberland* into French and Napoleon's interspersed comments were unmistakable.

How had the doctor's book found its way into Longwood? It was an outrage and an affront. He would investigate. Sometimes the children played with toys on the floor, interrupting the adult conversation with their high-pitched French chatter. The closed doors mocked him, and at this moment he knew moral defeat. Guard-houses, barriers and restrictions were as nothing; the fear of escape faded before the greater fear of Napoleon's prestige among the inhabitants of the island, and, beyond them, the world outside. The 'man of destiny' was becoming an island legend.

A housemaid from the Governor's own establishment rode to the guard-house, put over a tale to the soldiers that the Governor had forgotten to give her the necessary pass, was let in and, being 'saucy' and attractive, had herself taken all through Longwood; she begged for a sight of the great man and in fact peeped through a door and caught a glimpse of him before the door could be closed.

Later, the youngest Miss Johnston, equally daring, walked around the garden, encountered Montholon, who gallantly "escorted her, on his arm, and perceiving the Emperor approaching presented her". She went off carrying a rose he picked for her from one of his own bushes.[10] Mr Raffles, on his way from Java, admitted that his curiosity to see the Emperor had become extreme, and his satisfaction was complete when he took his leave, for though it was not one of the Emperor's best days and he might well have pleaded indisposition, curiosity prompted his agreement to the meeting and the feeling was mutual, Mr Raffles having no words to express his delight at the manner in which he had been received. Napoleon asked him endless questions about Java, saying, "The Dutch have represented it as a pestilential climate"; and the visit continued for a considerable time, only concluding on Mr Raffles's departure to rejoin his ship at sundown on her voyage to England. Napoleon spoke of Java to Dr Warden and remarked, "I believe a more favourable opinion is now obtained of it." Raffles had given the full picture. They talked of the ex-Governor's home, a Georgian-type mansion set in parklands on which deer grazed near the then capital. Colonial Governorship was fully maintained by Mr Raffles and the Javanese guards were clad in British uniforms, suitable only for a cold climate.

When the doctor arrived at Longwood, after the visitor's departure in the late afternoon, he found the whole suite preparing for an outing, which Napoleon delayed in order to speak about Mr Raffles and Java. The doctor voiced his vexation at the delay he was causing which lent some embarrassment to the Marshals, Counts and Generals, hats under their arms, and the ladies, whose petticoats were "playing about from a smart and rather unmannerly breeze", but Napoleon was disposed to continue the talk further. Not often did he receive two visits in one day. Presently Warden was given a seat in the carriage and asked to recount all he could about the East, where his naval service had occasionally taken him. He did not like the tropics. "Have you ever seen a case of plague?" Napoleon enquired of him. "Do you know the disease?" "My only knowledge of it is from what I have read." "The Army of Egypt suffered much by it and I had some difficulty in supporting the spirits of many of those who remained free from it, yet in two years I continued to keep my soldiers ignorant of what I myself knew. The disease can only be communicated through the organs of respiration." Warden observed that actual contact could convey it. "No," said Napoleon, "I visited the hospitals incessantly and touched the bodies of the sick to give confidence to their attendants. At the same time I always took the precaution of visiting after a meal and a few glasses of wine, placing myself on the side of the infected person from which the wind blew." Napoleon once told William Balcombe, as well as others, that in 1792, when a colonel of artillery at the siege of Toulon, he contracted what doctors then termed "a malignant type of scurvy", attributing the cause to a gunner similarly affected who was killed beside him while serving his gun. He said, "Whilst commanding a battery of two guns at the siege of Toulon two cannoneers were killed by my side, in consequence of a discharge from one of the English gunboats. I immediately seized a ram-rod which fell from the hands of one of the soldiers. The man happening to be afflicted with the itch, and the ram-rod falling warm from his hand, I received the infection and in a few days found myself completely diseased. I accordingly had recourse to bathing, which seemed to answer the desired end, but at the expiration of five years I had a second attack of the complaint, which I suppose must have remained undestroyed in my blood; a cure however was speedily effected, and I have had no recurrence of the disease since that time."

Corvisart, the doctor, among other cures, strongly advised 'cautery', but Napoleon said he wished "to keep his arm intact", and refused. Constant, his valet, commented that during those years he appeared emaciated, sallow and bilious, and had a cough. Talking of the doctor's treatments, Napoleon said Corvisart's directions were to reject anything that tasted bitter or disagreeable and it had now become a habit. He took it to mean that the doctor feared poison. And in St Helena he reacted violently to the bitter coffee first served him at the Briars, and also later to young Alexander's proffered pills which he threw up.

The attention of Sir Hudson Lowe was constantly directed to a reduction of the expenses at Longwood.[11] Finding by their calculations that the existing establishment could not be supported for less than £14,000 or £15,000 per annum (it rose later to £20,000), he sent Gorrequer to Count Montholon to state to him that it was possible that the British Government had not been warned of the size of General Bonaparte's establishment when it fixed £8,000 per annum but he would undertake on his own responsibility "until the instructions on handling should be received" to allow expenditure to the amount of £12,000, including all charges; that Mr Balcombe must arrange this matter with Count Montholon. Napoleon, hearing this from Montholon and incensed at the possible curtailment of his living conditions, declared that he would sell his plate in order to obtain food and proceeded to make the *maitre-d'hôtel* sort out portions not in use, as well as other pieces kept for the Bertrands' table. Montholon, in a note, not shown to the Emperor, informed Major Gorrequer of this decision and implied that for some obscure reason it was at his (Gorrequer's) suggestion that Napoleon was forced to contribute towards the cost of the upkeep of Longwood. The startled Gorrequer denied any such thing and Napoleon, realising Montholon was running true to form in broadcasting a literal interpretation of a fit of anger and pique on his (Napoleon's) part, entered into a storm of abuse and excuses.[12]

Bearing on this there is a memorandum of a conversation between Major Gorrequer and William Balcombe on 15th September 1816. Major Gorrequer writes, "I called on Mr Balcombe at the Briars and found the Admiral [Malcolm] there, the Count and Countess Montholon and Las Cases, beside Mr & Mrs and the two Miss Balcombes. After the party left the room to go into the garden, I took the opportunity to ask Balcombe the purport of his conversation with General Bonaparte the last time he was at Longwood. He told me that about four days before, he went up there. [He was sent for by Bonaparte, who wished to speak to him.] He found Bonaparte and Las Cases in the billiard room. The General said to him that it was his intention to send some plate down to town for him [Balcombe] to sell as he found that the retrenchments lately made in the supplies for his table rendered it impossible for him to exist upon them and that the quantity fixed upon was quite insufficient. Mr Balcombe remarking that he hoped he was not in earnest about selling his plate, he answered, 'What is the use of plate when you have nothing to eat off it?' and said he could do without it and it was essential he should sell it to provide himself with what was necessary for his table. He then went on to talk about his obligations to the Admiral for putting up his tent and told Balcombe that his house, the Briars, was within bounds and he could visit him without an English officer. On leaving Napoleon, William Balcombe said he found the day's supplies had just arrived from Jamestown, a list having been given to Montholon, who remarked, however, he would give no more receipts. The purveyor immediately turned back and went in with it to Napoleon." Nothing is recorded of the interview, but there is a later note by Major Gorrequer in the Lowe Papers, "Montholon told Mr Balcombe this day that they wished much to see him at Longwood and asked him to come tomorrow, but Balcombe excused himself on account of his foot [he had gout], and said that he didn't know when he night be able."

The whole incident showed the jealousies, disagreements and frustrations. The empty hours that bred such suspicions and doubts were producing enemies where the Emperor desperately wished for friends.

Eventually Bertrand sent for the purveyor and the question of the plate was settled — the price five shillings per ounce, fixed by Sir Hudson Lowe. The urns and massive pieces were beaten out, thereby losing great intrinsic value, for good prices would have been paid for them by passing visitors on ships, and even from the inhabitants of the island. But Lowe was adamant; there were to be no souvenirs, the silver must be sold as silver. A few of the eagle tops to the bowls were surreptitiously saved and are extant, but the rest, hammered into shapeless lumps, were weighed out at the sum required by the Governor.

For a while there was a coolness between Montholon and Balcombe — not that they had ever been on very close terms. Later, Montholon openly abused Lowe to all and sundry, and his comments went back to the Governor, always very sensitive to criticism. He, in turn, was insolent to the Bertrands, whom he met at Lady Bingham's, the Admiral's wife, saying, "You people don't seem to understand your situation very clearly. You think you can grumble the way Napoleon does." So Bertrand reported the incident to Bonaparte, who wearily sent for Montholon. How stupid and petty everything was! Lowe, eventually, repenting his outburst to the innocent Bertrands, unbent and, on Madame's comment that the new cottage being erected was very small, added a square wooden veranda, mostly windows, that made an attractive drawing-room, even if it did look on the Barn and the soldiers' camp below.

CHAPTER 17

The King of Rome

The affair of Colonel Lyster became yet another thorn to prick Bonaparte, who was at the time suffering one of his recurring bouts of ill-health; it ended by absolutely precluding further visits from the wives of officers of the camp to Madame Bertrand. Lyster, a regimental companion of Lowe's in past days brought to the island by him, had been assigned the duties of inspector of volunteers, with a local rank of Lieutenant-Colonel. Lowe conceived the idea of making him also orderly officer at Longwood, with a Lieutenant under his orders. Napoleon knew that Lyster held no official military rank, also that he had once seen service in a Corsican regiment and so was, in his light, a personal enemy. Furious at the implied insult, he instructed Bertrand to write a strong letter of objection to the Governor, who foolishly showed it to Lyster.

Lyster, having already quarrelled with O'Meara and now deeply resenting the tone of the communication which demonstrated collective distaste for him, issued a challenge to Bertrand, employing words of extreme vulgarity, also adding epithets about the Emperor. Bertrand did not reply, and the next day Lieutenant-Colonel Lyster followed up his communication with another letter threatening to flog the General if an apology was not forthcoming. Bertrand made no answer and the next day Grand Marshal Lyster repeated his threat "to flog him if he did not apologise". At that Bertrand despatched all the communications to Lowe with a covering note dictated by Bonaparte.

The quarrel had now reached the highest bracket; Lowe backed down, made excuses, withdrew Lyster, but did nothing further, nor did he report the incident to Bathurst, who was kept in complete ignorance of the affair. Irritated and frustrated, Lowe now vented his wrath on the Longwood folk as a whole; there was a measure of perturbation on his own account, for the affair might have unpleasant repercussions for him if it became known abroad. He instructed the officers of the regular army and their wives to "send Madame Bertrand to Coventry". He hoped she would give up and return to

France, trusting that the doting Bertrand would accompany her and that once the Grand Marshal went away all would be well; he was Napoleon's shield.

Madame Bertrand put in some miserable months. She became a solitary woman in a narrow community of males, saddened to see the island people scurrying past her during her infrequent visits to Jamestown; occupying her days by teaching the children (which she did indifferently), in an endeavour to bring them up with a modicum of knowledge and good manners. Napoleon loved them, played with them in the same boisterous manner that he used when joining in the Balcombe children's games, and became amused at the jumble of French and English they spoke, and the language young Arthur picked up among the soldiers in the camp. He dressed them in his famous jackets and gave them a tiny Java horse to ride.

It has not always been fully emphasised that in the last years of his life Napoleon fought two battles simultaneously, each vital to him in his restricted surroundings. That he did not develop into a misanthrope, racked by regrets, lonely, unsatisfied, his ultimate mission in life incomplete, is surprising. He surely knew all these emotions. The sleeplessness, the brooding solitudes, were bred from hours of anguish, but during the long five years he displayed a rare fortitude and a spirit that met Lowe's vindictiveness with something of the resolution, the courage and resource of his prime.

An incurable disease had now begun to ravage him, to undermine his defences, to leave him weak, often in agony, but notwithstanding this handicap he joined battle and in his defeat and death perhaps reached his finest hour.

In retrospect, the minutiæ of the sick room are forgotten: the ignorant medical men, the prowling Lowe — enemy to the end; the multiple, trivial details of the confined existence on a far-away island. With a clear intelligence and a fighting spirit, he put his house in order, personally writing his directions and compensating his suite, and prepared to die with only the inadequate Arnott and Antommarchi as doctors in attendance. Acquiescing but not attentive to the Church from which in life he had derived no consolation, he asked for a *chapelle ardente* on his death. His was a brave and questing spirit. Evaluating in death the worth of his earthly activity, he accepted the inevitable with a soldier's stoicism and with a faith that acknowledged pre-destination, if not much else.

The figure of Lowe shrinks behind this great personality.

Lowe manifested his power by having the young men of the regiments, who formerly delighted to pay their respects to Mme Bertrand and Mme Montholon, informed that "it would not be to their advantage to be seen at the residence". Reade became busy seeing that tradespeople gave no credit to the Longwood exiles.

A web of intrigue and surveillance stretched over the whole of the household. Sir Thomas Reade's strictures on Napoleon were voiced in rough terms. "If I were Governor, I'd be damned if I wouldn't make him [Napoleon] feel he was a prisoner." On O'Meara's observation that the Governor could not do much more than he had already done, short of putting him in irons, Reade retorted, "I'd take his books from him. He's a damned outlaw and a prisoner and the Governor has the right to treat him with as much severity as he likes."

About that time, Mme Bertrand gave birth to a baby girl. The Emperor walked across to see her, when she took the child in her arms and presented it to Napoleon saying, "Sir, I have the pleasure of showing you a great curiosity, the first stranger that was ever allowed to approach Your Majesty in the island without permission from the Governor or the Secretary of State." The Emperor was delighted at the jest and laughed, by now a rare occurrence.

Betsy, Jane and their mother still came to the Montholons' and Bertrands' as the spirit moved them, and sought Napoleon, in the garden or the billiard room, the visit sometimes lasting all day; but even for them the times were changing. They knew that their movements, habits, and in the case of William Balcombe his financial dealings, were closely watched — the Governor being determined that St Helena should provide no outlet for his prisoner's escape. The barren shore, the patrolling ships, the sentinels, were not sufficient deterrents, and he watched closely the human element, knowing that sympathy could open a way.

The Governing Council of the island, of which, by virtue of his position, Lowe was head, obeyed his directions — if sometimes unwillingly. This had the effect of creating a rigid caste system. They influenced the townspeople's very livelihood, and deported, jailed and held the natives as closely as they confined their own slaves; the shopkeepers, mindful of the ban on trading with Longwood, obeyed to the letter, however much they pitied Madame Bertrand when, escorted by an Officer, she visited their shops and chose garments under his watchful eye, according to prescribed items already listed and approved by Lowe himself. It did not belittle her status — but Lowe's suffered. Small repairs were effected, and combs, needles, cosmetics and soap produced only if the items appeared on the list, although the money for their purchase was her own. Sometimes she changed from her riding habit into street clothes in Mr Solomon's shop, while the officer waited outside the door. She had acquaintances in the little town and welcomed a word with them — the commissioners spoke to her, naval officers, Mr Weston the town jailer, whose attentions were yet to be called upon for Longwood, the clerks at the purveyor's office; sometimes William Balcombe and the men in the customs shed. No word passed but was heard by the officer in attendance. Nevertheless the ride abroad proved a welcome break in the boredom of the days at Longwood and for a little while she felt at one with the outside world. More often than not, on her way home she turned right at the cross-roads and rode down the avenue of trees to the Briars, to wait until the worst of the heat had passed. There she could relax in familiar surroundings among friends, who gossiped freely about island happenings, while the officer lounged in the shade of the garden.

On one such occasion Betsy and Jane had something of added interest to tell her about what Betsy termed an excursion to Cruise Plain — she identified the host in her memoirs as Mr I. (his name was Ibbetson) and described a large cheerful picnic, "nearly all the inhabitants contained" at his home near Friars Valley, a long way distant. The party evidently exceeded all expectations, and the faint echo of the Ladder Hill Gun told the startled guests that the ninth hour had struck and "none had the counter-sign without which nobody must venture forth, unless they made up their minds to be taken prisoner!"

A consultation ensued and the most daring decided to run the risk and ride home, William Balcombe one of them. In Betsy's words, "being under his command, my mother, sister and myself and a larger proportion of the guests mounted their horses and set forward.

"The night was starlit, but the road so bad and unfrequented that for a long while the sentries placed about the heights were easily eluded — then we became lost and the horses commenced to stumble and fall among the loose stones. My father at length seeing a light, hailed it, and — most unlucky circumstance — a sentry appeared, and presenting his musket demanded, 'Who goes there?' 'A friend,' said my father. 'Advance, friend, and give the counter-sign.' But no counter-sign had we, and we were all marched to the guard-house, situated between the Briars and Longwood — to be kept there the rest of the night. We crowded into the little hole, eaten by fleas, mosquitoes and all sorts of horrible things, but even more despicable was the quizzing endured from our friends, who had been shrewd enough to stop at Cruise Plain." Not the least amused was the Emperor when Madame Bertrand carried the tale to him. It gave him a good opportunity to abuse the strict watch which was set to prevent the possibility of his nocturnal wanderings.

That a large community of island people, councillors, foreign commissioners and naval officers should be subject to this regimentation appears unrealistic. Only a man of Lowe's calibre would insist on such severity, but his almost hysterical apprehension made it impossible for the officer on duty at the guard-house to use his discretion and allow a party of tired revellers to travel the three and half miles to Jamestown. It became an incident for laughter, but did much to antagonise public feeling.

The party must have been memorable. Usually in her chronicles Betsy does not enthuse about entertainments, but in this case she did — perhaps Major Fehrzen had been there; it happened during a period when she was shunning Longwood, when Montchenu's gossip had borne fruit, when her notes held comments of the Major's visits and her own attentions to George Heathcote, the Ensign convalescing at Arnos Vale.

The Emperor made every effort to re-establish the old state of easy companionship with Betsy, who, though gay and friendly, had become somehow elusive. One day he sent specially for her to come and see what he termed "some pretty toys". She rode to the guard-house gate, there left Tom, and ran along the path to the billiard room, where she guessed he would be. The doors were open and a cheerful Emperor met her with his usual ear-pinching and enveloping embrace. On the table was a set of chessmen. He had laid them out in serried rows and pored over them with delight. With Lady Malcolm, a good player, he had sat down to play after lunch and he told Betsy the beauty of the little figures had put him off his game, Lady Malcolm having beaten him. The figures were executed with exquisite skill, the men representing all the trades of China. Napoleon, examining the lovely figures, told Betsy they were too nice for St Helena and he would send them to the King of Rome for him to play with. They were later despatched to Europe but never reached their destination — nor indeed did any of Napoleon's gifts.

Except for a lock of hair smuggled in by Marchand's mother for the Emperor, there was never any physical link between father and son. Welle, the botanist who accompanied the Austrian commissioner to St Helena, made arrangements on his arrival to meet Marchand, Napoleon's valet, who was son of the King of Rome's nurse. Solomon's shop was chosen as the place of rendezvous, and after a brief conversation Marchand carried away a piece of folded paper on which was written, "I send you some of my hair. if you get the opportunity of having yourself painted, send me your portrait. Your mother, Marchand."

A golden curl lay in the paper. The Emperor Francis had forbidden any news of Napoleon to reach the boy and likewise kept the life and movements of the child secret, but what others dare not do an elderly French *bonne* contrived with a minimum of trouble and with the help of an under-gardener.

Lowe, from the grapevine, heard of it, castigated Welle and threatened the gallows. He was expelled from the island — even though the Austrian commissioner assured Lowe, "Welle did not see the Emperor — in any event he could have told him little other than that his son was well and had still his old nurse". Welle was forbidden the Longwood plateau and the coast during the remainder of his stay.

What he transmitted as well as the lock will never be known. It is to be hoped he gave some comfort and bore good news; but the probabilities are that he could tell the Emperor little that would ease his mind and heart. He already knew of the King of Rome's whereabouts, of the Germans who surrounded him, of the removal of all French influence and of the Empress's distraction with Neipperg. Yet no whisper of it ever formulated in his remarks to his companions. That final blow and insult went too deep for human ears to hear the true agony of his soul. The child represented to him his ultimate triumph or failure; loss of pomp and fortune, of his fabulous career, went for nothing before the fact that this living symbol of himself would be prevented his birthright. His one hope had been in the boy as an apotheosis of his faults and failure. Welle without doubt had conveyed to him all there was to tell and thereafter only a glimmer of hope persisted. When at the Briars, he used to talk sadly to Mrs Balcombe of his son, measuring young Alexander to the little known, much beloved child. He dwelt on the habits of little boys in the bath, at play, going to sleep. He had watched, sitting on the Pavilion steps, while Alexander and his older brother, and perhaps Betsy, became absorbed in some interesting object, or argued with Toby, or harnessed up the little goat to Alexander's carriage.

One morning at Longwood the Emperor called Mrs Balcombe in, from her way to the Bertrands' new cottage, to see the marble bust of his son which he concluded had been sent to him by Marie-Louise.

The history of the bust's arrival made lively comment throughout the island. When the *Baring* anchored at James Roads, it became known that a sailor on board was entrusted by someone to deliver the marble to the Emperor. The Captain reported the fact to Lowe, and as the sailor in question was ill of "inflammation of the brain and his head shaved" no explanation was likely to be forthcoming from him. Sir Thomas Reade wished the bust smashed and dropped over the side but eventually it arrived intact at Plantation House, where Lowe kept it. None of this was missed by Cipriani, who in turn passed on the information to the Emperor. Lowe found it expedient to hand over the marble, though after some weeks' delay, his excuse for the seizure being that if constructed of plaster it could have been designed to convey clandestine letters. Napoleon drew Mrs Balcombe into the bedroom, where he had placed it on the mantelpiece. From his bed he could look at it constantly. It portrayed a lovely child and Napoleon gazed at it with the eyes of a doting parent. It also was a good piece of sculpture, though the artist had patiently endeavoured to produce an angelic expression on what were the features of a normal little boy. However, Mrs Balcombe declared it beautiful, that he should indeed be a proud father. The Emperor's eyes filled with tears, as he hung fondly over it, tracing his own lineaments and those of Marie-Louise in its marble roundness. The bust was life-size and on the base had been inscribed: NAPOLÉON FRANÇOIS CHARLES JOSEPH. It bore the decoration of the Grand Cross of the Légion d'Honneur and Napoleon told her he took it to be a silent token of the unchanged affection of Marie-Louise. Vain thought, or perhaps a calculated statement; she was then far removed from French influence, remaking her life as the Duchess of Parma and producing a further family of children, a fact known to Europe and perhaps wilfully disregarded by Napoleon, who must have been aware of the general situation.

The bust remained close to him until his death and Betsy knew it well as a lovely image of what he would never see again in life. She avoided looking at it, for it gave a kind of false promise and was part of the visionary hope that lingered in his mind, the ultimate triumph that was never to eventuate — the great day when France would receive his son as Emperor.

It barely fitted on the mantelshelf, and to the ultra-critical showed eyes a little close set and a slightly too thick neck. Later it became known that the enterprising sailor who carried it to St Helena was commissioned to do so with no other motive than that of gain, by some art agents, who placed the price of £100 upon it. Napoleon sent the sailor £300; he also received a severe fright from Lowe, who threatened him with imprisonment, and delayed the payment until the man reached England.

Napoleon turned to Mrs Balcombe as if ashamed of his emotion and said, "Madame, you have your children with you; they are not marble." Later two mezzotints of the boy found their way to one of the Jamestown shops; Reade discovered them and they were immediately bought by Lowe and hung in Plantation House before the suite had even the opportunity to see them.

From the distance of a century and a half, the story of the bust is trivial, its only significance the portrayal of the narrow outlook, intolerance and mean spirit of Napoleon's jailers, how ineptly a simple situation could be handled, and to what lengths of despotism Lowe would resort.

The general feeling of indignation over the incident persisted so strongly that Lowe, alarmed, wrote to the Secretary of State for the Colonies denying that he ever threatened to destroy the bust or that Reade had ever contemplated throwing it into the sea.

Another gift arrived soon after, though in a more orthodox manner: a guitar from the Emperor's sister, Pauline, in Italy, to whom he appeared to be devoted. It travelled in a heavy rosewood case, felt-lined, and its ivory inlay and graceful Italian form Napoleon, the Corsican, found very pleasing. He knew something of the type of instrument and strummed on it, singing unmusically. Betsy picked up the intricacies of the six strings and after a little instruction

Napoleon taught her to sing 'Vive Henri Quatre' and other tunes, to which she added 'Hortense's Song', a general favourite. The voices penetrated to the orderly officers' quarters, drifting across the gardens outside the billiard room, where Napoleon sat on the doorstep, Betsy beside him twanging the strings; and later the report reached Plantation House: "Napoleon sang and whistled this evening to the accompaniment of a guitar. A lady sang also." Later others of the suite joined in and a little festival was held in the gathering dusk before the appearance of the sentinels. (The guitar is still in its rosewood case and was played last year, though it was difficult to find a musician conversant with its six strings. However, an Italian succeeded and, between sessions of jazz and calypso, the nostalgic tunes of the era were revitalised by young voices. Napoleon gave the guitar to Betsy on her departure from St Helena.)[13]

CHAPTER 18

The Deportation of Las Cases

Commencing in 1815 and continuing for some time, a bitter controversy raged between two clergymen that equally intrigued the island and embarrassed the governing powers. William Balcombe, after the suicide of Huff, placed the education of his boys in the hands of the irascible Rev. Richard Boys, senior chaplain and headmaster of the Jamestown school, and became involved to a minor degree in the vituperation which was exchanged between that divine and the Rev. Samuel Jones.[14]

Mr Boys confined his religion to the sharp contrasts of black and white and used the privilege of the pulpit to protect himself from charges of libel. It happened that, after Napoleon's removal to Longwood, the incoming commander of the St Helena squadron, Admiral Plampin, a noted sea captain and fighting man, arrived on the island and, for a while, lived in the recently vacated Pavilion with a lady, by courtesy Mrs Plampin, who travelled with him. The women coldshouldered her with all the efficacy of a small community. Mrs Balcombe herself found the situation difficult and withdrew behind a barrier of distant politeness, and likewise restrained the family from visiting the Pavilion. The Rev. Mr Boys, acquainted with the irregularity of the union, thundered his disapproval from the pulpit — no extra-marital arrangement could elude Mr Boys. To a crowded and deeply interested congregation he exposed the situation in ringing tones, and with his castigations the whole island was, for once, in full accord; it being probably one of the few occasions on which they were unanimous, for in the plainest terms he exposed the moral lapses prevalent among his flock, and spared nobody. His verbal assaults alarmed Lowe, for Plampin happened to be a faithful adherent to the Lowe policy regarding Napoleon and the Governor could not afford to lose him. Also he knew what a commotion Boys could cause in England were he to send him home on account of his exposure of vice in official quarters. As senior chaplain it was Mr Boys's duty to enter in the parish register all the births taking place on the island, and when, as sometimes happened, he was called upon to record illegitimate births to slave women fathered by the men who were the highest and most trusted of Lowe's lieutenants, the chaplain did not hesitate to note in bold capitals the titles and positions of the sires. These old registers, still surviving to this day, betray frantic attempts made by means of blots and penknives to obliterate the damaging evidence. But Mr Boys wrote a bold hand, and the precise titles and positions of the fathers, in spite of the attempted erasures, can still be plainly distinguished. Mr Boys once refused to take in a corpse to the church on the excuse that the island people were full of superstitions and passed around the altar "littering the church with myrtle". Repeated in full to the Emperor, these island incidents intrigued him greatly. The narrowing of his mental horizon had begun and small things loomed large in the now circumscribed world. Mr Boys's final shaft was hurled when, one Sunday before Lowe's departure after the Emperor's death, he preached a sermon into which he poured his heart and soul, addressing the Governor with special violence. It was the culmination of a burning sense of injustice which had grown over the years. He had known the Emperor, and they had talked together, Napoleon being grateful to him for his assistance in the burial of Cipriani, and he had expressed anger at the forced return of a snuff-box gift from Napoleon. They found common ground in their opinion of Lowe. Boys was a passionate upholder of justice; it governed his life and was the code by which he functioned.

He pitied the exile, but even more disapproved of the jailer's methods and expressed his disapproval with a fanatical violence. Addressing Lowe and his staff from the pulpit, he thundered at them, "Verily I say unto you, publicans and whores shall enter before you into the Kingdom of Heaven."

In November, 1816, Napoleon received the first assault on his little army of personal adherents. It was Las Cases who became the victim, and it saddened the Christmas season, made poignant already by homesickness.

The weather was fine and not over-warm. Napoleon, who had been busy all day long at what he called 'fortifications' — which meant — he had commenced to plan the banks and earthworks on the wind-swept side of the garden for protection, was in good humour from exercise and change of thought. Even though the breeze still held the chill of the south he sat, disregarding it, on a tree stump, talking with Gourgaud, the two Las Cases' and Montholon. Their subject was the Admiral, Sir Pulteney Malcolm, and his wife, who had just returned from the Cape, and whom Napoleon had received that day. St Denis crossed the lawn from the house bearing oranges, sugar and a knife — the fruit being the first of a case that the kindly Admiral had procured for Napoleon from Capetown, along with a welcome bundle of newspapers. Piontkowski, they learnt, was still at the Cape, borrowing money and trying to impress people with his account of his intimate friendship with the Emperor.

Napoleon cut an orange into quarters, gave a portion to young Las Cases, now grown a little more robust than on his arrival, but still an immature, grave youth daily employed by his father in interminable transcriptions of the Emperor's notes. Napoleon, with the Las Cases', presently passed into the billiard room, where they commenced to work on the mass of papers and reference books now accumulating in an ever-growing pile.

Napoleon had arbitrary habits with books and documents; he threw them when finished on the floor, where they lay until a servant gathered them, to add to the heaps around the room.

The Emperor commenced to dictate, walking up and down, hands behind his back, his voice animated, while the older Las Cases waited pencil in hand — this was the usual prelude to a session, an overall formation of ideas, the marshalling of facts, the incidents set in train. An unexpected sight of a troop of horsemen on the boundary interrupted Napoleon's pacing and he passed into the drawing-room to watch them ride up, with nodding plumes and jingling accoutrements, "like a troop of South Sea islanders after their quarry". He made out the Governor, Bingham, Reade, Captain Blakeney, Gorrequer, Rainsford (the new Inspector of Police), and two dragoons; quite a cavalcade. From behind the shutters he watched Lowe and Gorrequer draw rein while the others came on, and almost at once Gentilini, the footman, announced that Reade wished to speak to Las Cases. "Go and see what that beast wants with you, my dear fellow," the Emperor told him, returning to the billiard room. Soon Marchand, in the greatest excitement, ran in to inform him Reade had arrested Las Cases on the charge of sending clandestine correspondence overseas, and that all his papers were being seized. Napoleon hurried to his peep-hole, presently to see Las Cases marched off between Reade and a soldier, while Emmanuel followed, escorted by Blakeney and Rainsford. With them went two trunks of papers.

Longwood was in uproar. Napoleon called for his officers and they discussed the situation.

Shortly before, Las Cases had asked permission from the Emperor to write to Lucien Bonaparte and Lady Clavering, a friend in London, using as bearer a young mulatto, James Scott — once Las Cases's personal attendant and currently employed by a St Helena resident about to depart for England. The Emperor's immediate comment, "It would be madness," had appeared to have squashed the idea, but, conferring anxiously with his officers, Napoleon decided that Las Cases must have gone on with it. It was ascertained that Scott had called to say good-bye, when Las Cases prevailed on him to conceal in the lining of his coat two communications finely written on taffeta, to be delivered by Scott to Lady Clavering in England. Scott's father, English by birth, discovered this and immediately informed Lowe.

An angry Bertrand declared that Las Cases had asked for what he got and added, "I have other worries on my mind." The Montholons similarly showed little distress at their colleague's misfortune. Dinner, ordered for the Emperor and his three remaining officers, that evening became a quieter meal than ever under the blaze of candles, served by the same number of men in royal livery. Napoleon went to bed, but later O'Meara returned from Jamestown and sent in his name. He had met Reade on the road, accompanied by his troop, and Reade called sardonically as he passed, "You will find your friend Las Cases in safe keeping." Napoleon was staggered, not so much by the arrest, but at the gross stupidity of Las Cases. He assured O'Meara he knew nothing of the letters, and his anger redoubled when he realised that many of his own papers were now in Lowe's hands. "I shall have to burn everything I have written," he declared passionately. "It was a pastime for me in this dreary place, and it might have been interesting to the world, but with that Hangman one has neither security nor guarantee. There is no law he would not violate. His eyes were shining when he came here because he found a new way to torment me. When he surrounded the house with his staff, I was reminded of so many South Sea cannibals dancing around prisoners they were about to devour."

Bertrand rode to Plantation House next day and saw Lowe, placed the Emperor's protest before him, and in due course was shown the offending pieces of taffeta covered in minute writing. They constituted a résumé of the whole time spent on the island — indeed the history commenced from the day Napoleon left Malmaison. The Emperor, learning that St Denis had transcribed most of Las Cases's diary, sent for him that night; he was extremely apprehensive as to its contents. "How did it treat Admiral Cockburn?"

"So-so, Sire."

"Did it say that I called him a shark?"

"Yes, Sire, but it also says that Your Majesty is aware of his honesty and cannot refuse your esteem."

"And Sir George Bingham?"

"It speaks very well of him, as also of Colonel Wilks."

"Does it mention Admiral Malcolm?"

"Yes, Sire, it treats him extremely well."

"The Governor?"

Ali's face broke into a smile. "It says a good deal about him, Sire."

"Does it repeat what I said, 'He is a low character, and his face is the meanest I have ever seen'?"

"Yes, Sire," but he added that, "the language was often more moderate."

"Does it say that I called him a Sicilian …?"

"Yes, Sire."

"Well, he is!"

Among the papers was Napoleon's personal diary, and his descriptions of the Italian campaigns, but Emmanuel Las Cases, a bright boy for all his nervousness, when told by Reade to produce the papers, spread them haphazard in the room, and contrived to hide the most valuable under cushions and chair seats. The diary was taken, however, and Bathurst ordered Lowe not to let it out of his hands. It was only through the efforts of Lord Holland that in 1821, after Napoleon's death, it was returned to Las Cases.

Hutt's Gate was used as a lodging for the first night; then Las Cases and his son, both ill from excitement and apprehension, were transferred to Ross Cottage. There they were comfortable enough, but young Las Cases showed signs of a heart ailment, which O'Meara diagnosed as mainly of a nervous order. From the little home they could see Longwood, separated from them by gullies and chasms. They could, through glasses, distinguish the figures of their friends, the comings and goings of servants and all the life of the place they had now begun to look upon as home. The little cottage was not bad, however. "The building small," writes Las Cases, "but at least very liveable." There were trees and grass and, nearby, quantities of fowls raised for Longwood consumption. To Lowe, Las Cases presented a formal protest on their arrest, ending the document with a strange contradictory statement, "Today you could not send me back to him [Napoleon]. I have been sullied by being seized almost under his very eyes. I could therefore be of no consolation to him. In his eyes I would be merely a blemished object and a painful memory." Lowe immediately became suspicious and sought some hidden reason.

Las Cases played a good hand, however, though later, caught unawares by their mild treatment, he began to talk perhaps too much. To Reade he expressed his opinion of the Emperor's health. "He must be looked upon as a sick man. Great allowances should be made for him." The Las Cases' by now were jailed in the Castle, the 'common' jailer, the mild Mr Weston, taking them under his wing. They suffered from nothing more serious than lack of visitors, the Governor making sure they were *incommunicado* as far as possible, and at the same time pondering what to do with them. Las Cases, however, for his own reasons, did not wish to return to Longwood. His knowledge of his potential usefulness to the Emperor in Europe combined with his desire to escape from the growing tension among the staff. Gourgaud in his diary commented on a fervent urge to kick the Secretary if he walked in front of him to dinner again, and it can be certain he did not fail to let Las Cases know of his feelings.

Queen Hortense's diamond necklace came into the picture. On the *Northumberland* one evening after dinner, Napoleon while walking with Las Cases drew the chain of glittering stones from his pocket, and told the Secretary to wear it round his waist for safety. Las Cases took the necklace, put it in a belt, and habitually wore it on his person. In the excitement of arrest he forgot it, and only when at the Castle did the realisation dawn that he would probably be deported with the necklace still on him.

He saw none of the suite and was closely attended by sentries at all times. Despair threatened, when "an Englishman", who had business at the Castle, came in. Las Cases assured him in an undertone that "it would in no way impair his honour to his country if he returned the jewels to their proper owner". After a moment's thought the visitor said, "I shall walk very slowly past you when I am going out," and subsequently from the pocket of his coat the necklace found its way into Napoleon's hands. This is a family anecdote.

Las Cases never returned to Longwood although, as Lowe's deliberations turned out, he might have done so. After detention at the Castle he sailed for Cape Town.

Autumn in St Helena brought little change in the climate, only a reddening of a few trees. The majority, being sub-tropical, disregarded the passing of the season and still put out flowers. Fogs rolled in and hung like curtains around the sharp peaks. It rained more often, rendering the roads sloppy, while clothing became limp from the damp. It was a period of intense boredom for the Emperor, who, enveloped by the mists on his walks, returned muddy and irritable. Bickerings in his ill-assorted family never ceased, the damp affected their nerves and the mildew on the walls offended their sense of smell. Only the billiard room kept a normally dry atmosphere, and there they congregated on one pretext or another. They measured themselves against the door-jamb — the marks are there still. To whom did they belong? The Emperor's, at five feet two and a half inches, was an easy one to identify, though others were scored near him. Betsy's, also small, was probably the line beneath.

Betsy and Jane were invited to lunch, only a family party, yet conducted with shabby state — servants in knee-breeches serving good things on silver salvers, the Sèvres china out, the room hushed while the Emperor ate; even Betsy's spirits became so subdued as to render her silent for the first few minutes, but she recovered, trying with her chatter to dispel the gloom, until

Madame Montholon rebuked her for speaking at table before the Emperor opened the conversation. Remembering the meals at the Briars, when everyone talked simultaneously and Napoleon had to raise his voice to be heard by her father across the table, she pulled a face behind Madame's back, which Napoleon saw and gave her his first smile of the day. Afterwards he put sugar in her coffee cup with his own fingers, and brought it to where she sat — a sign of great approval.

They spoke of the Skeltons — friends of the family and much liked by the St Helena people — who were going home, and whose departure was a genuine cause for regret. A few days later, the Balcombes gave a farewell ball at the Briars, and the night, as if to make a last good impression, was unusually clear and aglow with stars. Lanterns marked the paths on the knoll, where the Pavilion was, while the waterfall, swollen by rain, took an appearance of quicksilver. Music filled the garden. The Bertrands returned to Longwood enchanted by the scene, the friendliness of island life — they were becoming very lonely, and recounted everything to an interested Napoleon, who knew many there. Gourgaud came back in a bad humour. His efforts had somehow gone awry; his account therefore was tinged by his feelings. "It was a bourgeois affair. Betsy wore her one evening dress. She is a flirt." They had pitched a marquee near where the Emperor's had formerly stood. The crown was still cut in the turf; the wine had been better than that provided at Longwood, so Gourgaud said.

Napoleon told him to ride to Jamestown to lose his ill-temper.

The Skeltons came to say good-bye and the Emperor presented Mrs Skelton with a Sèvres cup. She secretly undertook to deliver a letter to Cardinal Fesch, Napoleon's half-uncle, and so was able to send to Rome the first real news of the exiles. It was a fine gesture on the part of the Skeltons, for Napoleon's arrival had cost them their post, the position of Lieutenant-Governor not having been carried on.

The weather continued foggy and wet, and Napoleon stayed indoors unseen by the orderly officer. Sir Hudson Lowe began to show anxiety and summoned up Bertrand to demand that in future the orderly officer should view the Emperor daily, but this suggestion did not get very far, for Napoleon, suffering toothache, remained invisible.

A day or so earlier Lowe had called Dr O'Meara to Plantation House and questioned him closely on a variety of matters concerning the Emperor, including the exile's health and habits. Napoleon immediately got wind of this and in anger wasted no time in summoning O'Meara to him to enquire whether in their future intercourse he was to consider him in the light of a spy and a tool of the Governor or as his physician. "During the short interview that the Governor had with me in my bed-chamber, one of the first things he proposed was to send you away," Napoleon told O'Meara, "and that I should take his own surgeon in your place. This he repeated and so earnest was he to gain his object that, though I gave him a flat refusal, when he was going out he turned about and again proposed it." Napoleon gathered that O'Meara had provided the Governor with a very comprehensive survey of his physical condition. He was incensed.

Looking over the diaries, and the Lowe letters, reading the opinions and re-living the final years (and, for me, also going through Betsy's memoirs), one can be almost sorry for Sir Hudson Lowe. Yet much of the obstruction and unpleasantness that he encountered in the first stages of his term of office was of his own making.

The choice of a Governor with such a temperament and background was, to say the least of it, an unfortunate one. The Prince Regent had done better in appointing Admiral Cockburn in the first place and fate had been kind in that the worthy Admiral was on leave in London at the moment when he was wanted. In Lowe's choice, the British Cabinet's action showed all the lack of tact that marked its official life. It is said that the majority of the documents and papers relating to the St Helena incidents, with the official letters and private correspondence, were afterwards purposely destroyed. If it had not been for the copies kept by Lowe, the story of the captivity would largely have been hearsay, but the Governor's son in 1856, after his father's death, sold the whole collection, comprising over one hundred volumes of script, to the British Museum, where they remain in the archives, a strange study in human relations. The personal sentiments and characteristics of the writers, so widely divergent, create a picture that only begins to take life after a period of assimilation in the Manuscript Room of the British Museum, and then the Napoleonic era appears as close as yesterday. The Lowe collection of papers contains a mass of documents: directions, intrigue, French objections and complaints about their maltreatment, the purveyor's reports and accounts, O'Meara's quarrel, with here and there the record of a kindly act rising from some British citizen's goodness of heart (Lady Holland for one, sending material to the French ladies, toys to the children and books to the Emperor, her gifts frowned upon by Plantation House).

Admiral Cockburn, though relinquishing his post as keeper of the exile, remained for a short time, only to see his carefully considered regulations drastically reviewed. The thin-lipped, narrow-headed new Commanding-General, with the help and advice of Sir Thomas Reade, uncompromising and 'John Bullish', reconstituted the field to their own liking. Sir Hudson Lowe's hand was not only directed towards Longwood; he made alterations to the pleasantly-yellowed brick Plantation House, with its deeper-toned orange creeper that in spring makes a feature of the front wall. He subjected it to a thorough facelift and built an extra room, a library where once had been a courtyard with flowers. Here he put a marble mantelpiece to frame the iron grate of the period and lined the walls with bookshelves, while windows opened on to a flower-border. Today the room is possibly more pleasant than when it was first built. Time has taken a hand and mellowed the wood, dulled the polish on the marble and faded the furniture into anonymity, leaving an authentic scrap of a past generation, and possibly nothing has been altered since the time of the Lowe tenancy. Although high-level controversies still continued with the Allies about Napoleon, Lowe was not concerned. He showed no desire to be friendly or co-operate with his charges; he came as a jailer, a cold impersonal instrument of the law as he understood it, later to add a personal animosity that tinctured the whole British administration of Napoleon's imprisonment with disgrace. The final chapter of his dealings with the Emperor are disturbing inasmuch as they leave a memory of unnecessarily close surveillance, of persecution and annoyances that debased the status of both men. William Balcombe's comment on the situation was that it became painful to see an intellect such as Bonaparte's reduced to exercising its powers on the trivialities and tormentings of a man of Lowe's calibre, one to whom in the ordinary course of his life he would not have given a minute's thought. To circumvent his orders became an obsession with the Emperor, and the victories that he won with no weapons but his astute wits were cheap and added nothing to his comfort or his peace, nor indeed his stature. Granted the times were noted for rough and blatant realism, but the normal British outlook was never truthfully depicted by the meanness of Lowe's administration and thus he did unhappy service to his country. Later, intoxicated with power, he went so far as to suppress the knowledge of certain incidents from Lord Bathurst, his immediate chief, altered and added to the doctor's medical reports on the Emperor's condition, and translated Government repressive measures into even stricter sets of regulations of his own. British memory is notoriously short where a defeated foe is concerned and after Napoleon's death there stirred in England an uneasy national conscience that effectively precluded Lowe from reaching the summit of his ambition.

The periods spent at the Bertrands', in their new little home, were happy for Betsy; she made herself useful and was an unqualified success with the children, who followed her as one of themselves, united in mischief and chatter, speaking indiscriminate English and French, roaming the grounds in front of the Bertrands' garden, where below lay the Deadwood Plain, or watching the completion of the new Longwood house, most of it having come in sections from England in a store-ship. Varying sums from £60,000 to £80,000 were supposed to be the amount spent on this new home for the prisoner, and the iron fencing aroused adverse comment not only on the part of Napoleon but by the island community, who considered fences redundant and an iron barricade an offence. One Sunday morning Napoleon, having rather furtively walked around the new building, neither the position nor the plan to his liking, came bustling into the Bertrands', to find Betsy reading to her sister and the children. Enquiring what book she had and why she appeared so grave, he was informed they were learning to repeat the Collect of the day and that if they were not word-perfect their father would be very angry. "It is not for us," the Bertrand children piped up, "but we learn all the same." Bonaparte summarily put an end to the reading and Betsy remarked, "I suppose you never learnt a Collect or anything religious, for I am told you disbelieve in the existence of God." He seemed displeased and answered, "You must have been told an untruth. When you are wiser, you will understand that no one could doubt the existence of God." Mrs Balcombe, who heard him and was herself a religious woman, enquired if he were a pre-destinarian, as was generally reported. He admitted he was. "I believe that whatever a man's destiny calls upon him to do, that he must fulfil," he told her. Later he questioned Betsy on her opinion of Madame Montholon. Did she not think her beautiful? "Not to me", she replied bluntly. Perhaps something more than mere outward appearance called for unequivocal judgment. Napoleon assured her that as a young girl Madame had been really lovely and he sent for a miniature on a snuff box that gave an unrecognisable portrait of the lady as she now appeared — languid, subdued by many miscarriages, often bed-ridden. From the beginning Betsy and she had held nothing in common, their temperaments being completely divergent, but Betsy enthusiastically went on to say that Madame Bertrand was the loveliest woman she had ever seen: carriage, face, personality — she felt nobody could conduct herself better. Indeed William Balcombe, after his first visit to the *Northumberland*, had told his family on his return that he had been tremendously struck by her charm and dignity. In truth she was not strictly beautiful, but possessed a flair for wearing clothes that was Jane's despair and delight. Her house became a home — even the modest Hutt's Gate, perched on the lip of the valley, and in her time not sheltered by trees, caught something of her exigent personality. Her presence peeps out of diaries, requisitions and letters — "gauze for the children's rooms" (did she mean mosquito-netting?); remarks on a chair coveted by the Emperor; beds of such comfort that Betsy wrote of them with enthusiasm, as she did of her breakfasts. Scraps of admiration float down through the years, as do the remarks about her appearance at a ball and, in the case of J. Metcalfe, the carpenter, her surprising language when she wished to know "Why beds are being made for the Montholon children when the Emperor wishes my chair to be copied," adding "or else I shall lose my chair". Then, illogically, she asks the price of the beds and if they are good, and orders one for her own son at £40.

Hers was a very devoted family; Bertrand, returning home for meals on all possible occasions, drew comment from the Emperor; but nothing interfered with his domestic arrangements, only his family made the exile of St Helena bearable to him. Bertrand shared his life between Napoleon and his wife, and Napoleon, though jealous of the divided allegiance, reacted to the happy influences of the newly-built cottage and came there often and stayed for long periods. He met Betsy there, sat on the comfortable chair, gossiped and watched the Deadwood scene below through his spyglass. Extracts from her notes say, "The Emperor has been setting races for the children — prize, a sugar plum," "Napoleon has come from gardening." Unlike Hutt's Gate the new cottage was only a few minutes' walk from Longwood house.

CHAPTER 19

Betsy and the Ensign

The hospitable 66th Regiment gave a series of balls in Deadwood Camp — long-drawn-out entertainments on account of the curfew that necessitated guests remaining until the daylight gun (unless provided with the countersign). The insecurity of the roads in the darkness, moreover, became an added hazard, since most of the visitors were forced to journey on horseback carrying their finery. But nobody minded and Betsy's description of one of these functions remains; on that night she wore her 'other' evening dress — a very adolescent garment, but considered by her mother to be chic enough for an army ball. She was staying with the Bertrands and had received an invitation to dine at Longwood before setting out. All the suite had been invited to Deadwood, but only Madame Bertrand was going and Betsy arrived to find Madame had decided to make a magnificent toilet ... her hair brushed up with combs and withdrawn from her temples in the true Parisian fashion of 1816. Betsy with her untidy curls presented the appearance of childish adolescence. However, Josephine, an accomplished hairdresser, after completing Madame's coiffure addressed herself to Betsy's locks, tweaking and pulling the curls into some resemblance to a woman of fashion.

Betsy commented, "She pulled my hair so hard my eyes took a Chinese slant." When she caught sight of the completed effect she was horror-struck. From the waist down she looked a child — demure in black dancing slippers, white stockings and little short 'leno' frock, while, above the puffed sleeves of an off-the-shoulder neckline rose the coiffure of a lady of the French court, in prescribed extreme Parisian style and bedecked with Madame's diamond combs. There was no time to pull it down and she crossed the short space between the cottage and Longwood in dread of the shout of laughter that would surely come from the Emperor on seeing her starting eyes and straining hair, the pantaloons starkly noticeable below the childish skirt — but instead he declared "it was the only time he had ever seen her hair wearing the appearance of anything like neatness". When his eyes fell on her frock it was a different story — he pronounced it to be 'frightful' from its extreme shortness and demanded the hem to be let down immediately, twitching it and pulling at the tucks — until Josephine was summoned — when with the help of the Emperor, she undid both tucks and hem until sufficient length was achieved. Betsy's diary records, "I knew it was useless resisting when once the fiat had gone forth, but the effect was dreadful."

The meal ended with the Emperor's usual abrupt movement from the table "as if he had received an electric shock". "If Balcombe had been here he would want to drink one, two, three, ah! *cinq bouteilles*," he announced to them, holding up his fingers. He, as always, remarked at the want of gallantry of Englishmen in letting the women leave the table alone while the men drank port. "*Cinq bouteilles*," he nodded — nothing less was ever mentioned. Betsy felt glad it was only five. "I should be very angry at being turned out," he told Mrs Balcombe, "to wait for two or three hours while your husband and his friends make themselves drunk and get gout. Bah!" It was no use protesting or contradicting, so *cinq bouteilles* became one of the family phrases.

Napoleon happened to be in a good mood and, ignoring the silver tongs, helped the ladies to sugar with his own fingers. They lingered over Le Page's perfect coffee, and later the Emperor escorted them to his carriage that was waiting to take them down to Deadwood. Mme Bertrand and her baby not being able to be left, Mrs Balcombe, Jane, Betsy and General Gourgaud, disconsolate at the projected departure of the lovely Laura Wilks, all squeezed in with difficulty. Archambault, slightly inebriated as usual, laid on the whip, and the two wild Cape horses tore past the guard-house sentries and down the track, to the sound of Madame Bertrand's lusty screams. Nothing made an impression on Archambault's ears, however, and the pace increased as the road dipped, until finally a check was administered by a gum tree on one of the sharp turns. The passengers threw themselves out with thankfulness and in wet and foggy conditions they walked the intervening mile to the camp. Madame Bertrand later appeared in a dress of Mrs Baird's: the diary notes "half a yard too short", as "unrelated to the rest of her toilette as mine had been an hour or so earlier". The sophisticated head-dress and juvenile length of skirt, however, in no way detracted from the lady's innate elegance. Madame Bertrand's training rendered her capable of carrying off any eventuality, and the ball went happily for them until the guns from the forts announced the break of day.

"We cared less for the walk back through the rain and mist, for a large breakfast awaited us and comfortable beds in the Grand Marshal's cottage," was the diary's comment, and "Napoleon complimented me on my dancing and appearance at the ball which he heard were much admired, and told me I was considered very like the Baroness Sturmer and might be mistaken for her own sister".

Major Fehrzen was away, but Ensign Carstairs had been in evidence at the ball, immaculate as ever. Betsy avoided him; his censure at the race meeting and his slights at the parties following were incidents hard to forget. "He is too aristocratic for you," Napoleon had warned. She remembered the words as she caught sight of the young man's tall elegance. Napoleon's comments were always apt, nevertheless; she had been very attracted to the Hon. George. Youth called to youth. To dance with him had furnished moments of sheer delight and the garden outside the Briars house never looked more lovely in the moonlight than when she had strolled there with him. Betsy sighed: the faithful Fehrzen of the 53rd was older, but though considered attractive and a conquest, he fell short of the standard of the 'scented dandy', as the Emperor dubbed the Ensign. A growing awareness showed Betsy that the Imperial exile was himself a kind of yardstick in her mind, that over-riding his age and corpulence was an invincible personality that made others appear pale and ineffectual. He blotted out mental pictures of slim young officers, dances, moonlit gardens and rides over winding paths. She turned away from where she could see Carstairs; that episode at least was over and she was glad. His hands were the only part of him that still attracted her — strong, sinewy, capable hands for such a dilettante figure. Napoleon's exquisitely-kept nails and dimpled knuckles did not compare favourably. Somehow they warred with his impelling personality. She never liked his hands, they were in contradiction to what she knew him to be.

When next she saw George Carstairs, it was aboard the *Newcastle*, where Admiral and Lady Malcolm held a fête, that the young people of the island might meet the naval officers who came to James Roads in increasing numbers. As it happened, Betsy was placed under the chaperonage of Lady Lowe. Charlotte Johnston, her daughter by a former husband, had become friendly with the Ensign Carstairs and he went frequently to Plantation House. Betsy studiously avoided him while on the barge that ferried them across to the ship, nor did she approach that part of the deck where he stood holding a kind of court among the island girls. His poise was "elegant, yet in the extreme". "He's too aristocratic for you," sounded in her ears. The young strength of the naval men around her and the devastating Napoleonic shadow in the background were becoming potent enough to swamp the Ensign's fleeting influence, yet she was impatient and bewildered, a little sad; the grown-up world had come too quickly.

Charlotte Johnston caught up with her at the culmination of a dance "to a fiddle and a pipe" and told her she was wanted in the Commander's

cabin and pointed the way. During the day Betsy had noticed Charlotte and
Carstairs had remained much together, at lunchtime, later during the dance,
and when the sailors put on a hornpipe display. Evidently his charm was
being appreciated in the Plantation House circle, equally as in the days of the
former Governor. Carstairs found officialdom his métier and had hopes of
becoming an A.D.C. to Sir Hudson.

Betsy obediently ran down the steps, to check suddenly when she saw the
Ensign alone waiting for her. To one of her calibre, the fact that she had been
tricked into a meeting was infuriating, and to have a temperamental dandy
approach her with supplications and explanations of his cavalier treatment,
yet with the smug airs of an assured conqueror, aroused her undisciplined
spirit to quick retaliation. As he went to grab her she administered a series of
sharp slaps. What she did with the Emperor's horse was her own affair, she told
him breathlessly; the fact that he listened to gossip and censured her actions
was an impertinence and an insult. She cut short his protests and, glad to see
the colour rising to his check where she had attacked him with some vigour,
she turned and left the cabin precipitately, a half-uttered sentence lost in the
flurry of departure. "Why did you want to trap me with him?" she demanded
violently of Charlotte, who, curious, had lingered in the passage. Half-afraid
of the rage in Betsy's face, Charlotte hastily excused herself, putting the blame
fully on Carstairs, who had spent the morning soliciting her help. Not that
she had much wished to assist him to regain Betsy; the Ensign's guns were
socially big enough for her to be jealous of his attentions to someone else,
and it had not been pleasant to fix this meeting in the cabin, adding insult to
injury. Betsy's anger now reduced her to a state bordering on tears.

The Captain's quarters happened to be close by, and, retaliation always a
first thought in times of stress, Betsy gave the girl a smart push through the
open door, and slammed it, turning the key. When, panting, she regained the
deck, she found the whole party preparing to leave the ship, some of the ladies
even then being 'whipped' over the side to the waiting barge. Ship's officers
were gathered in a group to say good-bye, and the guns from the fort and
men-of-war at anchor commenced to thunder a salute for Lord Amherst, who
had just arrived in James Roads in the *Corsair*, from India. In the excitement
and noise Charlotte's imprisonment completely went out of Betsy's mind,
with the result that the girl was not missed until the barge had almost reached
the shore. After much commotion and scolding, it was found impracticable to
send the barge back and finally Carstairs was deputed to return in a row-boat
and rescue the prisoner. Lady Lowe administered a severe reprimand, telling
Betsy "to try and use her reason and not be so childish". Later, when he heard
of the incident, the Emperor remarked that he wondered at the lady's lack of

perception for giving Betsy credit for something she did not possess. He had already been in possession of the facts before she had opportunity to tell him, and was not too pleased at Carstairs's renewed attentions. Later, developing a dog-in-the-manger attitude, he took active measures in influencing Major Fehrzen from paying court to Betsy, the one man who might have superseded him in her heart and who could have given her a happy life .In the brief sketches and word portraits of the period, perhaps Major Fehrzen's character stands supreme. He was known as "a gallant officer, with all the points of a good soldier, plus breeding, looks and high intelligence". He was a password for all that stood high in nineteenth-century standards of manhood.

Betsy and he had no great affinity in tastes and inclinations, yet his departure with the 53rd to India, where later he died of cholera, was a blow she felt deeply. Here and there in chronicles one finds fleeting gossip linking their names ... whether Fehrzen would propose; whether she, madcap that she was, would refuse the eligible Major of the 53rd.[17]

In her diary she often mentions him, but from other sources it can be inferred that once she was removed from the influence of the Emperor's personality things might have been different and both their lives cast in kindlier lines. One contemporary writer records definitely that Napoleon expressed the hope that Fehrzen would not marry her, and it is attributed to him that he said she was not good enough, which seems at variance with his other comments. Possibly it was one of his 'gambits', at one with his remark to her that Carstairs was "too aristocratic", as in the same way he had a fixed routine when meeting people, asking their situation, their name, how much port they drank, "Une bouteille" or "*quatre bouteilles*" or in William Balcombe's case, "*cinq bouteilles*".

There were periods of calm, however, when she translated the English papers or obediently moved the red pins on the old war maps and the members of the household were correspondingly grateful. They groaned with ennui. Any break in the uneventful passage of the day was helpful and the 'rude hoyden' cheered them. They relied on William Balcombe and his family for so much — for strength and sympathy, for a normal outlook in the midst of the strange fantasia of their daily life, for additional delicacies for the table, and even adequate food. There are stories, possibly far-fetched, in some contemporary journals of Madame Bertrand borrowing food for breakfast from the soldiers in the guard-house.

CHAPTER 20

The Emperor's Decline

Before the full circuit of the roads was curtailed, it had been Napoleon's custom to ride in a type of jaunting-car in the afternoon. His horsemanship amounted to foolhardiness, although it had been widely circulated that he was of a cowardly nature. Betsy mentioned on more than one occasion the control he exercised over his mount of the moment, and how prone he was to ride into the most inaccessible places, and at great speed. Out of devilment he insisted on Gourgaud forcing his horse to rest its hoofs on the floor of the carriage in which he and Betsy sat, to demonstrate what could be done by perseverance and firmness. Her comment was that "I tucked my feet out of the way on the seat, and was frightened by the whole performance". One of the Emperor's foibles took the form of breakneck driving around the narrow mountain tracks in the jaunting-car, and if some rider happened to be approaching from the opposite direction the only course open to him was to turn round and gallop ahead of the approaching vehicle until an outlet on the side of the road could be reached. As three Cape horses were habitually yoked abreast to the Emperor's car in French style, the rider had no alternative but to retreat or fall over the precipice. "You are cowardly," Napoleon accused Betsy on one of these occasions, when she begged for a more moderate speed. "Josephine was also cowardly with horses."

One of Betsy's exasperatingly brief recollections is that once, when Napoleon was imitating London cries, she asked him if he had never been there incognito, to have acquired the cries so accurately. He avoided answering the question by saying that one of his *buffo* actors had introduced them in a comedy. Jane afterwards commented she was convinced he had visited London.

(As a matter of history, Napoleon did visit England once, lodging in a house in the Adelphi, in the Strand, remaining there for a short time about 1793. The object of his journey was not known to the General who accidentally met him there, but Jane's surmise had evidently been correct.)[16]

Betsy informed him she had heard that Talma, "whom as an actor Napoleon admired very much," had given him lessons in sitting upon a throne. Napoleon remarked complacently, "*C'est une signe je n'y tiens bien.*"

The Wilks family finally left the island — the pleasant Wilkses, whose kindly manners and sympathetic actions during their term had endeared them to all people. The Balcombe girls joined the crowd on the dock and waved farewell to the *Havannah* as she set sail. Betsy, who was again a guest of the Bertrands, rode sadly up the curving road to Longwood and found the Emperor sitting in his favourite chair in Madame's room. Seeing her in low spirits, Napoleon enquired what could possibly have happened to drive away what he called "the dimples from your *riante* face. Has anyone run away with the favourite *robe de bal*, or is old black Sarah dead?" He was in a pliant mood, gentle and persuading, the tempers of the past weeks gone. Betsy told him of the Wilkses' farewells and the genuine grief at their departure, how all ranks and ages had gathered at the Castle and crowded the dock to wish them "God Speed". It resembled more a funeral than a leave-taking and, as the frigate spread her canvas, groups of saddened women wandered, watching from under the trees until she became a white speck.

Napoleon listened with interest and some curiosity. He had met the former Governor and appreciated his manner and sound intellect, but the fact of his great popularity — for he was a quiet-spoken man — was something he had not expected. He learnt more of the English character every day, a strange mixture, to his mind, and he told Betsy he sincerely regretted not having been better acquainted with so amiable a lady as Mrs Wilks. He pondered on the unpredictable British — Betsy always something of an enigma; O'Meara's Irish personality; William Balcombe's blunt, factual approach; Captain Poppleton's ingenuous charm; Major Fehrzen's military gallantry (none wore a uniform better); the tacit acceptance of command of Admiral Sir Pulteney Malcolm; the obedient, hard-treated sailors — all these intrigued and puzzled him. Napoleon remarked that in France they could never use their sailors so harshly. He also said, "Whatever British sailors take in hand, they never leave undone. As a race they lack much of the glitter and poise of continental nations but appear to possess a tough core; even the women."

He wound Betsy's curls around a plump finger and told her to cheer up, sorrow did not suit her. Madame Bertrand came in with a collection of things sent her by Lady Holland, who was consistently kind to both her family and the Montholons. They appreciated deeply the thoughts of another woman from an alien land — Napoleon called her "*la bonne Lady Holland*" — and they talked of her attentions to the Emperor "when abandoned by the world in the distant island". He told them that the Fox family "abounded in liberal and generous sentiments". Of Fox he said, "He was sincere and honest in his intentions and, had he lived, England would not have been desolated by war. He was the one Minister who knew the interests of his country. He was received with almost triumph in every city of the French Empire and fêted and welcomed."

The records of certain incidents often recur in the history of Napoleon's captivity. A dozen books give almost similar versions of the story of the bust of the King of Rome, of the six meetings of Lowe with the Emperor, Betsy's attack on him with his own sword and the story of Toby, the slave. In some ways trivial, they yet have caught a century of public interest by their human angle and have lost nothing in the telling. More sinister incidents remain hidden, possibly of necessity, until a sufficient period has elapsed when they, too, can be ventilated. The rumour of the attempted assassination of the Emperor remains an uneasy conjecture, as does the plan of his escape, his intrigues to gain his removal to England, his illnesses, his methods of circumventing censorship and even the mystery of the papers hidden in Longwood — these may all eventually be cleared up.

Gourgaud's desertion created the second gap in the Emperor's retinue. Napoleon showed great forbearance towards his aide-de-camp, as indeed he did towards all the suite when at times tempers became frayed and they quarrelled and sulked. Gourgaud was more vocal and explosive than the others and the Emperor tried with added softness to divert him from his tantrums.

Gourgaud fell into an obvious trap from his very boredom and discontent — aided to some extent by the Emperor, who encouraged him to go out among the people whenever he had an opportunity. The Governor invited him to dine and he met with unexpectedly pleasant conditions — an unusually affable Lowe as well as the three commissioners and an amiable hostess. It did not take long for Gourgaud to become an *habitué* of Plantation House, joining in the social activities of the Sturmers and the Misses Johnston, finding a certain pride and satisfaction in the fact that the Governor treated him better than he treated the other exiles. Major Gorrequer mentions him several times in the Lowe Papers on the occasion when Baxter and Reade talked with him about the Emperor. He recounted all he knew, which, however, wasn't much more than they had already gleaned from Captain Nicholls, but which was in the nature of a confirmation. Also he remarked that "the Emperor's health was no worse than when they arrived in 1815". A statement which even Dr Baxter considered an exaggeration, having read O'Meara's comments over the months.

So eventually Gourgaud received permission to sail to Europe, not unduly regretted by the Longwood fraternity, bearing a letter to Lord Bathurst and preceded by a lengthy correspondence of a private nature between Lowe and the Colonial Minister of State; which caused the latter to write back that they had "picked up" Gourgaud while in the Channel and brought him to London, where he had given them a full description of Napoleon — had indeed told them his health was no worse than when he first landed on the island, and "confessed" to a great deal more. Gourgaud was allowed the freedom of England as long as he behaved himself. He had bought his immunity and, in consequence of his 'confessions', Lowe tightened rather than relaxed the restrictions on Napoleon's movements.

Bathurst, notwithstanding Gourgaud's assertions, had begun to be concerned about the apparently authentic reports of the Emperor's physical condition. Politically he feared a hardening of public opinion if Napoleon's state of health were further disregarded by his jailers. He guessed there was a system of communication between the island and the continent, and it did not need Lowe's suppositions and fears to apprise him of it; the London newspapers presented evidence enough. Lowe cast suspicion on everyone who had the smallest contact with Longwood — the guards at the gate, the infrequent visitors, the Chinese workmen, but primarily on the two Englishmen whose duties took them almost daily to the Emperor's presence. In the office of Balcombe, Fowler and Cole he installed a quick-witted agent, who, however, discovered nothing incriminating; he examined the books and could give no more information other than on the weekly needs for provisions and requisitions of the exiles. This proved exasperating to Lowe, sensing intrigue around him yet completely baffled, and a letter from Bathurst, written on the 10th May 1818, did not mitigate his frustration.

"Private. 10th May, 1818.

"... General Gourgaud had no difficulty in avowing that there has always existed a free and uninterrupted channel of communication between the inhabitants of Longwood and this country or the Continent transmitting letters, receiving pamphlets, money and other articles.

"Mainly to General Bonaparte through Englishmen who visit St Helena and are glad and willing to convey letters brought to them by Napoleon's servants. Merchant ships' captains and East India Company ships would give passage of articles any time if wanted. Napoleon owned a sum of money in Spanish dollars of £10,000 at the very time that he disposed of his plate. On question, he (Gourgaud) assured me that neither Mr Balcombe nor Dr O'Meara were in the above."

For all his exaggeration, some affirm that Gourgaud's journal is the most truthful of the St Helena period, except where his personal feelings were involved.

As an aide-de-camp on active service, he was keen, intelligent and useful, but the inactivity of life on the sub-tropic island became torture verging on madness, and he vented his distress and temper on all around him.

His journal reiterates ennui, the ever present feeling of isolation, the anachronism of court life in a cottage.

Later in England he fell foul of Sir Walter Scott, who had hinted that he played a double part, being a kind of agent for the British Government, whereupon Gourgaud wanted to 'call him out'. He hotly declaimed he had never even spoken to Sir Hudson Lowe — which was manifestly untrue, for, apart from the admissions in his journal, half the island had seen him in conversation at one time or another with the Governor.

Gourgaud subsequently retracted all he had previously said, to be unceremoniously packed off "to Hamburgh" — but the damage to his master's cause had been done and the gloomy pattern of Napoleon's existence was fixed for good. Others of the household followed his departure. Santine, Rousseau, the *lampiste* and one of the Archambaults were all considered 'unsatisfactory', and Cipriani, the *maître d'hôtel*, was removed by death. The malady to which he succumbed became the subject of suspicion, for the diagnosis "inflammation of the bowels" seemed vague. O'Meara perhaps feared to voice his thoughts, especially as two others in the household, a woman and child, had died in similar fashion. Napoleon saw Cipriani carried to his room in agony and wept for him.

He and many others guessed how much more lay behind the death of his *maître d'hôtel*. Thus officially listed, Cipriani had never been prevented, since the first day of their arrival, from visiting Jamestown on household business. He was known by Lowe, however, as one of the Emperor's former spies; indeed the Governor had reason to remember a Capri incident in which Cipriani figured, when 'intelligence' materially affected the success of the British adventure. He had been the prime mover there. It is surprising that Lowe, on his arrival, did not have the man recalled immediately, but probably this last incident served better to close the chapter.

Meanwhile Napoleon had a close check made on the kitchen routine. It was noted that even with the family at the Briars he had shown apprehension of poison — the bitterness of the coffee had been suspect, and young Alexander's innocent presentation of an aperient-pill as a sweet had considerably shaken him. Later when routine took shape at Longwood, fears diminished, but Napoleon himself remained always on the alert. Now, after the quarrels with the Governor, the added curtailment of liberty, the refusal of visitors on the old scale, and finally Cipriani's death, his old apprehension was redoubled. It is possible that O'Meara had by then repeated to him the Governor's conversation, with its hints on poison; his meaning had been definite enough.

Lowe at that period was a vengeful jailer and antagonist, and Napoleon did not underrate him. Grieving over Cipriani, he openly expressed strong suspicion that something sinister had taken place, that the death was not an act of God. His distress was manifest to all, and his appreciation of the Rev. Mr Boys and his assistant who officiated at the burial — there was no Roman Catholic priest — found expression in a sum of money for the little church and the gift of snuff-boxes. With reluctance, Mr Boys felt it incumbent upon him to return his gift, remarking that he was only obeying so called laws.[17]

The Emperor spoke to O'Meara of Cipriani: "Where is his soul gone — to Rome perhaps to see his wife and child before it takes the long final journey?" He was to be a loss, not only because of his ability to find out what was going on, but for his rough humour and the kinship his nationality imparted.

Allusions to poison continued to circulate among the household and accentuated the ever present underlying dread of some overt act resulting in the Emperor's death.

Previously Cipriani had recounted all kinds of Jamestown rumours and had picked up more than one veiled hint, and amid the gossip of shops and tavern he had heard speculation on the time and on the method to be employed to effect Bonaparte's demise.

In the Lowe folios can be read several ambiguous references to the same subject, making it clear that the Governor himself dwelt on it, and Sir Thomas Reade's uncensored statements even now must arouse speculation.

Subsequently, the Emperor, after a conversation with O'Meara, ate nothing that was not shared by the others. Even towards his death he maintained that rule, and, having ordered two special dishes, retained the English Doctor Arnott with him so that he might taste them first. His apprehension must have been very strong. It manifested itself as early as May, 1816, during the third interview with Sir Hudson Lowe when the latter came to inform the Emperor of his intention to remove O'Meara from his household and to replace him by Mr Baxter as Doctor to Longwood. (Baxter, once surgeon to the Corsican Rangers, had accompanied Sir Hudson Lowe to St Helena.) Napoleon was indignant and immediately objected to the proposal, perceiving in it insult as well as something more sinister. He told O'Meara afterwards that Lowe, with signal lack of tact, had stressed the point about Baxter on two occasions during the interview, and even at rising to leave referred to it again. The Emperor then discussed at length the probability of O'Meara's expulsion from the island and its bearing on his own future safety. He trusted O'Meara and, though sometimes impatient, evinced a great liking for him. The doctor did not unduly stress his personal fears to his patient, but he now pondered at length on Lowe's cryptic remarks at Plantation House which took place during one after-dinner stroll on the sloping lawn, out of earshot of anyone else. Lowe openly discussed the benefit that Europe could derive from the death of the captive. He avowed his intention of being revenged on Bonaparte and making him feel his status. He observed again that he considered "Ali Pasha as a much more respectable scoundrel than Napoleon". It fitted in with the even more outspoken statements of Reade, who remarked that, "The Allied Powers have missed their aim; they should have throttled Napoleon's son, who, as long as he lives, will be an object of unquiet to the Allied Powers."

O'Meara's reaction was swift and uncompromising and roused the lurking suspicion in Lowe's mind as to his loyalty; his vindictiveness now temporarily shifted from the French members of the suite to centre on the cheerful Irishman. He had volunteered for service to Napoleon while aboard the *Bellerophon*, when the latter's own doctor did not sail with him to exile. O'Meara spoke fair French, a great advantage to the Emperor, who trusted his knowledge of medicine as much as he trusted anybody's. Admiral Cockburn had not disliked him — on the contrary he found him accommodating; and there appeared to be no disharmony between the doctor and authority until Lowe's arrival.

O'Meara diagnosed Napoleon's ailment as chronic hepatitis, an island complaint bred of careless sanitation, aggravated by lack of exercise and by mental frustration. These last appeared to him to be natural enough in the Emperor's case, though on occasions he had remarked to William Balcombe that Napoleon might perhaps inherit the malady that had attacked his father. Dr O'Meara's narrations of his interviews with the Governor intrigued Napoleon vastly. "I would rather be a jackass or a spy," O'Meara told Lowe bluntly "than an informer for you or for anybody". "What do you mean, sir?" the Governor thundered. "To be a spy or an informer?" On that O'Meara retorted that in informing an ordinary conversation, he would be just that. In a paroxysm of rage, Sir Hudson Lowe told the doctor he was to consider himself under arrest, and prohibited him from holding any communication with Bonaparte, except of a medical nature. He was beside himself, walking rapidly about as was his custom, touching ornaments and articles in the room. O'Meara asked for the order to be put in writing. This Lowe refused and told the doctor to wait outside the library door. In about a quarter of an hour, he was recalled by the clerk and told to "continue as usual". O'Meara took his leave without further conversation.

Napoleon listened to the details of the interview and dismissed it with a shrug. What could be expected? They were all suffering under the domination of an unbalanced mentality, one not sufficiently insane to warrant the man's detention or recall, but sinister enough to cause apprehension. It added to the weariness of the life they lived; the loneliness, the blowing winds, the sickness and malaise. He said to O'Meara, after one bout of indisposition, "I feel that the machine struggles, but cannot last" — an unusual observation since at that time he did not consider death imminent from natural causes. Later Lowe again called O'Meara before him. Had he not ordered articles of clothing in Jamestown for Mesdames Bertrand and Montholon? It was against regulations. Had he not written to someone in Jamestown to send them basins, chambers, and other utensils for household use? What business had he to do it? If Madame Bertrand wanted anything, let her apply to the orderly officer. Dr O'Meara answered by saying, "Cleanliness is necessary to prevent sickness," and "as all things ordered are of a medical nature, Madame Bertrand can hardly be expected to go to the orderly officer to request chamber-pots etc." Lowe shouted; he would not let O'Meara thwart him in his capacity as Governor, even in the matter of chamber-pots. How dare he order things from the King's Store? Lowe ended with "very coarse remarks about French ladies". O'Meara notes "he was very violent". He now ordered him to appear at Plantation House twice a week to report on Napoleon's condition. This O'Meara refused to do, saying he would not come to be insulted. An altercation ensued, during which the Governor shouted that he had power to send him away and give no reason, if he so desired. O'Meara afterwards told Napoleon that after a scene of incoherence and temper, "He crossed his arms, looking at me with an expression which I shall never forget, and said, 'This is my office, sir, and there is the door leading to it — when I send for you on duty, you will come in at that door, but do not put your foot on any part of the house, or come in at any other entrance,' which had no bearing whatever on the subject under discussion." The doctor also told Napoleon that Mr Hobhouse's book specially sent to the island for him and seized by Lowe, because of its dedication by the author, was lying on the library table; Napoleon remarked "that it was a *bêtise*" for the Governor to leave it about after he had illegally retained it.

During his service as Napoleon's physician, O'Meara personally dispensed the medicines and prepared the draughts in a little room off his bedroom. When he left Longwood, he handed over all he could, with instructions, to the valet de chambre (along with the care of the clocks, also his charge), but for a long period after that the Emperor refused to take anything medicinal and relied on abstinence and a hot bath to curb his stomach upsets.

There is not a great deal of data after O'Meara's arrest, which took place in December, 1818. He rode with his guards down the valley to the castle — an angry man, and sick at heart. Two days saw him away, his luggage in the meantime ransacked, valuables stolen, but the majority of officers from

Deadwood Camp were on the dock to see him off, and watchers in the hills identified them in order to report their names to the Governor. His revelations in *A Voice from St Helena*, written after the death of Napoleon, caused a major stir. However no actual lawsuit for libel was preferred by Lowe; time and disinclination combined against it, but a smear campaign that lasted a century, on no concrete evidence, rendered the statements in O'Meara's book to some degree suspect. My family stoutly maintained that he was absolutely factual, his Irish exuberance reacting unfavourably by English concepts. Great-grandfather and he had stood together to temper the wind to the exile, and the doctor's loyalty to England, in William Balcombe's opinion, was unchallenged and unchanging — while as a surgeon he could do no more.

Mr James Hall, surgeon of H.M.S. *Favourite*, in a signed statement on the 25th December 1818, at Ascension, declares, "Dr O'Meara stated if he had complied with Sir Hudson Lowe's wishes, he did not think Bonaparte would be alive. He also hinted I might not find Bonaparte in existence some months hence. The sense of his expressions was that Sir Hudson Lowe had wished him to act improperly, from all which expressions I drew an inference that Sir Hudson Lowe had wished him [O'Meara] to poison Bonaparte or to indirectly put an end to his existence by withholding medical assistance from him. I heard Lieutenant Coppage say that O'Meara had had a similar conversation with him, and Lieutenant Coppage had drawn exactly the same inferences as I had, and he stated it to me."

O'Meara, on his way home, among the captains and medical officers of the British fleet then lying off Ascension, gave details of Lowe's regime he would not have dared to mention while on St Helena. He told of his refusal to leave the Emperor's medical history with the Governor, as he considered it not to be medical etiquette, but said he would give it to the Secretary of State on his arrival in England. He told Lieutenant Coppage he had been "packed off", and his luggage searched. Coppage asked what Bonaparte had said on parting. O'Meara replied, "Poor fellow, he has been taking calomel these last six weeks for the liver complaint, and when I left him he said there was no doubt my removal was a prelude to assassination, but 'they did not like to embrue their hands in my blood'." O'Meara honestly felt his removal was a precursor to Bonaparte's death, either by poison or from want of proper medical advice, and he would not venture to say Bonaparte was alive at that moment.

Apprentice-Surgeon Robert Malcolm at Ascension on the 5th January 1819, in H.M.S. *Griffin*, wrote a statement that O'Meara gave an impression to him that he was removed from St Helena in consequence of refusing to do away with Napoleon Bonaparte. Even the barren outlines of Ascension island must have spelt freedom to the intrigue-haunted O'Meara.

CHAPTER 21

The Balcombes Leave
St Helena

Sir Hudson Lowe never ceased to keep the Balcombe family under surveillance; they were suspect because of their position on the island, their close friendship with the exiles, and later on account of the leakage of uncensored correspondence from Longwood. Indeed, but for the interference of the Prince Regent, William Balcombe would have been expelled much earlier merely on suspicion, as were others, but for the time being Lowe was content to order a watch by Sir Thomas Reade's intelligence agents and to await some definite proof.

Lowe, deeply apprehensive, ventilated his fears in despatches to Bathurst — he disliked O'Meara, but he feared Balcombe more. To a milder degree the Admiral and his wife were also suspect, mainly because of the Emperor's liking for them. A letter found in a bundle of papers long afterwards illustrated the terms of brevity between Lowe and the Admiral, routine alone prompting their exchanges.

"Sir,
"I have the honour to inform your Excellency that the *Julia* is arrived from Ascension. Mr Folkstone, Master of the *Byrea*, Store ship, unfortunately fell overboard and was drowned. Captain Jones does not bring any news.
"Yours obt.,
"Pulteney Malcolm"

Such of William Balcombe's letters as are included in the Lowe volumes are mainly trivial, showing in most cases a strong combative spirit in their answers to Lowe's demands. Yet in spite of these disagreements Lowe placed in his hands large sums of money for negotiation on the exile's behalf, and by order of the Governor the money for the broken-up plate Balcombe alone was permitted to administer.

Finally, by elimination, Lowe pin-pointed the firm Balcombe, Fowler and Cole as the intermediaries linking Longwood with the Bonaparte family. He could discover no other avenue through which contact might be made, with the exception of O'Meara. Only the Balcombes and O'Meara had constant access to Longwood. He always considered the doctor too inconsequent and ignorant of business to handle drafts and bills, but feared his fluent pen and Irish exuberance.

Lowe's hatred of the Emperor embraced all of the French; they experienced a feeling of apprehension every time they caught sight of his spare figure and Balcombe knew the unhappy tension among them, felt also by O'Meara and himself. From Sir Thomas Tyrwhitt in London had come the first warning that Balcombe's own actions were under review, and that it would be as well to send his family home. However, Sir Pulteney Malcolm on his arrival contradicted the message and they remained. Now Balcombe considered taking a leave of six months. His wife had been ill with hepatitis and the convalescence proved slow; he would take her home for the restoration of her health and make it an opportunity to obtain some alleviation for the Longwood people. He had personally borne enough interrogations, orders and arrogance from one he honestly considered to be half crazy, whose unreasoning spleen was directed towards anybody kindly disposed towards the captive. A sailor by training and a factual man, with an almost fanatical regard for what, in his opinion, stood for fair play (which had led him into troubles before), he undoubtedly assisted in the transfer of letters to the captive's supporters overseas — more than possibly to the hand of the Regent as well. That eventuality Lowe feared above anything else. Lowe conveyed his apprehensions to Bathurst and the Secretary of State for the Colonies wrote in answer asking "for all information regarding the Balcombe family". With Reade to assist, Lowe compiled a dossier, containing distorted facts and some truth, which is still to be read. Up to that time, however, there was no actual evidence to act upon, and Lowe held his hand.

No actual proof that correspondence passed through the firm has ever come to light; but the trust imposed in William Balcombe by Napoleon rankled in the Governor's mind, and it became increasingly clear that Lowe would do all in his power to prevent the continuance of what he considered a dangerous friendship.

In answer to a letter of enquiry sent by Bathurst, Lowe wrote, "What makes my suspicions fall the more strongly on these persons [the Balcombes] is the particular intimacy subsisting between them and Mr O'Meara, now deported, which long since made me caution Mr Balcombe against adopting him as a medium of interpretation with the persons at Longwood ... Mr Balcombe is very warmly protected by Sir Thomas Tyrwhitt, his father was drowned by a yacht, in which the Prince of Wales embarked, running over a boat in which he was sailing at Brighton ... Sir Thomas wrote to him at the time of the *Newcastle* arriving here to send away his wife and daughters, but Sir P. Malcolm advised him not to do it seeing he had seen Sir Thomas subsequently, and the letter was written by him under some wrong impression. Mr Balcombe never connected to me the letter Sir Thomas wrote to him.

"The attention shown by both Lady, as well as Sir P. Malcolm, towards Mr Balcombe and his family is without all bounds ..."

He wrote on the 14th March 1818, "Mr Balcombe has applied for leave of absence to go to England. I have no particular reason to suppose his application is connected with any circumstance of General Gourgaud's departure, as he sometime since manifested an intention of applying as Mrs Balcombe has been seriously ill, which has been assigned as the reason of his present application. In a former private letter I spoke of circumstances which was supposed to influence Sir Thomas Tyrwhitt's particular notice of Mr Balcombe ... in fact it is difficult to learn Mr Balcombe's real history, the only certain thing is Sir Thomas' protection of him which commenced long before Napoleon Bonaparte's arrival here, and has been always accompanied by the very best advice. He is generally ever considered as an indiscreet, rather than a designing man, liberal, and even profuse, living apparently a good deal beyond his means, keeping literally open house, in particular for the Navy, to whom he is much attached... . He talks sometimes very largely, and gave out a few days since he had been left £2,000 per year at home ..."

Gourgaud's statement to Bathurst in the Lowe folio read, "Mr Balcombe had never made money transactions or betrayed the trust reposed in him, but that did not necessarily mean letters. There was no difficulty in eluding the sentries — in short escape was in no degree unpracticable."

Lowe considered the departure of the Balcombes a convenient occurrence and planned to obtain a new purveyor once they had sailed. Montholon commented in his book, "The departure of Mr Balcombe for Europe afforded the Emperor an opportunity of causing his short sojourn at the Briars to be remembered by an act of imperial munificence. To the Commissions with which he charged Mr Balcombe he added a bill for 72,000 francs drawn on London and a pension of 12,000 francs, saying to him, 'I fear that your resignation of your employment in this island is caused by the quarrels and annoyance drawn upon you by the relations established between your family and Longwood in consequence of the hospitality which you showed me on our first arrival in St Helena. I would not wish you ever to regret having known me.'"

Montholon went on, "Mr Balcombe soon after his return to England was appointed Purveyor-General of New Holland. He was a worthy man, and rendered us many services, but without ever failing in his duty to his sovereign. It was said in the island that he was a natural son of the Prince of Wales."

Mrs Johnstone, Betsy's daughter, appends a footnote, in the third edition of her mother's memoirs, "With regard to the last item it would be unjust to my grandfather's memory not to remark that not a *sou* of this money was ever received, though, under no circumstances would it have been accepted, as the following anecdote more than satisfactorily proves ... When my Grandfather went on board the ship that was to carry them to England, a messenger gave him a letter from Napoleon, and in it he found a blank cheque with a request that he fill it out to any amount. He took it to my Grandmother, who was leaning over the bulwark, she glanced at it, and without a moment's hesitation, tore it to pieces and tossed the fragments into the sea... . This was the fate of the kindly gift." There is evidence also from their later straitened circumstances to show that no intrinsic gain was derived from the Balcombes' association with the exiled Emperor, and Mrs Johnstone comments, "His devotion was the downfall of the family fortunes, for Lowe never ceased until he had him forbidden to return to St Helena."

Lowe feared not only Longwood communications passing to French supporters but that Carlton House might also receive them — through the agency of William Balcombe's equerry-brother, thus by-passing Castlereagh and Bathurst. There was also Sir Thomas Tyrwhitt to be considered, who was "very close to Carlton House".

It was shortly after the Balcombe family's arrival in England that Lowe discovered letters and messages transmitted under cover of three differently addressed envelopes to the St Helena firm of Balcombe, Fowler and Cole. In the Lowe papers is a copy of an intercepted private letter from William Balcombe to W. Fowler, forwarded by Captain Shannon of H.M.S. *Leveret*, which concerned the Governor very closely — and which made him act with despatch.

"I send some newspapers to Barry O'Meara. If he should not be there, endeavour to give them to General Bertrand. I have this moment heard from London that Sir Hudson Lowe is recalled. Keep this to yourself and Cole. I have been with Cabinet Ministers. Of course I told the truth. Whoever comes out as Governor, you will have strong letters of recommendation to from different quarters.

"I find Mr Holmes, Barry O'Meara's friend, is an excellent fellow. He is coming down to stay with us.

"Sir Thomas Tyrwhitt has been very kind.

"(signed) W. Balcombe".

Mrs Johnstone, Betsy's daughter, appended a further footnote to her mother's recollections of the family's departure from the island, "My grandfather's visit to England was contrary to the advice of his wife and all his best friends. His journey home was preceded by secret letters from Sir Hudson Lowe, in which he insinuated that my grandfather's attachment to the Emperor was so strong that his return to St Helena would be scarcely advisable. The Government acted upon these suggestions, contrary entirely to the opinion of the Prince Regent." Mrs Johnstone also contributed something of a picture of her grandfather, giving a verbal description of the man — in the main bearing out the comments of Montholon and Lowe. His build and mannerisms were duplicated in a later generation, a grandson in Australia.

It was with him Mrs Johnstone corresponded, forging a last link with the scattered family, and from her came the Napoleonic relics now in our possession. When elderly, she presented my mother at the Court of Queen Victoria, and, as a young woman, made a pact with the Prince Imperial of France to elope with him to America after the Zulu War. He was killed in Africa, another story and hardly known to us except for half-forgotten comments on my mother's part and its recital at greater length in Princess Bibesco's book, *Prince Imperial.*

Even though regulations now demanded a pass for Betsy to visit, Longwood, this did not deter her from going the day before she sailed to say farewell to the Emperor. It is probable she ignored the insistence on the pass altogether since there is no reference to their last meeting in any of the other reports. In her own notes she displays more emotion than ever before, interlacing her story with miscellaneous observations: that Toby was weeping; she would lend Tom, the pony, to Miss Mason; Sarah had packed for them all, and was coming to look after her mother on the voyage; the geraniums were blooming in the front of the home and the crown was still noticeable in the turf by the Pavilion.

She felt a growing tension in response to the atmosphere of restraint as she entered by the Bertrands' gate — apart from Napoleon's ill-health so apparent to them all, Lowe's strictures and the lessening of hope were almost tangible. Flat, stale and unprofitable had become the days and nights, while the noisy children, rough from lack of discipline and little education, combined with Madame Bertrand's illness and now constant depression and the narrowing circle of familiar faces to create a desolation, where once had been, if not hope, at least a semblance of gaiety. She would miss the usual greeting, "*Betsee, qu' as tu?*" — "The rude hoyden", Las Cases's disapproving appellation, had remained even though he had gone. "*Betsee, es tu sage?*" was Napoleon's usual remark. His smile of extraordinary sweetness, his forbearance with the rowdy games and the unceremonious treatment whilst at the Briars, their meeting at the Bertrands' — were all past. And the ageing man in the billiard room who rose to greet her seemed a shadow of the Emperor who had ridden out of the sun to their door, and who had stood, hands behind him, gazing from the Pavilion towards Jamestown.

He kissed her with great affection, and then sat and talked for some time of widely separate things and everyday thoughts that came scurrying to impede the single fact that loomed larger and grew closer as the minutes passed. Presently he led her to the garden where once they had leaned against the wall and watched the seventy-four beat upwind to James Roads. With a sad smile he pointed to the ocean, spread out like flat silk. "You will be sailing over the rim of the sea towards England, while I stay to die on this miserable rock." Rising emotion made him gesticulate wildly — "Look at those dreadful mountains, they are my prison walls. Soon you will hear the Emperor Napoleon is dead."

Oblivious of the sentries and gardeners, she put her arms around him and felt the damp skin of his forehead on her cheek and the flabbiness of his arms and shoulders. The green coat had ceased to fit him. Age and illness had wrought marked changes and he was more corpulent than before, his once neat ankles now shapeless.

She held in her arms a travesty of the man who had been followed by kings. Betsy wept bitterly and felt in vain for her handkerchief, which as usual she had left behind in her saddle, so the Emperor gave her his, scented with eau-de-Cologne, and, as she took it, said, "The only things we have shared are tears and the same handkerchief. Keep it, Betsy, in remembrance of this sad day."

Betsy turned blindly away, to what future she did not know, her short life being a concentration of emotions and scenes created around the island and its captive. Oblivious of everything but the fact that tomorrow the *Winchelsea* would take her "over the rim of the sea", as he phrased it, she realised she was going from him and everyone she knew. The fact of her departure suddenly made Napoleon's vision more acute. He saw beyond that horizon the piled glories of his lost world, and now passed with it the English girl with the loving heart.

Somehow, in the confusion, Betsy's arms recalled the embraces of Josephine — they were strong arms holding him tightly, her tears upon his face; young, resilient, faithful Betsy grown up, shapely, tidy, with a bonnet on her curls — not, as was her usual habit, hanging by a ribbon; Betsy, a beautiful woman, fragrant with youth, bidding him good-bye, yet one more in the lengthening procession of those who were to leave him. He felt terribly alone as she ran down the path to the gate and Betsy heard the well-remembered voice calling her once again, "Betsee, Betsee." Turning she found him holding out his hands in supplication, tears on his cheeks, probably the only time in his existence he had been a suppliant. She saw only a shadow of his once self-reliant and determined personality. Fate, illness, bondage, the indignities of Lowe, the frustrations of memory, all had joined to quell the soaring spirit, and she ran back and held him close again, trying to instil something of her own strength and vitality into his decrepitude, her youth transcending his age; her hope beating against his despair. She could only murmur half-words, hopes and prayers. "I shall return:" But even as she finally broke away and turned to where her horse was tied, her straightforward mind accepted the inevitable as one accepts a blow. She would never see him again.

CHAPTER 22

The Suite at Longwood

In September, 1818, Deadwood held another race meeting, and on this occasion it was not Betsy but Archambault who caused the diversion — by riding down the course in a drunken condition. Dolly and Regent, two saddle horses from the Longwood stables, had been entered in the events; the excitement proved too much for the groom, who careered on Dolly among the spectators and was chased off the course by a steward, after a horse-whipping.

Sitting upstairs in the Bertrands' house, his spyglass poked through the window, Napoleon witnessed the scene and the family heard him laughing. Archambault's indiscretions could at times be painful and even dangerous but on this occasion he afforded comic relief in the robust style that appealed to the Emperor's sense of the ridiculous. The race meetings, still run by Captain the Hon. Henry Rous, were now looked upon as fixtures in the calendar, horses being regularly shipped from the Cape to take part in the events. Captain Rous remained on the station for several years, transferring from ship to ship, finally to the command of the *Mosquito*. Racing must have been to his taste, for after he left St Helena he became a power of the turf in England, in whose more decorous atmosphere such incidents as the pursuit of Archambault down the course and the earlier performance of the female Imperial jockey, in the person of Betsy, could be recalled only as fantastic.

From his vantage point Napoleon saw distinctly the bright dresses of the women, the tethered riding horses and the activity around the saddling paddock. He could even make out familiar figures — the Doveton family, Lowe and his A.D.C.s, stout Sir Thomas Reade, some of his own household, naval men, Lady Lowe's barouche and the carriages of others that with the improvement of the roads had recently been brought to the island. Groups gathered around to drink tea and gossip. The skirts of the women's habits were long and pointed, and some of the women wore feathered hats, as there was some flamboyance in the dressing. The soldiers from the camp of the 66th nearby had lent regimental tents for the day, and the red coats could be picked out among the more sombre clothes of the civilians in the betting ring. Sounds floated up, confined by the sprawling bulk of the Barn immediately opposite.

Life, wanton, inexorable, demanding, went on — a gift from the Power that equally took away, as it had done from Napoleon now sitting in a small bedroom, looking down on this tiny expression of its propulsive force. He thought of Betsy. She, too, had gone from him, removed by the incomprehensible law of life and fate, which, as a predestinarian, he accepted. As not so long ago she had ridden his Mameluke, she could today have been among this crowd, doubtless once again the successful candidate for the honour in the ladies' race. He remembered her habit was bottle-green, and that she had ridden hatless, with Fehrzen in attendance. The Emperor remembered, as the lines of a play, how he had told her Fehrzen was too old — as he had said Carstairs was too aristocratic. He realised his strictures must have been a quirk of jealousy, born of loneliness; an ageing man seeking to retain the fleeting favour of a youngster. As conqueror, Emperor, man of destiny, how many women had he charmed? This last girl had not been moved by material things, but, in spite of defeat and the detriment of captivity, she had loved him. The realisation eased his bruised pride. He remembered Mameluke, the red trappings with the gold imperial cypher, the little silver trophy laid before him, the recital of the story of the race that accompanied it at the dinner table.

They had all gone — the family into whose happy circle he had entered, with whom he had shared love and human companionship, from whom he had accepted hospitality and help — perhaps too generous help on William Balcombe's part, for although he had applied for and obtained leave to depart, Napoleon knew that the suspicions raised about him made return problematical. They were nearing England now, and had become one with the other shadows, growing as dim and insubstantial as the rest, leaving only a memory of an outline, some trick of characterisation or a note of laughter, but creating also an ache of loneliness that became one with the physical pain marking his growing illness. His days were as monotonous and undeviating as the rollers beating on the rock base of the Barn. That the distant view of Deadwood races could divert him seemed almost an affront, from its very triviality.

Not long after this, a doctor, discussing Bonaparte's condition, told the Governor that only one thing would cure him, "The sight of a seventy-four coming to James Roads to take him away."

As it was, he watched with envy the store-ships and frigates as they passed into view around the great bulk of the Barn, graceful as wide-awake birds, anonymous symbols of freedom and movement.

He lapsed into one of his moods of almost trance-like immobility; nothing seemed tangible; the race-meeting below took on the instability of a dream; bright colours faded; galloping horses, crowds, shouts and merriment became as remote as the happenings of years ago and no more substantial than the marches, the battles and the pageantry, the heat of Egypt or the Moscow winter. He was surrounded by an insubstantial world. At these times the suite left him alone.

Presently he passed down the terrace steps of the Bertrands' cottage, turned to the left through the gate without a glance at the new Longwood home, and crossed the grass to the passion-fruit arbour and the sunken paths of his own garden, his steps still brisk, his green coat and white breeches distinctive enough for the orderly officer to register a 'sighting'.

Although Bertrand played a decisive role in the shoddy drama of Napoleon's last years, the Controller's natural, quiet observance of duty removed him from criticism, excepting that which always came from Plantation House, where a solid wall of negation and incivility met his every approach. Bertrand passed the period of captivity with the calm assurance of an admirably balanced man. Only once did his emotions overflow his barrier of calm — in the affair of Lyster. Madame Bertrand's domestic sense, her devotion, which had grown out of what had been an arranged marriage by Napoleon, made Bertrand ever anxious to return home after his day in the Longwood house. He dined only rarely with the Emperor, and Madame made excuses of the distance to be walked afterwards. Napoleon grumbled at this divided allegiance. Madame Bertrand and the Countess Montholon were not compatible. She had had her own ideas as to what was going on. They kept apart, and later when Montholon, his wife gone, came even closer to Napoleon, Madame Bertrand went less and less across the green field dividing the houses. However, during Napoleon's final illness she begged to nurse him, and towards the end he invited her to come and see him. Her Irish temperament manifested itself in her homemaking proclivities; to her, the family, her husband, the few friends around her, and the garden she had personally planted were her whole world, while in Bertrand, adoring, solid, unimaginative, immensely dependable, she possessed a perfect complement. But for him the Longwood household would have fallen apart. When necessary, he made demands, and on those occasions Lowe found him a determined, astute opponent, who stood his ground before all insults, completely un-French in his calm.

Lord Charles Somerset visited the island in 1819, arriving on Christmas Day. Although he had behaved well to Las Cases and his son and entertained them as 'guests' in his handsome house in Cape Town, yet he prevented their early passage to Europe with purpose, fearing the information they would spread and the sympathy they could arouse for Napoleon. The Emperor knew this — indeed, understanding its reason, the long delay of Las Cases in Cape Town had considerably angered him. Therefore, when Lord Charles Somerset announced his wish to call on Bonaparte, and Major Gorrequer rode over to convey the request to Montholon, Napoleon did not even answer.

The next day a cavalcade set out, consisting of Sir Hudson Lowe and orderlies, Lord Charles and his two daughters and Captain Nicholls. Captain Nicholls has left a description of what occurred, "They first went to see the new Longwood house and grounds, a barren adventure for the furnishings were not there and the garden unmade, while the view of the Barn lent no charm to the outlook. Also, it had become warm and sultry." Voices came from the Bertrands' home and there were figures on the little terrace but the cavalcade did not visit there. The Imperial snub had registered in Somerset's rather inflated head. Lowe, however, was for showing the sights and took them into old Longwood grounds. Nicholls writes, "At the moment Bonaparte was at dinner in his garden under the oak trees with Count Montholon. The Governor, Lord Charles Somerset and the young ladies passed around the garden into the wood. However, as soon as they were perceived, the General rose from his dinner and ran into the house. The dinner was carried after him into the house. Lord Charles did not know that General Bonaparte was out, having only walked around the large garden, and did not intrude near to the home out of delicacy to General Bonaparte. After Lord Charles' party had left Longwood, General Bonaparte immediately walked out."

During the last eighteen months there is a gap in the chronicle of the Longwood household, due possibly to a self-imposed censorship. Napoleon, who had no medical adviser for ten months, remained out of sight for weeks at a time, suffered, took baths for relief and walked unobserved in the dusk. Another purveyor was in command. Betsy had said what Napoleon guessed was a last farewell, for he told her that when she returned he felt he would not be there. Admiral Pulteney Malcolm and his wife were in London. Gourgaud, Las Cases and Cipriani no longer came to his call. One of the 'elevated' Archambaults as well as the *lampiste* was in America. The shades were closing in and Napoleon knew that, but for his ill-health, Montholon would have gone also, following his wife, who, succumbing to the climate, had sought the waters of Baden.

The pin-pricks of Lowe, the spy David in the garden, the lack of visitors and news, of human companionship except that of his suite, were becoming less irksome only because bodily pain engrossed him, sapping any desire to dictate — indeed to move. The apathy of illness held him for hours, silent, in a chair or in his bed. Marchand gave him perhaps the only real comfort, for he anticipated his every want, watched over and attended to him, withheld the minor problems of the household just as Bertrand staved off the outside pressure of Lowe, the commissioners, the sentries, the demands of the orderly officer and the inadequacies, as far as it was possible, of the provisions.

One day after reviewing his clothing, now showing definite signs of wear, he walked up the steep little stairs to the place where Marchand slept, to find a mahogany cupboard filled with half-forgotten uniforms, brilliant with gold lace and fantastic trimmings — a mute testimony in regalia to past majesty, now hanging shrouded in sheets against the plateau damp. Marchand had brought them all. Napoleon drew them out one by one and made a close examination — this had been worn at Marengo, this at Austerlitz — he uttered an exclamation, shook his head, and went slowly downstairs; they were no longer for him.

It was with an emotion of relief that the Governor learned that Professor Antommarchi had arrived on the 20th September to take over the medical regimen of Longwood. Chosen by Napoleon's uncle, Cardinal Fesch, the young Corsican possessed fair qualifications but an unfortunate manner that immediately alienated the Emperor. The Abbé Buonavita and a young priest, Vignali, came also, with a new *maître d'hôtel* to replace Cipriani, and another cook. In these Napoleon displayed no interest. His conduct in shutting himself away from all visitors had a dampening effect on the whole household. Madame Bertrand, the only woman left, felt the situation keenly, and approached Lowe in desperation to ask that she might see some of her own sex. Forsyth's book says, "Lowe courteously consented", but after remarking that she was very agreeable, and had been a remarkably handsome woman, went on to say that they wished they could see anything so favourable about her husband, whose influence was invariably exerted for evil, and his behaviour to the Governor himself intolerable. Bathurst had written to Lowe, "The conduct of Count Bertrand makes it unfit that you should any longer address yourself to him."

The Corsican, Antommarchi, did not fit into the accepted picture of medical adviser and at no time achieved the Emperor's confidence. No one could have been less fitted for his task — more of a surgeon than a physician, he was quick, impatient and unsympathetic. Napoleon made him work in the garden with the others, and invited him only once to his table, though sometimes he lunched with him under the trees outside. The Abbé Buonavita, an aged priest who suffered a palsy, the result of a stroke, retired after a few months, unable to support the climate; Vignali, blatant, illiterate and impulsive, remained, his fate being to lose his life in a duel when he returned home after Napoleon's death.

Napoleon roused himself enough to plan a chapel in one of the rooms that he had once used for dining, and Vignali made the necessary arrangements and found the altar cloths. There are notes on this in the Governor's letters to Bathurst. The list of requisitions amplifies them. "The senior priest wants a stove set up in his front room, the same as the surgeon has got in his room." This last request was sent from Mr W. Darling to Colonel Gorrequer. Mr Darling also commented on the 'fauteuil-de-malade' and the length of time taken in its construction. Antommarchi never impressed the Emperor, either in personality or by his degrees, but he was at least better than Baxter. There are descriptions of the Emperor during that time that truthfully highlight his condition, outlook, his growing irritability and restlessness, the periods of inconsistent action that mark the sick man. After Antommarchi's arrival, he appeared to take more interest in his surroundings, possibly because of a subconscious feeling of security stemming from the presence of a doctor close at hand. Vignali had embarked on the study of medicine as well as the service of the Church, but Napoleon made it clear to him that he was at Longwood only in an ecclesiastical capacity. His collection of Napoleonic relics was sent for sale to New York in 1958: bedroom curtains with a green band on the cream nankeen, on which William Balcombe's wife had remarked in 1815 — "single-width curtains are too unimportant for an Emperor's room"; the silver cup out of which he had taken his last drink; his knife and fork; his clothes — shirts and monogrammed handkerchiefs; in a little leather jewel case, a parcel of hair from his body and head; the principal tendon of his body; bed linen; a bundle of documents; a codicil to his will, leaving money and altar cloths to Vignali (the materials yellow with age); his breeches, their wide band very noticeable in relation to their length — a forty-inch waist measurement. It was a far cry from these relics (now in the possession of Rosenbach the antiquarians in New York City) to St Helena, of Napoleon's last days, the one hundred and forty years bridged by a comment of my great-grandmother's on the imperial inadequacy of single-width curtains.

Vignali busied himself about the chapel, made the arrangements and showed initiative.

Presently the old Abbé Buonavita returned home, filled with rheumatism and pains, and Napoleon hardly missed him. By then the resounding past had become an episode in a life — a phase — a memory; the final chapter held no place for the Abbé. Even as it was, its narrow stage seemed crowded with extras hovering about the principal character, some ill-cast, others reluctant performers, others men of Lowe's placing, all dwarfed by the still tremendous personality sinking into death. The records show how grimly Napoleon fought his last enemy. An earthy man, brave, determined, selfish, no force of arms could help him here. He faced the enemy alone and empty-handed.

Towards the end, Montholon appeared to be nearer to him than any other — nearer even than Bertrand — the latter always having the dual interest of his family living across the grounds. Montholon, now alone — his wife still taking the waters in Europe — attended to him constantly. Marchand and the other valets likewise surrounded him with such comfort as they might be able to bring, but at the late stage of the disease that ultimately killed him there was little they could contribute towards his well-being. He suffered intolerably. No drugs alleviated the pains. It is problematical whether, even if Antommarchi had obtained any, the Emperor would have consented to swallow them, so averse to medicine was he; in any case, knowledge of even the simplest of pain-killers was, in those days, almost nil. The final records, dating over eighteen months, present a clear medical picture of the Emperor's decline to any physician of today. It makes dull reading in its entirety. Repetition of bouts of pain, malaise, sickness, swelling, debility, then a return to a kind of normal existence, each bout leaving the victim a degree lower in health. A losing battle, yet tenaciously fought. Lowe's letters reveal it, though Lowe himself appeared to be in ignorance, reporting the appeals of the suite to Bathurst without comment, and relying on Gourgaud's 'confession' in England as a correct appreciation of the situation, "That Napoleon was as well then as he had been when he first came to the island." Lowe still firmly chose to imagine that Napoleon was malingering in order to obtain concessions, to be allowed to live in a sheltered valley, to be unrestricted in rides and visitors. He did not see the wood for the trees. He fought immaterial problems and failed in his duty in treatment of, knowledge of, and forbearance to a dying man. By such, his name goes down marked in history. (In a subsequent parliamentary debate, a Minister of the Crown, speaking on an Irish appointment, remarked, "We must not get a Hudson Lowe for the post.")

And so Napoleon, in unsympathetic hands, was to die in Imperial squalor, his name and greatness illumined by the very contrast of the circumstances.

Ships passing through from India heard only rumours of his growing ill-health. During the years, he had of necessity withdrawn himself from the knowledge and sight of island visitors. Prevented by the refusal of passes and the bayonets of the guards around Longwood, they could only glean news of him from the infrequent appearances of the suite in Jamestown. There are a few notes remaining of that period of trivialities and tragedy. Marchand requested a new set of green curtains for Napoleon's bedstead; later Pierron asked that the floor of the back pantry be covered with flat stone; Marchand wanted a wash-house built, "the sod walls of the cookhouse are a great harbour of rats"; "Shirts were eaten and the buttons belonging to the surgeon, and the night before last a great part of a coat belonging to the Emperor."

Darling noted, "it will cost £10 or £20 to erect a house of the description Marchand wants." Montholon sent written complaints to Colonel Gorrequer, "The bread has much fallen off; beef not so good, beer not so drinkable — and there never was anything like sufficiency of fish. The burgundy has become sour and can no longer be drunk."

CHAPTER 23

'Sighting' the Emperor

Captain Nicholls, when orderly officer, wrote in his diary:

"*September 5th*, 1818: This day was appointed Orderly Officer to General Bonaparte. Captain Blakeney and myself waited on Count Montholon. I have received positive orders from the Governor to make my conversations through Count Montholon in preference to Count Bertrand, in consequence of Bertrand's improper conduct to Colonel Lyster, and I acquainted him that Sir Hudson Lowe had been pleased to appoint me Orderly Officer to General Bonaparte, and begged him to have the goodness to announce the same to the General. Count Montholon bowed, but made no answer. The Count was likewise to inform Napoleon that I should at all times be ready to attend on him. Montholon was very polite, and I was not introduced to General Bonaparte.

"*September 7th*: I took possession of my quarters at Longwood and also commenced on my new occupation and consequently relieved Captain Blakeney, but was not introduced to General Bonaparte. I met Count and Countess Bertrand walking, and was introduced to them by Captain Blakeney. The Count was polite, Madame Bertrand said in rather a peevish manner, 'So, Captain Blakeney, I see you are determined to leave us.' I propose to mention the particular days on which I may hereafter see General Bonaparte, in this journal.

"*September 8th*: Deadwood races commenced today. It was mentioned to me that General Bonaparte was seen on his veranda with a telescope in his hand, viewing the sport.

"*September 10th*: Sergeant David has just informed me that he saw Napoleon at his dining-room window; that Novarrez told him that Napoleon had been sick yesterday and vomiting; that he was then going to take a bath.

"The Governor now gave notice that 'the orderly officer must see General Bonaparte daily, come what may, and may use any means', and 'That if he had not set eyes on Napoleon Bonaparte by ten o'clock in the morning he was to enter the hall and force his way into Napoleon's room.'"

The Emperor's reply, through Montholon, was brief, that "there was no question for him of any choice between death and an ignominious condition of life", the implication being clear that he would resist such treatment until death if necessary. It was known he possessed five pairs of loaded pistols in his bedroom. Lowe came to Longwood to withdraw his instructions, but outwardly it made no difference; the miserable orderly officer was stimulated secretly to further efforts, and sent equally plaintive messages back to Plantation House as before.

"Napoleon still keeps himself concealed. I have not been able to see him since the 29th ult."

"I have again waited on Montholon and told him I could not see Napoleon. He appeared surprised and said that they had seen me. I was nearly twelve hours on my legs."

"I believe I saw Napoleon today in the act of stropping his razor in his dressing room." Later Captain Nicholls reported, "I have been upon my legs upwards of ten hours endeavouring to procure a sight of Napoleon Bonaparte either in his little garden, or at one of his windows ... during the whole time I was exposed to the observation and remarks of not only the French servants, but also of the gardeners and other persons employed about Longwood ... I have frequently experienced days of this kind."[18]

Daring souls periodically offered Napoleon the prospect of escape but he disregarded them; a precarious voyage ending in a problematical welcome in Europe did not excite his interest. Even Canada and America offered small inducement.

He knew it would end in assassination. He once told Betsy it was untrue he wore a coat of mail. Betsy had informed him it was stated that, besides wearing armour, he made a practice in France of never sleeping in the same place twice in succession. He remarked that these were fabrications, but he gave her a description of two near assassinations: one by a sculptor, Carracchi, who returned on the pretext that he wished to take a further model but was foiled because Napoleon had not the time to sit; the other at the hands of a fanatic, who followed him to chapel with the intention of killing him at the elevation of the Host. He felt certain the current Government of France would have him knifed if he returned and he once told Montholon, "I should not be six months in America without being murdered by the assassins of the Comte d'Artois." He had only just escaped death in Elba; now middle-aged, he was prepared to await developments. Nicholls writes, "On New Year's day he stayed outside until gunfire [9 o'clock] looking at the boys and others firing crackers. The next day he amused himself with the pipe of the fire engine, spouting water on the tree and flowers."

"His morning dress at present consists of a white gown and straw hat with a broad brim but in the afternoon he appears in a cocked hat, green coat and white breeches, and stockings. He walks a good deal in the afternoon in the garden, accompanied by Montholon or Bertrand, and often pays a visit to the Bertrands in the evening. The one-eyed cooper came up from Jamestown with a large tub, 12 feet wide, for the General's Garden, to serve as a reservoir. He was very much pleased and gave the cooper a glass of wine with his own hand. The old man was delighted."

Formal state continued to be kept up in the original Longwood manner, notwithstanding the narrowing boundaries, curtailed amenities and facilities, and lack of companionship. Napoleon, always a martinet, severely dealt with a situation arising from four Chinese gardeners, whom he caused to be summarily removed for grumbling at an order.

Antommarchi on his arrival commenced to visit Napoleon in "ordinary morning dress with trousers and boots", but not for long. Soon he changed into black breeches, silk stockings and shoes. He arrived at the General's bedroom in this attire at ten a.m., paid his professional call, which took about ten minutes, then, free for the remainder of the day, changed back into ordinary clothes and did not see Napoleon until the next professional visit. Napoleon never liked the Corsican, marked him as a mountebank. Eventually it was to Dr Arnott he sent for advice.

Lowe reported to Bathurst, "Bonaparte has observed that Europe presented no further hopes for him," but added *"Il n'y a que l'abîme qui me reste"*. [There is nothing left for me but hell.] The Governor added that the suite had put in a requisition for a fishing-boat — lack of fish at Longwood had prompted this action, but Lowe, fearful of some ulterior motive, vetoed the request.

At the beginning of spring there came a marked change in Napoleon's conduct. It appeared as if a last flicker of the tremendous energy that formerly drove him flared up where hitherto lethargy, *malaise* and inertia combined to imbed him in stagnation. The garden called, and once again the scene became animated and not only the suite, but Chinese labourers worked under his eye. Antommarchi may have had something to do with the change, for, after the first examination of his patient on his arrival, he immediately prescribed exercise and Napoleon roused himself sufficiently even to ride a little. The boundaries had not been extended but were wide enough to give him an hour's canter on roads untroubled by sentinels.

Nicholls's life became more bearable. Lowe, writing privately, told Bathurst, "General Bonaparte continues to show himself daily and is now occupied in directing little improvements to his garden principally of such a nature as to procure shade with retirement and hide the view of his windows."

Once long ago in the school gardens at Brienne he had worked on a little plot of ground, only one-third of it his own; nevertheless he made a fence around it and woe-betide any who interfered with the place of his solitude. Had this expression of youth, this desire for a garden, remained buried in his mind to revive and calm the last dragging years at St Helena? For the planning of the Longwood grounds became the most pleasant of his activities, such as they were.

Antommarchi applied for permission to attend the Jamestown Hospital clinics in order to study the prevalent diseases of the island; he resented the order that he must be accompanied to and fro by an officer, and the fact that he and the Abbé Buonavita were arrested by a sentry while returning from a walk on Deadwood, after gunfire, brought a tart protest from them both to the Governor. Between the Bertrands' cottage and New Longwood stretched a length of fence, which Antommarchi and the Abbé climbed through while the sentry loaded his "fire-lock, having charged them already with his bayonet". Their dignity was assailed, if not their skins, and as a result of that action they changed from neutral observers into partisans. Antommarchi, who demanded a wider scope for his patient's rides, told the Governor that the Emperor would not expose himself abroad because of apprehensions that he might be interfered with, as it was known in Longwood that the sentries had orders to shoot Bonaparte if he were seen going beyond the stipulated boundary.

Captain Nicholls's diary notes, "The Emperor is pleased with the progress of the garden. Spade in hand, he walks among the Chinese servants or amuses himself with the Bertrand children among the flower beds, which by now are filled with bloom."

20th November: "General Bonaparte out at work in his little garden at 7 o'clock with a spade and five or six Chinese and valets. The two priests and the surgeon were likewise employed. Afterwards they breakfasted together in the garden. Count Montholon is unwell today: most probably he caught cold working so hard yesterday."

During this period, Captain Nicholls's diary breathes relief and satisfaction — the long endeavours at 'sighting' for the moment had ended.

Later came more accounts of the "bustle and activity which has been recently displayed by General Bonaparte in giving directions about his flower garden and superintending the workmen employed at it. He is hemming it in all round with as many bushy trees and shrubs as he can get transplanted, and with sod walls so as to screen himself as far as possible from external observations. He dined and took coffee under the trees, watching the bigger trees arrive from other gardens on the island, and constructing a small reservoir. He is seen turning the cock of a cistern to allow the water to run over the flowers in one of the little garden's beds. At 5 a.m. in the morning he throws a stone on Marchand's window upstairs and work commences".

On the 6th December, Nicholls saw "General Bonaparte in full dress, with a star on his side, walking with Count Montholon. At present he does not mind anybody seeing him, provided they do not stand looking at him. He appears completely occupied in gardening and planting, and writing and study seem quite out of the question — the Governor and his two daughters-in-law came to Longwood this afternoon. The young ladies wanted to see General Bonaparte but he did not seem inclined to give them the opportunity. After they left Longwood, he had dinner under the trees in his favourite garden with some of his family.

"General Bonaparte this afternoon in one of his little gardens, in his dressing gown. They are doing nothing but transplanting trees. Even this day — this Sunday — they are moving peach trees with fruit on them. They have been moving young oaks in full leaf and the trees probably will survive, but the leaves are falling off as in Autumn."

The satisfaction was short-lived however. On the 25th January he reported being "sorry that I have not been able to get a sight of General Bonaparte today. Since 8 o'clock this morning I have passed six or seven hours walking Longwood garden in order, if possible, to obtain a view of him — General Montholon dined in General Bonaparte's quarters today, and I believe I heard him reading half an hour ago in the General's billiard-room."

In the Forsyth chronicle it is stated that Sir Hudson Lowe "saw almost as little of the prisoner as if the ocean had rolled between them". Forsyth declares that, after the last interview in 1816 when he was so grossly insulted, the Governor never attempted to visit Napoleon again, and continues, "Delicacy prevented him from seeking opportunities of seeing Napoleon unobserved, merely to gratify his curiosity." This would hardly appear to be correct for there are frequent references in many of the contemporary books, telling of Lowe's visits to Longwood, his interviews there with the suite, his walks about the garden, his unannounced appearances at the Bertrands' cottage. Forsyth appends the following incident, which he copied from a letter of Lowe's to Bathurst, prefacing it with a comment that, "This sight of Bonaparte on the 4th August, 1819, was an accident."

Lowe wrote to London, "I had on the 4th instant, a most distinct view myself of his person. I had repaired to Longwood to give directions about some alterations he had himself desired in his garden, when I suddenly found myself quite close to him. He had his back turned to me, and he had a long stick, like a wand, in his hand. [It was a billiard cue.] He was dressed in his usual uniform, looked as lusty as I had ever seen him but walked with a gait that bore somewhat the appearance of infirmity. The children of Count Bertrand were with him——"

Reading Lowe's confession to this itinerant peeping, one cannot but feel a certain sympathy with the prisoner, that here in this restricted little patch of ground, laboriously raised to the level of a country garden, he could not walk without the knowledge that a spy was watering some nearby plant or the Governor might encounter him on the turning of a path. On walking the narrow confines of the actual garden, it becomes evident that this fear must have produced a reaction of claustrophobia. The general feverish activity to rebuild and re-shape the grounds, throw up earthworks, lower paths, hide like some distracted animal from a hunter, is understandable. Here, in the now tranquil piece of ground, a mental battle for very sanity must have been enacted.

Forsyth continues in his book, "It is needless to add that not a word of recognition passed between them. Napoleon had observed Sir Hudson approaching and moved away, — as Captain Nicholls often remarked in his reports, 'made play up the path before the Governor came to the spot where he was standing'."

It became impossible to get into the hands of the Emperor any letter or document which the Governor required him, to read, and on one occasion the luckless Nicholls, given a packet to deliver to 'Napoleon Bonaparte', tendered it in vain to Montholon, Bertrand and Marchand, who all refused to consider it, the result being a direction to Nicholls from Colonel Wynyarde, "Finding you cannot gain admission into the house by the principal entrance — I request you will enter the house by the offices [behind the Montholons' quarters] and proceed towards his dressing-room — knocking at every door that may be closed before you enter it — and should you find them barred or bolted, or any personal obstacle opposed, merely put the letter down on the table——" Bertrand did not help the situation when he told Nicholls that Napoleon would consider any person an assassin who should enter his private apartments without his consent. Nicholls, well aware of the loaded pistols, considered himself to be running a certain risk, although, in Lowe's words, "remaining outside his — Napoleon's — doors exposed to the inclemency of the weather, in the worst season of the year, sometimes for 10 hours' duration, was almost as, if not more, dangerous."

Poor Nicholls recorded, "I saw General Bonaparte this morning, a quarter to eleven, up to his neck in water in a bath. He had a most ghastly appearance, Marchand, his valet, attending him." This sighting was accomplished at the suggestion of Bertrand (who had begun to feel sorry for the hard-pressed orderly officer), by peeping in the little window of the bathroom through which the buckets of hot water were passed.

About this time, Napoleon asked that Mr Stokoe, who had once attended him in a medical capacity soon after O'Meara's departure, and who he understood was returning to St Helena, might attend him again "or would the Governor authorise some other English doctor to come, providing he sign similar conditions as had been accepted by Stokoe in the past". A complaint also went with the request over the "violation of the privacy of his house by the orderly officer——"

Dr Veriling was sent immediately to Longwood, but ended up in Bertrand's house, and, Montholon being ill, he offered his services there, to be told he must accept the Emperor's conditions agreed to by Stokoe if he were to attend to him. Stokoe by then was approaching St Helena, having returned under orders from England for court martial on his conduct in connection with Bonaparte (which was, of course, unknown to the Emperor).

Dr Arnott also saw Count Bertrand and made an offer of his professional aid. The Count took out a series of conditions from his packet and Arnott, reading them, said he would not consent to anything more than professional ethics demanded.

Immediately after, Mr Stokoe arrived at St Helena, was put under arrest and tried on varying counts — seven in all. The whole was found proven. The third indictment read, "That he had signed a paper purporting to be a bulletin of General Bonaparte's health, and divulged the same to the General and his attendants contrary to orders," and the seventh, "That he had contrary to his duty, and the character of a British Naval Officer, communicated to General Bonaparte or his attendant an infamous and calumnious imputation cast upon Lieutenant-General Sir Hudson Lowe. etc. by Barry O'Meara, late surgeon in the Royal Navy" (also now dismissed) "implying that Sir Hudson Lowe had practised with the said O'Meara to induce him to put an end to the existence of General Bonaparte."

Stokoe, though dismissed the Navy, was put on half-pay. At Stokoe's treatment Napoleon, enraged, now refused the services of both Veriling and Arnott.

Captain Nicholls, in the meantime, was still not doing so well. Sightings proved intermittent and he finally asked to be transferred back to the 66th Foot — after a residence of seventeen months at Longwood. Of the 421 days Napoleon was said to be in seclusion, Nicholls was assured of his presence "sixty-eight per cent of the time" — which says something for his zeal and tenacity.

In February, Captain Lutyens of the 20th Foot, who succeeded Captain Nicholls as orderly Officer, wrote, "I saw General Bonaparte today at his favourite amusement, viz. Gardening. He was himself employed placing sods on one bank. In short, his sole amusement at present seems to be building sod walls, making reservoirs to hold water, etc. and pulling down today that which he has reared the day before. He shot three fowls on the 6th for trespass, two of which belonged to his valet Novarrez; this so offended his faithful follower that he wished to leave his service."

Bonaparte went through a period, happily brief, in which he used his gun with effect. No animal straying in the garden was safe — Madame Bertrand's goats, the laying hens or later the rabbits. The Emperor took pot-shots at them all. This 'bad practice', as it was called, caused concern in the minds of Sir Hudson Lowe and the Marquis Montchenu. Lowe called it "*tres inconvenable*" for a person in Bonaparte's situation. The Marquis assented and laid coals on the fire by remarking that it must have crossed the Governor's mind that if a man were shot instead of Madame Bertrand's goats he had no power to do anything with the Emperor, but perhaps shut him up more closely. "He is the prisoner of Europe," he reminded Lowe. Lowe said he felt sure Bonaparte would take care, but when Montchenu left Plantation House he penned a letter to Bathurst asking what was the law in the circumstances. It appeared to be a poser to the Secretary of State, for as answer he sent an opinion from the Solicitor-General. As it happened, there were only two other victims after that, one a bullock that had strayed and which Napoleon shot through the neck, the other a goat.

Count Balmain, finally recalled to Russia, and about to leave the island, spent an afternoon with Madame Bertrand. He said to her that Montholon reported that things were going smoothly and there was nothing at the moment to complain of but ennui. He also asked Madame Bertrand why she had never called upon Lady Lowe. "My situation is very peculiar," she said. "You of course know that no English officer speaks to my husband." She told him of Lowe's warnings to the officers of the garrison that there would be repercussions if they were seen near the Bertrands' house or the Montholons' quarters at Longwood. "It is only rarely I have a visitor now," she ended sadly. No woman dared come. The pleasant days when the island people welcomed them in their homes had long since passed. Balmain judged the situation to be quite intolerable, and suggested she submit the names of fifty of the people on the island that she might see. Lowe showed an unyielding front and complained bitterly to him of the constant attempts made by Bertrand and Montholon to infringe regulations and send packets of letters abroad. Count Balmain was lenient. "They are prisoners and of course will avoid your regulations, just as it is your business to prevent them. You cannot hinder them from intriguing."

"I could turn them off the island," Lowe told him angrily. "What good would that do? It is precisely what the Count and Countess desire; they are anxious to return." Appreciating the force of his argument, Lowe said no more, and Madame Bertrand remained in her lonely state.

CHAPTER 24

Exiles in England

Two or three months before Napoleon's death, Lowe was advised by Bathurst not to direct any prosecutions against the *Morning Chronicle* or Mr O'Meara's publications. "Not because I feel any indifference on the subject," he wrote, "but because London juries are very uncertain in their verdicts and one ill-disposed juryman would be able to acquit the parties, which would give occasion for triumph and appear to justify the complaints made against you.... . You are acting With great prudence in avoiding, if possible, any scene with Bonaparte... . You will find, I think, Abbé Buonavita a very harmless man. The surgeon is reckoned very intelligent and I think will not be disposed to be troublesome, as he is apparently inclined to make advances to the Government.... . With respect to Mr Balcombe, will you let it be known that in the event of his arriving at St Helena, you have orders to send him away. His partners must not be allowed to continue their contract if his name is in it."

Lowe's thoughts shied away from Balcombe: an unfortunate episode, the wrecking of a family in this manner, but his duty — or was it? On what evidence? Had malice entered to warp his judgment or had Sir Thomas Reade swayed him? He was aware that William Balcombe and O'Meara had judged his harshness towards the Emperor as unnecessary, as did Admiral Pulteney Malcolm; that the threat of escape was nebulous, that apart from ill-health the Emperor was far too astute to launch himself in a half-baked scheme that would inevitably bring disaster upon himself. His frank remarks, that he would return to France if and when he was sent for by a nation wanting his return, had been relayed to the Governor, as was his reiterated and immediate desire to leave the island and live in the English country, or even, as he told them, "in the Tower of London".

The distance from his family, the solitude, the immense spread of sea, and the frowning mountains of St Helena appalled his spirit. Several methods of escape were put before him from America and Brazil over the years. Ships' captains, for a consideration, were ready to receive him. Schemes had been prepared and only awaited his acquiescence. He listened, nodded and shrugged his shoulders, and made no comment. Once, in the midst of discussions, he asked for a book and commenced to read.

Judging by the Lowe Papers, following William Balcombe's return to England there was considerable correspondence in reference to his actual whereabouts. Had he gone to France? It was feared he carried messages to the Bonaparte family on the Continent. His letters to St Helena were closely scrutinised on their arrival. About that period the Lowe Papers reflect a growing uneasiness on Napoleon's condition. Faked bulletins by surgeons other than O'Meara had been circulated since November 1817 to the different courts of Europe, as well as to England, and bore Dr W. Baxter's name on the margins of some. Bathurst was not to know of their specious quality, but Balcombe certainly did, and as a consequence his correspondence, conversations and movements were checked at Lowe's instigation.

No diary has been found that refers to the family's movements after they left St Helena nor is it known what William Balcombe did once he reached London. Did he confer with Sir Thomas Tyrwhitt, on whose judgment he greatly relied? Did he seek presentation to the Prince Regent to report the true condition of the captive? Did he speak to the leaders of other political parties than the parties in power in the hope of securing fair play?

On 2nd October, Lowe, still harping on the subject, gave Bathurst extracts from an intercepted letter, saying, "Mr Balcombe in a letter to O'Meara refers to 'our friend Bony' and said he has got Sir Pulteney Malcolm and Sir George Cockburn 'on our side'."

Later he wrote about a confiscated letter, "Under the circumstances Mr Balcombe's letter to Mr Cole, I thought it best not to deliver, considering the fact that the persons whose names are spoken of in it could not approve of my giving any expressions of Mr Balcombe's remarks regarding them." One of the 'persons' mentioned, 'Charley' Ross, was subsequently removed from the Navy by Lowe's command, for no ascertainable reason.

Though the fear of clandestine correspondence greatly exercised the Governor, his ruthless search of the St Helena mails yielded only miscellaneous scraps of news, mainly of private and unimportant matters.

Baffled by the leakage and still unable to pick up direct evidence, Bathurst took a hand and "invited Balcombe to give such information as he was able to afford". A detailed minute may still be read of what passed at the Colonial Office at a Sunday meeting in November, 1818, between William Balcombe, Earl Bathurst, Viscount Sidmouth and Viscount Melville, a minute which was later forwarded to Lowe.

Balcombe in answering their questions asserted that he had not been concerned in any correspondence of which he was 'ashamed' and that he could give no information. Bathurst then informed him that he actually had a confiscated letter of his, written to Dr O'Meara, and Bathurst went on to tell Balcombe that they knew that on his departure from St Helena he had left letters at Ascension Island. Balcombe admitted that this was the case, the letters in question being copies of bills of exchange — a usual precaution. He gave an unequivocal denial that he was commissioned by anyone in St Helena to act in London or elsewhere. Sir Henry Goulburn, in previously writing to Sir Hudson Lowe on the form the proposed interview should take, stated, "Lord Bathurst considers that our best chance of making further discoveries rests in concealing the extent of those which we have made." When hinting at the possibility of his holding other information, Bathurst described it as "correspondence of a very serious nature".

He also remarked it gave him pleasure "to find Mr Balcombe had shown more unwillingness to take an active part than others who were engaged in it!" The three Ministers in turn pressed him to disclose any information about letters addressed to Paris and was again told he knew nothing.

(O'Meara's statement in the press on the St Helena situation read:

"The actual state of matters is now appalling and will probably produce a most unpleasant situation both in England and in Europe.

The Governor may perhaps reflect upon the terrible responsibility which weighs upon him if (as it is possible and soon very probable) Napoleon, deprived of assistance, was to die before the expiration of the five or six months which are required to obtain an answer from England.")

Sir Henry Goulburn, from Downing Street, wrote to Lowe, saying, "Mr Balcombe was evidently alarmed, but, as you will observe from the enclosed minute of what passed, declined to give any satisfactory reply to the questions which were put to him. He has subsequently written to the Colonial Secretary and given outlines of the bills of sales posted at Ascension Island."

It was an inconclusive interview and one that elicited no information yet betrayed a certain uneasiness on the part of the Cabinet. It can be gathered that the Balcombe family were living quietly in the south of England, but Lowe's suspicions, plus O'Meara's friendship, and the intercepted letters all added to something of intrigue — something suspicious, unsubstantial, yet disturbing. If, uninfluenced by Lowe's exaggerated fears, Bathurst had exercised ordinary common sense, he must have realised that, as a potential menace, Napoleon was by now of little account, yet the witch-hunt persisted. At the beginning,

O'Meara's articles and his disclosures had only caused mild uneasiness in the public mind, but opinion hardened and the Cabinet, not over-popular in any event, looked upon the doctor's outpourings with personal alarm; they "proceeded by false representations to combat the statements of the voluble Irishman", for they accepted Lowe's disclaimers at their face value. It suited them to be represented by a man of Lowe's calibre and mentality. If it were ever expedient, he could be relegated usefully to the role of scapegoat. Meanwhile the Cabinet would protect him from the clamour that O'Meara's outspoken reports had aroused.

Sir Hudson Lowe, on his return to England after the Emperor's death, collected many affidavits to substantiate his denial of maltreatment of the exiles. It is said that he obtained one from William Balcombe — but the letter does not appear in the folios, although I made a personal search; I found only an ambiguous answer to a request to confirm his (Lowe's) treatment of the slave Toby. Perhaps that is the letter indicated. Not far along in the miscellaneous bundles of what appeared to be answers to Lowe's 'requests for help', I discovered a forgery, a letter purporting to come from William Balcombe — illiterate, ill-composed and signed, 'H. Balcome'." Besides being completely dissimilar in handwriting and diction, as well as lacking the 'b' in the name, it was a veiled confession and an appeal couched in terms that the irascible William could never use. One wonders whether Lowe invented or forged the missive. He sustained objections to Balcombe's advancement, a condition that lasted for four years, and it was generally known that his accusations, even though not proven, sufficiently influenced the Secretary of State for the Colonies to close the purveyor's business and break up the family's life at St Helena. While the ban lasted he could never return there, could no longer hold the position of Naval Agent or be Purveyor to the Emperor, yet when the need of assistance in the forthcoming lawsuit against O'Meara arose, Lowe did not hesitate to seek it. Many of the affidavits sworn in Lowe's favour were of trivial importance, one example being "that he never prevented the Officers of the 53rd Regiment from visiting Madame Bertrand" and there were others of equal trumpery. It is stated that William Balcombe "declared in his favour". A formal letter found in Balcombe's handwriting is the reply already mentioned to a request for an affidavit about the treatment of Toby, and, with all the stamp of Balcombe's personality, it may be what they mean. It reads:

St. Omers, Oct. 11, 1822.

"Sir,

"In reply to your letter of the 5th inst. received this morning requesting me to state as far as lies within my knowledge to you what foundation there may be for that part of the statement which says, in a book entitled *Napoleon in Exile*, Bonaparte had 'directed me to purchase the freedom of the slave' etc.

It has been asserted that you prohibited the sale of the slave. Bonaparte mentioned to me more than once, either through Le Conte Las Cases or Bertrand, to purchase Toby my gardener and give him his freedom and place the amount to Longwood private account or Bertrand's, I don't remember which.

"I have no recollection of having mentioned the subject to you before, but I do having done so to Sir Thomas Reade.

"The first paragraph was brought to the police and an investigation took place, I think before Col. Skelton, the then sitting magistrate, and I believe the result was sent home to the Court of Directors.

"I am, Sir,

"Your obedient servant,

"W. Balcombe."

There is another and typical letter written by him for black Sarah, Betsy's maid, to take back to St Helena, in which he gave her implicit instructions as to her conduct on her arrival on the island. Both are in the Lowe Papers, the last having been taken from Sarah at Jamestown. It is endorsed by Lowe with the record that she was interrogated as to the Balcombe family's whereabouts in England and who went to visit them.

Apart from Toby, Sarah, a comfortable, middle-aged African servant, had at once caught Napoleon's interest when at the Briars — possibly because of her infectious smile, or it might have been because of her devotion to the children. There were other negro servants. Homes such as the Briars were stocked with them — but Sarah, being older, stouter and a woman of personality, attracted him.

She 'minded' the children and she is mentioned in their recollections as going with the family to England and enduring the cold of two winters. This letter reads:

London, 10th April 1819.

"Sarah Timms,

"In sending you back to the island of St Helena, your native country, you must understand that I do it upon the condition that you do not take charge of any package, parcel, or letter whatever, and that you do not undertake to convey any such, or any message, to or for any person whatever on the island, and further that on your arrival you conform yourself in every aspect to the regulations of His Excellency, The Governor, and I also desire that in case any parcel or letter should come into your hands, either on board ship, or otherwise, that you will instantly give up such letter to Captain Locke or the Officer Commanding to be conveyed to the Governor. You will show these instructions to Captain Locke when you go on board the *Larkin*.

"(Signed) William Balcombe."

Lowe kept a curt note among the papers from Mr W. H. Holmes, the agent who negotiated bills in London for the exiles, complaining that he, Lowe, had unceremoniously dispossessed him of his property — namely three cases of books. Holmes states, "The legal arrangements that you were pleased to establish in St Helena might in that country have justified intervention of private rights, but, as the Laws of England do not sanction such acts of outrage, I request that you will immediately send the three cases of books to my brokers.———"

Possibly the confiscation of the books was the outcome of an earlier action when a case opened at Jamestown uncovered a letter from William Balcombe to O'Meara, inserted inside one of the volumes. The suspicion already aroused about the family immediately hardened, and contributed to the ban on William Balcombe's return. In the meantime Gourgaud's 'extravagant' confessions were being discounted one by one ... and Napoleon had died.

Napoleon's observation that those close to him seemed to encounter trouble was probably the remark of a man obsessed by disaster, yet in some manner it was borne out by results. He had been the focal point of violence and movement for years, and even on St Helena the quietest of lives reacted to his presence.

In the case of the Balcombe family, it diverted their history from a relatively commonplace way of life in Naval and East India Company employment to conditions far removed. Unable now to return to his East India Company post and his property, William Balcombe lived in England until objections hitherto placed in the way of his advancement were overcome, and a Government that, on Lowe's advice, prevented him from resuming his life on St Helena transferred him as Colonial Treasurer (the first) to Australia.

He sailed in the early part of 1824 for Sydney, with his family, only Betsy, who had by then married, remaining in England. The *Winchelsea*, the ship that had conveyed the Balcombes to London in 1818, once again received them for the longer journey south to the almost unknown land — scarcely twenty-five years colonised — a convict settlement.[19]

Jane died on the voyage, tuberculosis being probably the cause, her romance with Dr Stokoe summarily ended.

Of Betsy's subsequent history only small items, and those widely spaced, have been recorded. Her marriage turned out unhappily. She was left without means, and taught music to educate her one daughter. Of her husband there are few data. A relative of the Nevill family, and reputed to be an extremely handsome man-about-town, he became a brief and evidently stormy interlude in her life, passing out of it after a few unhappy years. This I learned from the late Lord William Nevill, who cherished a deep affection for Elizabeth Johnstone, Betsy's daughter, and whose London flat held many memories of her in the form of Napoleonic relics.

It is characteristic of the habits of families who migrated to the Colonies in the early 'twenties that, whether from negligence or accident, most of their previous history is forgotten.

Few personal documents have survived to provide any record of their varying fortunes. The exigencies of nineteenth-century travel, the primitive dwellings, the lack of facilities in which to store possessions, all contributed to the destruction of data which were mostly trivial, from a contemporary viewpoint.

In many instances the past was gladly buried and forgotten — possibly in the Balcombe family's case some of this feeling persisted. William left no personal record of his life, dying a few years after his appointment as Colonial Treasurer. One or two formal letters in his handwriting remain in the Mitchell Library, in all cases referring to Treasury matters.

There is a record that Betsy and her daughter rejoined her family in Australia for a brief period, and the Government *Gazette* of 1829 notes that she belonged to a committee of the female school of orphans under the presidency of Mrs Darling, the Governor's wife.

Only one personal letter survives, a closely written folded sheet, frank-stamped as was the custom before the days of envelopes, and it is now in the possession of the Mitchell Library.

Sent from Edinburgh in 1826, it was written by George Heathcote, the convalescent Ensign who had received frequent visits while at Arnos Vale from the Balcombes, and by whose bed Jane and Betsy had read for his amusement.

Contemporary maps show Arnos Vale to be a valley adjacent to the Briars, a similar fold in the volcanic spread of mountains.

From the tone of Betsy's diary, George Heathcote rated as a disregarded suitor — his personality paling before the still effulgent glow from the famous figure at Longwood.

However, her charms remained deep in the young man's memory. "I want to hear more of your situations in that far-off country," he wrote. "My mind had been much deformed and kept backward from every species of knowledge and useful service by the company I was forced to keep on board ship.

"Mr Stokoe has just been here, sends his kind love and desires me to say he is thinking of going to Joseph Bonaparte in America. He was extremely distressed at the news of poor Jane's death.

"His feelings however had not been so dreadful as mine for after I had mourned for you, dearest Betsy, I had to lament the loss of Jane — God bless you and preserve you.

"Dearest Betsy, where is this husband who I heard treated you so cruelly? Do you feel lawfully bound to him still?

"What is his name and where does he live? — Forgive me, dearest Betsy, if in asking these questions I hurt your better feelings and believe me I do it with more affection than you can conceive and my love for you and yours must plead my excuse ...

"I want to hear about my young friends Alex and Tom, who now, I suppose, don't remember me. They would not remember reading by my bedside in the home at Arnos Vale.

But they cannot forget that beautiful vale itself, where their young limbs were strengthened by climbing the mountainous sides — nor can Betsy forget how often in her 'more gentle' moods! she knocked me down on the grass, flat, and delighted herself with my weakness and her own strength ..."

CHAPTER 25

Napoleon's Last Phase

Meanwhile on St Helena the tragi-comedy went on. In the end, Montholon sought leave to join his wife in Europe, but Bertrand remained uncomplaining, notwithstanding 'Emmy's' claim that they must go for the sake of the children.

Napoleon saw the breaking up of his restricted world. He made no further effort to throw off the lethargy that enveloped him. His decline had been slow, only half-appreciated by the staff, and Lowe's concession in enlarging the boundaries came too late. Napoleon, however, wanted to take advantage of the wider field and, mounting Hope, he rode to the outside limits, to return utterly exhausted, to be helped off and supported to his room, where he lay on his bed. From then on, even carriage driving became difficult for him to bear. Stubbornly he told himself that, not being seriously ill, he had allowed want of exercise to aggravate his condition. He caused a kind of seesaw to be erected in the billiard room — a weight on one side — that by manipulation he might exercise his legs. A sorry picture it presents: the one-time ruler of Europe and eighty million souls, reduced to forcing his legs to operate a plank and weight.

Chronic hepatitis was still generally accepted as his complaint. He had asked again for removal to a more temperate part of the island, to the Briars for choice, but that request, along with the dreams of a home in the English countryside, or a return to France, or asylum in America, had long since been abandoned. Now his life consisted of a defence against Lowe. This shadow of a hate somehow had shifted, from the nation that held him to the jailer himself.

Napoleon's last caller from the outer world he received on the 2nd April. It was Mr Ricketts, a member of the Calcutta Council, returning home from India, and, incidentally, a relative of Lord Liverpool. Napoleon told Bertrand to seek him out and invite him to Longwood. This, through Plantation House, he did. At that late hour in the Emperor's heart a wavering hope awoke again that some change, some alleviation, might come from the pleading of a new voice. A change of scene meant life! He hoped that Ricketts, so near to the Prime Minister, would press his request for a kinder climate in which to live; for he genuinely believed these St Helena conditions would kill him soon. Ricketts was received in the Emperor's little bedroom — he found him lying on his camp-bed. Deeply interested, he took full notice of everything he could see — which was difficult, for the usual storm lantern, shrouded by paper, gave the only light in the room. Hudson Lowe's warning kept returning to the visitor — not to be led astray by the captive's persuasive powers. Lowe had not come himself, but, since probably he did not want it discovered on what bad terms he was with the household, he sent Ricketts, primed with warnings, escorted only by an orderly. Napoleon was propped on pillows, one arm passed through the frame of his bed to help his movements, which evidently caused him pain. He had tied a coloured handkerchief around his head and his checks showed the dark growth of a three days' beard. Ricketts later wrote, "He resembled that picture of misery, leaning on the capstan of the *Northumberland* — not exhibiting any particular marks indicative of his being afflicted with the liver or any other severe bodily complaint." He and the Governor must evidently have discussed the Emperor's condition beforehand.

Lowe had warned him, he added, of Napoleon's abrupt manner. His own report was that Napoleon's sentences were well-turned. He spoke rapidly and became animated, gestured often, giving his visitor little time to answer; it was a one-man show, the onlookers shadowed in a darkened room.

Ricketts, the recipient of this last appeal for clemency from the failing prisoner, was a biased listener, too small a personality to combat the machinery of what then passed for British justice. The interview lasted four hours and its record of Napoleon's part in the conversation shows incoherency, as if the words burst from a pleading, overburdened mind. "Tell Lord Liverpool that I should like to leave the island, which is fatal to persons suffering from my trouble — I have been ill a long time. There is heavy mortality among troops in the garrison. Put me somewhere else — in Europe — no matter in what country. Your Government has already spent £1,000,000 in watching me and there is no end in sight. Lord Liverpool probably has not the faintest idea as to how Hudson Lowe is persecuting me — a police system that reminds one of Sicily. If I do not appear in person before an orderly officer, my apartment will be entered by force. I am living in these wretched rooms under lock and key — they shall cross this threshold only over my dead body. As the height of folly, they are now building a house that will cost a huge sum and which I shall never occupy — I hate its location, bare of trees and facing the camp. I could never put my nose against the window-pane without seeing red-coats — my ears would be dimmed by all the drums — I would even hear the challenge of the sentries." He ended the tirade with a pathetic sentence, "Yours is a generous nation: in the end it will grow indignant." It was both an expression of misery and supplication — the two sometimes unrelated, shaming to the listener inasmuch as it betrayed to what limits imprisonment had brought the most compelling man in Europe; but it was received only with the foggy comprehension that characterised Mr Ricketts, who took his leave of the Emperor in his stuffy sick-room and returned with thankfulness to the formal comfort of Plantation House. He related to Lowe that he found the Emperor "stout", "normal" and "not particularly dark under the eyes". At first the visitor was disposed to be touched at the Emperor's plight but only until he returned to Lowe's influence; and the latter immediately took him in hand — a long talk at dinner, the candles, the port, quietude and the shelter of the pleasant house induced other impressions. Lowe declared the interview was staged, the illness strictly diplomatic, the harangue, which Ricketts faithfully recounted, so much eyewash in an attempt to be removed from the island. Ricketts reported in due course to London and dutifully advised Liverpool in Lowe's words. An ironical letter came back from Bathurst to Lowe: "Nothing could have been more fortunate than Mr Rickett's visit to St Helena; he has given the most satisfactory report concerning the real state of the business."

Now Napoleon began to stir out less, often staying in bed for most of the day, wrote spasmodically, rolled the billiard balls aimlessly about the table until finally he had the table removed to the servants' room. He talked of his battles, his edicts, his schemes of government, sometimes of his followers — but even they, loyal adherents or renegades as the case might be, became little more than figures in a play, defeat and disaster in war now overlaid by the present stagnation of body and the trivialities that surrounded him. Ill-health preoccupied him. He changed from bed to bed, and to the sofa 'with the white drape, seeking ease from the altered position; writing, dozing, sometimes calling Marchand to talk to him, even sending at night for Bertrand, who came from his cottage accompanied by sentries with fixed bayonets. Rarely were the windows opened, the fear of draughts persisting. At those periods he kept completely out of sight, though by voice and whistling he let the orderly officer know he was there, a small action that Lutyens noted gratefully.

The suite registered the decline of his physical condition and the unsympathetic Antommarchi made comments on certain aspects of his routine of life and continued to order exercise. One day Napoleon called for the carriage and, assisted by Montholon and Marchand, made a sudden decision to visit Sandy Bay and the Dovetons, on 4th October. Sir William, now growing elderly, was walking in the garden before breakfast when he saw several people on horseback coming over Stitches Ridge. It was unusual to receive visitors at any hour and he went for his spyglass, to recognise the party from Longwood. The cavalcade stopped at the door and Mrs Greentree and her father welcomed them. The Emperor asked if he might "come down and rest himself". He dismounted on the lawn, as did three servants, Count Bertrand and Count Montholon. Sir William noted that Bonaparte stood for a moment, looked around and appeared to be greatly fatigued. He asked him to come to the house and the Emperor turned to the steps, to be assisted to climb up them by Bertrand's arm. It was a difficult progress. Sir William brought forward an armchair, but the Emperor preferred the sofa. He immediately noted the change of furniture since he had last been to the home, so long ago, in the days when there had been some hope. He remarked that there were now two sofas. Sir William informed him that as he had left the East India Company's service, and now having no residence in town, the furniture had all been brought to Mount Pleasant. He added, "Things have changed." The Emperor asked whether he liked England, as Sir William had spent some time there since their last meeting. He answered truthfully, "A fine country," but he was satisfied with St Helena for himself. He begged the Emperor to share breakfast with the family, having noticed that during the conversation the servants, under Montholon's supervision, had put up a table under a tree on the lawn and spread a breakfast they had brought with them. He showed him the dining-room, bright in the morning sunshine, and told him here was butter and honey, the best in the island. Napoleon smiled, gave him a gentle pinch of the ear, a glance of approbation, but shook his head and asked Sir William to join him on the lawn instead.

Mrs Greentree had butter, jelly, eggs, radishes and watercress sent out and Mount Pleasant water to drink. The Emperor's table held cold pie, potted meat, cold turkey, curried fowl, ham and pork, dates, almonds and a very fine salad. They drank champagne and coffee. Sir William sat on the Emperor's right hand and was offered a slice of potted meat, then curried fowl with champagne. Coffee was served afterwards and Mrs Greentree came out from the house and drank some with them, finding it acrid. Afterwards the Emperor went again into the drawing-room, leaving his servants to eat in the garden. He had done that often before when at the Briars, leaving the Pavilion to the domestics after his own meal while he went for coffee with the family, with whist to follow, or gossip on the lawn. That seemed long ago but the domestic scene at Sandy Bay brought it back to him. The children's voices and the home of sane, ordinary people, living untramelled lives, warmed his heart.

He sat on the sofa and talked to Mrs Greentree and paid her compliments; the usual gambit: When was she married? How many children? Where was her husband? Seeing the children peeping at the door he called them in; holding one to him, he tweaked her nose and gave her liquorice from a small tortoise-shell box. Mrs Greentree went to bring her baby and Napoleon motioned her to sit beside him on the sofa so that he might examine it. She considered that but for his pallid colour Napoleon appeared to be in good health. She had not been present when, with Bertrand's help on both occasions, he had mounted the steps with difficulty, so did not judge from anything more than his outward appearance. His face was "astonishingly fat and his body and thighs very round and plump". Montholon whispered to her, putting his hand on his right side, that the Emperor had a liver complaint. Napoleon suddenly asked Sir William if he ever got drunk. Startled, the old man admitted he liked a glass of wine sometimes. Then, turning to Mrs Greentree, Napoleon asked, "How often does your husband get drunk? Is he so once a week?" Mrs Greentree hurriedly said, "No." "Once a fortnight?" "No." "Once a month?" "No," and, gathering her wits, she remarked, "It is years since I have seen him so." Napoleon, disappointed, said, "Bah!" As when at the Briars, he was always curious at the supposedly large amounts drunk by Englishmen. The habit of lingering over port, as ever, intrigued him. The joke of 'two bottles, three bottles' came back; and the joke about William Balcombe's gout.

Sir William noted that the Emperor kept his hat on during breakfast and also commented in his diary on the conversation, which took him aback, for the family were of highly religious and sober habits.

The Emperor rode away in good spirits, having eaten more than was his usual custom, his mind lifted from the monotony of passing hours by the influence of new surroundings and kindly people. However, by the time he reached the waiting carriage on the road he was barely able to sit his horse and went to bed immediately on returning to Longwood.

After that there were no more rides or excursions, only short walks in the garden, long periods in bed interspersed with very hot baths lasting two or three hours. Antommarchi's reports gave a descending scale in his patient's condition.

Stendhal, clerk in the War Office and perhaps the most measured and critical of all Napoleon's biographers, considered his banishment a cruel and shameful action on England's part. Stendhal's manuscript is still to be seen in the Grenoble Municipal Library; it was not published until after his death in 1842. He wrote, as he said, to refute the slander of a man who had been exposed to the vengeance of all the powers on earth. He did not live to see Napoleon's apotheosis, to feel the satisfaction in the final triumph of personality over prejudice, to hear the acclaim of world judgment. He saw only a military genius made the subject of malevolent jealousy, finally derided, and, as the last stroke of fate, interned upon a rock. Without mercy he told of Napoleon's shortcomings, his quickness of temper, his seeming inconsistencies, but all the while he held the balance of character, revealing the man as far as another human being could reveal human personality. Stendhal did not know Napoleon in captivity, where at the beginning his characteristics were all those of Stendhal's finding. He was not there to chronicle his finest hour, the hour of death, when he wrote his last orders, remembered those who had followed him, showed no tinge of rancour, but resignation and courage of the highest calibre in a long and drawn-out battle in which he knew he could not be victor.

Stendhal notes that, in his opinion, Napoleon's mediocre political genius at Moscow cost him his army. Napoleon had said, "if I succeed in Russia I shall be master of the whole world." He was defeated by his own pride and the climate, but firstly his own pride. The Moscow winter was not early, on the contrary was as fine as could be desired, for when the French left on 19th October there was superb sunshine and only three degrees of frost. Napoleon's perspective had gone, the balance that held him secure on the tightrope of his life had become impaired and the retreat from Moscow was the beginning of his journey to St Helena.

Towards the end of March there were good days and bad days, the usual chart of an ailing individual. The Emperor's hours became irregular. He sometimes worked at night, dictated, sorted papers, held conversations on one subject or another; once he walked up and down the rooms most of the night until stricken by a bout of violent vomiting, when the absence of Antommarchi in Jamestown again became a matter for censure. Frankly, Antommarchi did not believe the Emperor's sickness to be much more than a mental condition — an imaginary symptom to make himself appear worse than he was, for political reasons. Napoleon's calm appearance the next morning seemed to confirm the doctor's words. The Emperor became almost gay. He talked of Warsaw and Madame Walewska, and ceased his dictation to describe his meeting with her for the first time at a ball. He was with Bertrand and Louis de Pérregord, his Generals. "They were both hovering around her," he told Montholon. "Several times I found them in my path, particularly Louis de Pérregord. This at length became annoying and I told Berthier to send him off immediately to obtain news of the 6th Corps. I thought that Bertrand would be more clear-sighted, but Madame Walewska's bright eyes had dazzled him.

He never quitted her side, and during supper he leaned on the back of her chair in such a manner that his *aiguillettes* danced hither and thither on the beautiful red [pink] and white skin of her shoulders. I touched him on the arm, drew him into the recess of a window ... gave him orders to set out immediately for the headquarters of Prince Jérome (his brother) ... to bring me reports of the state of the siege of Breslau ..." He laughed — sighed — and became lost in memories.

Antommarchi was on hand at the next bout of vomiting and acknowledged at last the seriousness of the case, which he diagnosed as a gastric fever. He prescribed emetic lemonade. The next night Napoleon reluctantly drank what Antommarchi gave him and, after unsuccessfully trying to bring it up, rolled on the floor in agony. Antommarchi told Montholon the dose was too powerful "but it is the necessary remedy". Napoleon drank no more of it, giving his order to Pierron personally. When lemonade came he sniffed it with suspicion, asked Montholon whether it had a sharp smell and to drink some of it. Montholon did, and in ten minutes was seized with such a paroxysm of vomiting that, as he noted in his diary, he was hardly able to reach his quarters. Napoleon became excessively angry that his orders had been disobeyed. He treated Antommarchi as a murderer, and declared he would never see him again. Turmoil reigned until by a fluke of luck a box of books was delivered at Longwood and distracted him.

Montholon wrote that the old phobia of poison evidently lingered in the Emperor's mind. "People now rival in their respect the skill of Catherine de Medici," Napoleon told him. "I have escaped poisoning ten times if I have once." He related to him an incident with snuff. He was leaving the dinner table with the Empress Josephine when he saw what appeared to be his snuff-box on the salon mantelpiece. He took it up and half opened the box when the thought struck him that he had his snuff-box in his pocket after all. He took it out. They were both his. Suspicion awoke and the snuff from the two boxes was analysed. The one on the overmantel had been poisoned.

He now occupied himself with his will. The names of past friends, adherents, his family, his son, marshalled themselves across his vision, and he thought of them with poignancy, gratitude and love. For days he dictated — money, land, his medals, swords, his jewels, all came under review. How much less than he imagined! How had his earthly possessions shrunk! But finally the document was complete, witnessed by Bertrand, Montholon and Marchand.

Even so, at this late stage, a little sparkle of fun remained. The Bertrand children were sat upon the see-saw to replace the weight, and Napoleon spent his time in endeavouring feebly to shake them off. The children's laughter and cries were a welcome sound in a house filled with anxiety.

CHAPTER 26

The Emperor's Death

After September, the grip of disease became manifest. Bonaparte's strength diminished and he asserted that fresh air disagreed with him. He could not tolerate a lamp in his bedroom. He became deaf and giddy. Time was running out. Antommarchi, unaccustomed to the symptoms, tried futile alleviations that caused Napoleon to ask him, "Do you not think Mr Lowe has tormented me enough without you wishing to do the same?" This was when Antommarchi applied a blister and omitted to shave the skin. After administrating the treatment he then went for a walk to Jamestown, to find a tormented patient on his return. "How are you?" asked the doctor. "I do not know," the Emperor bluntly told him. "Leave me in peace. You have applied blistering plasters of the worst shape to my arms, and you did not shave my skin before applying them. A wretch in a hospital would get better treatment. It seems to me you could very well have left one arm free without treating them both at once. A poor man is not treated in this way. Go away; you are a fool and I a bigger one for allowing myself to be served like this." Nevertheless, the bout of anger, plus the burning, revived and roused him., and for a few days he braved the air out of doors. Soon his walks in the garden again made him ill, and he shut himself up in the billiard room. Food nauseated him. He only chewed the beef for the juice and spat out the meat. Madame Bertrand describing his meals said, "He takes a sup of wine, sitting on the sofa beside us in the dining-room. Mastication is painful, owing to his spongy gums." It is a sorry picture, tempered only by the unfailing respect and attention afforded him by Bertrand, Marchand and Montholon — faithful, trio, totally dissimilar and incompatible, yet held by a strong bond of love for the dying man.

It was on the 1st April 1821 that Antommarchi, at length unwilling to undertake the case alone, asked Bertrand to send for Dr Arnott on a consultant basis. The Governor acquiesced. From now on, Dr Arnott visited Napoleon, keeping a verbose diary of events and a singularly meagre record of medical facts. Antommarchi and he disagreed on certain medicaments. Bertrand reported that the Corsican had decided that at the moment Napoleon "*avait perdu ses sens*" they would apply for further medical assistance, and even Lowe now appreciated that Napoleon's condition was not a matter for politics.

It was life and death. He offered any medical aid necessary and the Navy wished to send their chief medical officer, but Dr Arnott plodded on, unassisted by a further opinion. Antommarchi did not oppose his proposition for administering a *lavement* — he knew Bonaparte would not permit it; they had been over that ground before. "He would not allow his bedclothes to be changed, even though his bed was wet through to the fourth mattress." To give him a *lavement* it was necessary to turn him over on his side, but how was this to be done when he would not suffer himself to be moved or touched? "He might expire if moved to another bed." Bertrand's notes went on, "Agitation produced a hiccup. He was experiencing weakness of mind; though sometimes clear, it often wandered and he refused medicine or nourishment, saying, '*Non, non,*' in a groaning tone.

When asked if he would permit the administrations of other doctors, he asked, "*Mais, est-ce que je suis mourant?*" Meanwhile, Dr Arnott, always one to look upon the bright side, continued to attend, and spread his optimism by day, while Antommarchi wrote sombre reports at night. But on the 2nd April, Arnott noted: "Found Bonaparte very weak and feverish, profuse perspiration and pallid."

On the 5th April he wrote, "Bad night but not unduly alarmed. Told Bertrand that Napoleon is in no danger whatever. Told Napoleon to rise and get shaved. Napoleon replied he was too weak at present; he would shave when a little stronger as he preferred to shave himself. His beard is very long and he looks horrible, but he has a stout heart and as much flesh on him as myself. His face has not fallen away; the colour is pallid and cadaverous; he has vomited. The bedroom is kept very filthy and particularly the bedclothes, occasioned by Bonaparte spitting upon them. He has a cough and spits a good deal, and never turns his head to avoid the bed linen, but throws it out immediately before him!

"7th: Bad night, coldness in extremities; pain and tension of the belly; headache and great restlessness, but I told Montholon I didn't think him any worse.

"8th: Shaved and better today.

"9th: Antommarchi desires to go away. Examined Bonaparte, who winced a little on examination of the liver — calls it a stab of a penknife. Found no hardness or swelling. More vomiting — am still not worried."

Napoleon remarked to Arnott: "The devil has eaten my legs." Arnott's next note was: "Extraordinary paleness, sometimes quite ghastly and horrible. He was assisted across the room in the arms of Bertrand and Marchand. A beard now shows some days growth. I still find no organic infection. A great part of the disease lies in the mind, the symptoms of hypochondriasis."

17th April 1821. From Gorrequer's notes: "Bonaparte again complained of the *fegato*, putting his hand on his right side and using the term above. Doctors not alarmed with his condition, but Arnott said, 'The dust of a ball would carry him off.' Dr Arnott added he felt more or less confirmed in the opinion that the disease was hypochondriasis. Dr Arnott noted a singularity this morning, Bonaparte's mind seemed particularly affected. He was sitting in a chair whistling when suddenly he stopped, opened his mouth wide — quite wide — projected it forward and looked steadily at Dr Arnott in the face for a short time with a kind of a vacant stare.

"The Governor asked if moving him into the new house might help, and Arnott replied, 'Anything to break the concentration would be good — in fact, if, for example, a 74 were to arrive from England to take him away he had no doubt he would recover. This would put him on his legs again directly.'

"Arnott was asked if he could walk alone and said, 'No, he could not move without assistance.' 'At least,' he said, 'I never see him move unless he has two persons assisting him.' He commented that Napoleon's followers were still afraid of him.

"20th April: Antommarchi reported that Napoleon was troubled at night with heat and choking and difficulty to swallow. Arnott's report was, 'I can see no difference whatever — decidedly not worse.' Montholon's letter on the same day says, 'Death seems to be impressed on all his features.' To his wife he writes, 'I conclude that this letter will reach you at some mineral waters, and it is unhappily probable that I shall be joining you on your return from thence. I say unhappily, for I shall very dearly pay for this meeting so much longed for, should I be indebted or it solely to the death of a man whose friendship towards me has for a long time past known no bounds and of whom his last moment gives me more proof of it than ever.'

"21st April: Dr. Arnott's report still *parrot-like* continued to, 'find General Bonaparte better.' But on the 22nd April he concedes that, 'My patient is not so well. Vomited undigested food. Better in the afternoon.' Nevertheless he adhered more and more to the opinion that the cause was hypochondriasis and that he 'could not give him that which would set him right.' Lowe asked what was that and Arnott replied, 'Liberty,' but still insisted he was better. 'He wears no shirt, only a flannel waistcoat, and when he gets out of bed, sits with his legs in a large flannel bag. He betrays great impatience with those who attend to him and breaks out in passionate exclamations against them. Arnott wrote without comment, 'Bonaparte vomited black matter like coffee grounds.' Lowe stayed in the new house to receive further bulletins. Arnott reported great exhaustion and weakness of voice and suggested further medical aid. He added, 'His obstinacy in refusing remedies ordered is most vexatious.'

"April 26th: At 4 o'clock in the morning Napoleon called Montholon and told him, with extraordinary emotion, he had just seen Josephine 'but she would not embrace me. She disappeared at the moment I was about to take her in my arms... . She was seated there ... she had not changed ... still the same — full of devotion for me. She told me that we are about to see each other again ... never more to part ... she assured me that. Did you see her? Montholon was non-committal; he had no desire to interfere with something that gave Napoleon comfort. The chair had remained empty to his eyes, no fantasy touched his senses, and he went about changing the Emperor's soaked garments, a difficult process not accomplished often enough. A comment in his diary read, 'Even the mattress was wet through.'"[20]

To Bertrand, coming at midnight, Napoleon said, "*Comment êtes-vous ici, Bertrand? Que voulez-vous? Est-ce vous vous êtes ennuyé à cette heure?*"

Lieutenant Croad, on 23rd January, wrote in his diary of a visit to Jamestown, "Montchenu and Montholon on the sofa: Montholon says with a shrug 'He, the Emperor, is just like a woman with child. Whatever he eats his stomach discharges almost immediately.' Montchenu goes on gossiping about the island, regretting there were no women as always; it filled him with ennui."

Once in his last days Napoleon slipped right down towards the end of his bed. Montholon asked him what he was doing, saw he was trying to ease himself up, and when the Count assisted him he complained of a pain in the stomach and fell down. Montholon said his eyes turned upward in his head and he lost all recognition for some time. This happened a second time, when he was raised and pillows were placed against his back to support him. Montholon said he no sooner had him *sur son séant* than he threw up his arms and fell down insensible again. They administered castor oil but he immediately vomited it, and between three and four in the afternoon Antommarchi came to Colonel Gorrequer, saying Napoleon was dying — might even die that day. Could Dr Shortt and Dr Mitchell be called?

Gossip, conjecture and consternation filled the homes on the island. The man who had been the lodestone of their thoughts for five years was dying. They felt a kind of sorrowful pride in him: his brilliant history, his defeat, his prestige, his gentleness. He had been an enemy, but they remembered the days when he had ridden about the roads, smiled at the children and given a napoleon to anyone who did him a small favour.

After some protest, the Emperor consented to change his room and have a bed placed in the drawing-room. The doctors thought he might get more air there. Napoleon, asking if everything was ready, with great difficulty got out of bed and, refusing to be carried, reached the other bed with the support of Montholon and Marchand, crying, "I have no more strength; lay me on the palliasse." His feet and legs were swathed in hot towels, as had been done each time a collapse appeared imminent.

As a great favour, Madame Bertrand was allowed to come in and sit a while. There had been a coolness since he found out that she was planning to leave St Helena and take her husband with her. He asked that she might sit by the head of the bed, and spoke of her recent illness. "You are well now," he said. "Your complaint was known — mine is not, so I shall die."

Most of the time his face was turned towards a little coloured print of the King of Rome, one of two that had come for sale to the island and been sequestered by Lowe and kept in Plantation House until the suite, through the grapevine, heard of them and they were eventually procured for the Emperor. Lowe's reasons for retaining them were obscure — perhaps the result of the unpleasantness over the marble bust; he wanted no more pictures to be exhibited or distributed.

Madame Bertrand talked little, and did not stay long with the Emperor in the darkened, stuffy room. There was a keen desire on her part to be allowed to tidy everything, to give him fresh sheets or move his pillows, but, knowing him, she felt anything she might offer would be refused. He was in the hands of the valets, who themselves did all they were allowed to do, his dominant spirit ruling them even *in extremis*. It was noted that even towards the end the household implicitly obeyed his orders and accorded him the respect of royalty. He looked extremely lonely, and when Madame Bertrand shut the door behind her she burst into tears. She came to him for a brief visit every day afterwards.

On the 20th, Napoleon said to Vignali, in Antommarchi's hearing, "When I am dying, you are to prepare an altar in the next apartment, expose the Blessed Sacrament and recite the prayers for the dying. I was born a Catholic — I want to obey its commands and receive the help it affords." Antommarchi's face was expressive of his feelings, and Napoleon, seeing him standing at the foot of the bed smiling scornfully as he listened to the conversation, called, "Your insults weary me. I can forgive your foolishness, and your lack of skill, but a want of reverence, never — get out!" He turned to the Abbé. "When I die you are to celebrate Mass and cease only when I am buried." Vignali dropped to his knees and kissed his hand, that now had the habit of lying over the side of the bed.

The doctors, for some unknown reason, decided as a last resort to administer calomel — ten grains. Marchand, reluctant, but fearing to object, mixed it in sweetened water. The Emperor swallowed it with difficulty, tried to spit it out, and turned to Marchand, saying, "You are deceiving me, too," but he was not distressed and later drank some more sugared water. He commenced to hiccup, the paroxysm lasting into the evening, and at night he vomited black matter, like coffee grounds, mixed with a little blood. Later the hiccup reasserted itself. None of the servants went off duty. There was subdued activity outside Napoleon's doors, the comings and goings of orderlies, doctors and servants. He refused to see Dr Shortt and the Naval Chief Surgeon. New faces would be of no avail and he had no hope of alleviation. Only familiar hands would bring him any physical relief, if relief were possible at all.

In his growing confusion during the final days, Napoleon muddled his doctors' names. He spoke of O'Meara and Stokoe, long since gone from the island. Suddenly he would appear perfectly composed. Once he called for a pen and paper and dictated a letter to the Governor, to be sent the moment he expired, "As he would have the honour to do." He also told Montholon that on his death he must show the Governor his will. Later, unbelieving, Lowe asked Montholon to repeat the remark.

Bertrand's appearance at unusual hours worried him still. It brought home to him that they, like himself, knew that he was about to die. It made the realisation clearer, and he flinched from it. Later Madame Bertrand remarked that he did not wish to die. Some lingering hope remained that somehow, somewhere, he would be reunited with his son. Marie-Louise had drifted from his thoughts to be more shadowy and unreal than the ghost of Josephine, who, he considered, was near him on occasions.

At six o'clock on the morning before Napoleon's death the shutters were opened. He had gone beyond the thought of draughts and too much light and was sunk in a coma of tranquillity, eyes fixed, mouth open, pulse just noticeable in a wrist that still remained plump, his hand over the side of the mattress, his face shadowed by the growth of beard they had not dared to remove. Madame Bertrand was called and sat beside the bed. Later the outdoor servants came to see their master for the last time and they kissed the chilly, inert hand, some gathering in the corner of the room to wait and watch. There was silence in the house, where for a week there had been activity, day and night, from the departure of grooms and the arrival of doctors and orderlies keeping the lamps alight.

On the road to Longwood at eight a.m., Sir Hudson Lowe received a communication from Dr Arnott, intercepting an orderly galloping on his way to Plantation House. "He is dying. Montholon prays I will not leave his bedside. He wishes I should see him breathe his last." Lowe rode on past the guard-house to the new Longwood house and walked about the empty rooms. A flatness of spirit kept him pacing uneasily past the still uncurtained windows. The iron railings so detested by Napoleon caught his eye. Now he saw them anew, symbols of detention, the serried rows of iron stretching almost around the whole building. As a concession, he remembered, the back quarter had not been enclosed, but in front he saw them as he went by every window, row after row stretching on either side. He began, now that it was too late, to consider if after all he had not made conditions too harsh for the prisoner. He had carried out Bathurst's and Castlereagh's wishes to the letter. The thought sustained him, but the spirit of the regulations bothered his conscience. He knew his actions had been neither better nor worse than their demands warranted and, now it was almost over, somehow he felt his prisoner was gaining a release at the hands of a greater Court of Justice.

He saw his orderly outside, with the tethered horses, testing one of the iron railings with his hand. No more meetings with Gorrequer taking notes, and Janesch later transcribing them in his beautiful script. No more requisitions for trees and bookshelves, for nankeen and horse-feed. A chapter was closing even as he paced up and down, and his thoughts centred with some relief on a triumphal homecoming to rewards, to laudatory remarks. He had done his duty to the letter. His nails, habitually bitten, were now down to the quick, and he chewed the side of his forefinger, the dark blemish on his cheek flushing. World interest would always focus upon this enigma, this strange vital character. No distance of sea made any difference; time playing on his side had brought victory to him — victory by death. France had begun to bask in the memory that once she had ruled the world, governed Europe, her greatness accepted unchallenged, under the hand of this failing prisoner. As the years passed, so he would gain in the estimation of posterity, and Lowe knew nothing could be done to prevent it.[21]

The house echoed to his footsteps and finally he rode away, glancing at Bertrand's cottage, where nobody was to be seen, and the Longwood garden, equally empty, and finally to the doors of Longwood — closed, as always, to him.

At three p.m. another note in pencil came from Arnott: "The pulse cannot be felt at the wrist now and the heat is departing from the surface, but he may last out some hours yet." More waiting; more thoughts. Re-planning and a certain growing excitement. Lowe and Reade conferred in the pleasant library at Plantation House, while Gorrequer once more took notes and issued orders.

At five-thirty p.m. Arnott again writes, "He is worse; and respiration has become more hurried and difficult."

A few minutes before six o'clock, just as the sun was setting, the following line was received: "He has this moment expired." He died at ten minutes to six, about the time of the evening gun.

From the standpoint of modern nursing, Napoleon received little skilled attention, his sheets remained unchanged, mattresses soaked, and windows tightly shut, any light there was coming from the storm lantern shrouded by paper. In that atmosphere he passed his last days. From the observance of his wishes, ordinary nursing care compatible with the times was not followed. He lay inert, or struggled from bed to bed: little camp-beds whose frames stood a few inches from the ground, his body raised perhaps eighteen inches by four mattresses; the green silk curtains draped so that any whisper of air was kept from him.

The Lowe-Bathurst Papers made particular note that Montholon, being close to him, heard his final words but that they were unintelligible. Evidently the legendary "*Tête d'armée*" came from some imaginary source — not from Napoleon's lips.

The watchers awaited the climax and when it ended, as the sun was setting, the Grand Marshal bent his knee beside the still figure and kissed his hand. Afterwards came all the members of his suite, in seniority, the servants, the women, the Bertrand children, who had been fetched from the cottage by their mother. Even the daughter of St Denis, a year old, was carried to give her baby salute to the cold flesh.

At midnight, in a stillness now made more noticeable by the absence of the usual household activity, Marchand, St Denis, Pierron and Navarrez attended to the body of their master and carried it from the death-bed to the second camp-bed, which was put in place of the one taken away. Vignali laid a crucifix on the Emperor's breast. Montholon observed that the Emperor presented an appearance of youth. His mouth was faintly contracted on one side and gave his face an expression of resignation, and he did not look more than thirty.

Two days after, when two death-masks were taken, the retraction of the flesh made him look older and, Marchand said, "spoiled his beautiful expression." Vignali states he did not leave the body until it was buried. He remained in the *chapelle ardente* praying until the coffin was finally carried out.

Most of the suite, exhausted, went to their rooms after the Emperor had drawn his last breath, but were awakened by a messenger who announced that Sir Hudson Lowe would visit Longwood at six o'clock. He arrived at seven with his entire staff, on horseback: the Admiral, the General commanding the forces on the island, the Commissioner of the King of France, Montchenu, several naval officers, doctors and surgeons resident on the island, an impressive cavalcade clattering past the guard-house, receiving and acknowledging salutes, brave in full regimentals, yet a dejected group. Lowe was conducted in to what was termed 'the room of death'. Bertrand and Montholon, already there, bowed to him and, with a gesture, motioned him to approach the Emperor. Montchenu was close behind and Lowe asked, "Do you recognise him?" The French commissioner turned his head to look and said, "Yes, I recognise him." Lowe's comment was, "He was the greatest enemy of England and of myself also, but I forgive him." The remark, its significance and delivery of tone, marked the man for what he was. He omitted, from some feeling that superimposed itself on his usual rudeness, to mention Bathurst, nor did he call the dead man 'General' any longer. History had taken over, bringing a new evaluation. A human being four times unanimously acclaimed by his people as a sovereign, anointed and blessed, now in death, no living power prevailed against his rightful place in history — the Lowes, Montchenus, Bathursts, Castlereaghs, took their proper positions in the picture, small voices blending into a background of sound that made the chief actor's exit a triumph.

Lowe watched Montchenu's expression and sensed the attitudes of all the men around him. They were paying homage to someone timelessly great. He roused himself almost in self-defence and turned to the group of silent officers to issue orders about procedure, the funeral, the sentinels around the Longwood house, the regiments lining the route to Geranium Vale, where he would be buried. There would be a post-mortem in the billiard room on a dining-table. At two o'clock Antommarchi began the autopsy, in the presence of Bertrand, Montholon, three British officers and seven doctors, Vignali and some of the Emperor's valets. The first report on the dissection of the body ran as follows:

"On opening the body, it was found to be very fat with extensive disease of the stomach. The ulcer, which had penetrated the coats of the stomach from the peloris, was sufficiently large to allow the passage of the little finger. The stomach was a mass of cancerous disease with a fluid resembling coffee grounds.

"The convex surface of the left lobe of the liver adhered to the diaphragm and the liver was, perhaps, a little larger than natural. With the exception of the adhesion, occasioned by the disease of the stomach, no unhealthy appearance presented itself."

Dr Shortt in his notes to Lowe (with Lowe's comments written in the margin) says, "The liver acted as a kind of cork to the perforation. The stomach was perforated through and through. In the centre of the small perforation the aperture was closed by the adhesion of the left lobe of the liver."

Sir Hudson Lowe did not feel authorised to give the heart to Count Montholon, but he directed that it should be placed in the coffin separate from the body. He ordered Dr Rutledge to remain on watch all night. Dr Rutledge left a memorandum of what occurred during his melancholy watch and said, "The heart and stomach, which had been taken out of the body, was put in a silver vase by me and I was directed by Sir Thomas Reade, according to the order of the Governor, not to lose sight of the body or the vase. To take care and not to admit of the cavities being opened for the second time for the purposes of the removal of any part of the body and not to allow the contents of the vase to be disturbed without an order from him to that effect." It was in consequence of the pressing solicitations from Madame Bertrand to be allowed to keep the heart and to take it away with her when leaving the island.

The autopsy over, Antommarchi desired to examine the brain, remarking that the sight of that organ should be of the highest interest. To this proposal Bertrand and Montholon objected strongly. The professor sprayed the opening of the abdomen with eau-de-Cologne and sewed the incision. However, somehow eluding the watching eyes of the English, Antommarchi extracted two fragments of bone from a rib and the 'principal tendon', which he gave to Vignali.

In later times, certain schools of thought maintain that the cause of death was not cancer, the evidence coming from the fragments of pitted intestine smuggled in to London to O'Meara. Those were given to the Royal College of Surgeons and became lost, it is understood, during the bombings in the Second World War.

Professor Sir Astley Cooper and Sir James Paget thought they detected cancerous nodules in them, but histological examination by Sir Frederick Evans, and later Dr Shattock, did not reveal any neoplasm. Professor Keith concluded that the "fragments present a lymphoid hyperplasia due to malaria". Another doctor concluded that Napoleon died of a gastric ulcer and in this a Helsingfors doctor concurred.

Yet another doctor considered it was an acute and chronic gastritis made fatal by corrosive 'incendiary' medicines, and one surgeon positively eliminated cancer and diagnosed suppurative hepatitis. The evidence remains conclusive that an ulcer was the actual cause of death; possibly two diseases — one superimposed upon the other — made an actual diagnosis difficult.

During the autopsy Antommarchi removed the liver and demonstrated as if to a class of students, You see, gentlemen, how this ulcerated part of the stomach has become adherent to the liver — what are we to infer? That the climate of St Helena has intensified the gastric disorder and has thus brought about premature death?"

The vote was taken, English against French opinion. At no cost must it be thought that the climate had been a factor in the Emperor's demise. Dr Shortt, Naval Chief Surgeon, was asked to draw up the report of Napoleon's death for despatch to Lord Bathurst. It was signed by Shortt, Burton, Mitchell and Arnott. On receiving it, Lowe became incensed and there was feverish agitation at Plantation House.

Dr Shortt in the report noted that "the liver was perhaps a little larger than usual". Lowe asserted that this would support the argument that Napoleon died of an affection of the liver due to the St Helena climate. He brought every pressure to bear upon the doctor to induce him to delete the offending words. Shortt objected vehemently, but afterwards succumbed, his patience giving out, and his apprehension of Lowe's influence growing, on the recollections of the treatment of others who had stood out against the Governor's orders. Under instructions he therefore made the correction and the second report went to Bathurst. The original draft is extant, showing the phrase relating to the liver scratched out and a note appended, "The words obliterated were suppressed by the order of Sir Hudson Lowe ... Thomas Shortt."

Longwood became a scene of pilgrimage. Soldiers, sailors, the townsfolk, farmers from the outlying valleys, "an immense crowd of people", came to file past the bed. An English officer wrote, "An enormous crowd came to see him yesterday — one of the most extraordinary sights I have ever witnessed — it was one long file on the Longwood road and included women and children, slaves, shocked, deeply moved and sharply aware that the great captive had at last escaped his jailers. They came in working clothes, in uniforms, in flimsy summer garments — for the weather was hot — and the procession did not cease to pass the peaceful figure until nightfall."

Captain Crokat put himself in charge of the proceedings — marshalling the crowd through the valets' hallway to the dressing-room and finally the room now hung with drapings as a mortuary chapel, then out into the dining-room, drawing-room and the billiard room. Most of them, aware of the part the latter room had played in the Emperor's life in his last days, and that yesterday it had been the scene of the autopsy, observed its details and the maps on the wall, the big globes, the pile of books and the cue in the corner — his walking-stick, the little peep-holes in the shutters; and many wrote of the scene.

The officers of the 20th and 60th came first to pay their respects and then followed the soldiers, the crews from the naval ships, afterwards the whole population. Piles of arum, the lily of the island, moonflowers and hibiscus were laid in front of the bed. A soldier said to his little boy, "Take a good look at Napoleon — he is the greatest man in the world." Those who were Catholic made the sign of the cross on the calm forehead. His hands appeared alive, small and white, lying on the blue cloak of Marengo, and his face retained a half-smile. Bertrand stood watch at the head of the bed — at the foot, Montholon and Marchand, Antommarchi, Arnott, Rutledge and the domestics, dressed in black, stood in line along the windows, leaving a small passage free to allow the throng to pass to pay their last tribute and lay their flowers, to pause, say a brief prayer and pass on.

The body was dressed in the uniform of Colonel of the Chasseurs of the Imperial Guard with gold epaulets, spurs, a sword, a tricorn hat, Star and ribbon of the Legion of Honour and two crosses.

They feared that Lowe might purloin the sword, so, for the time being, substituted Bertrand's.

CHAPTER 27

Obsequies — 1821 and 1840

There had been conjecture about the two death-masks of Napoleon. Antommarchi failed in the first attempt, but the second mask, attributed to him, but in reality largely made by Dr Burton, is still called the Antommarchi Death Mask, and as such is recognised. On the first occasion, Doctor Burton was not able to procure sufficient plaster of Paris; what he had was from pulverised church statues and Antommarchi could do little with it. For the second attempt Doctor Burton obtained gypsum crystals from George Island, a rock adjacent to St Helena, which he reached in a long-boat, at the risk of his life, with some sailors. That probably was the sole substance employed in the second attempt and it was Doctor Burton who made the successful impression. Both are to be seen at Longwood. The second is incomparably better than the first, which somehow resembles a carnival mask and is devoid of dignity — Napoleon's features appear blunted, and the moulding on the sides of the brow is incomplete. It was an unsatisfactory reproduction of a head and countenance that in death were majestic. Forty hours elapsed before the second impression was taken, and decomposition had then set in, facial muscles had sagged, bringing the cheek-bones into prominence, which gave him a tragic aspect; slightly opened lips showed teeth, which narrators called white, but which the factual Betsy said were habitually coloured by liquorice. Once more Novarrez shaved him, for the beard had grown, and opened the collar at his throat, and Burton covered the face with the pulverised gypsum he had personally prepared overnight. The attempt was successful. Archambault held the head while Burton took an impression of the back and neck, while Antommarchi assisted. A young Lieutenant passing through wrote a letter to his mother in England, "I went once again when they were taking the casts of the head but the stench was so horrible that I could not remain. Doctor Burton was taking it with the French doctors." By now the skin commenced to peel, so nothing further could be done, and in order to protect the body

231

from flies, that had gathered in swarms, it was covered by mosquito net. Novarrez writes that the body had now to be placed in its coffin without further delay, that it was so far gone that in the afternoon it was in a state of complete putrefaction. Under the supervision of Rutledge, it was lowered into the first shell. Indeed, Rutledge and Arnott, working in relays, had not left the body at any time, Rutledge especially guarding the heart and stomach, which Lowe was afraid might be carried off.

There is a family legend to add here. My grandmother told me that, during the watches of the night after the autopsy, a rat, attracted by death, crept into the room where the body lay and nibbled a portion of one ear, and that the heart was dragged half out of the silver dish on which it lay.

Lowe wrote to Bathurst during the days following Napoleon's death: "It was established a fact that climate and captivity had no share in contributing to his end. Bertrand and Montholon show no great distress; possibly the thought of the large fortune is a consideration. Napoleon expressed a wish that his heart might go to his wife and his stomach to be examined so that the doctors might learn and profit from the experience for future generations and his own son particularly." Montholon, Lowe commented, desired earnestly to take the heart to Marie-Louise. "Uninformed as I naturally must be in what light, after so long a cessation of any relations together, whether of a public or domestic nature, such request might be viewed, I, however, refused it."

The suite wished the inscription on the headstone to be, "*Napoléon, ne à Ajaccio 15 Août 1769 et mort à St Helena 5 Mai 1821.*" Lowe refused, unless the name Bonaparte be in the inscription, and so the grave bore no name.

Forsyth, Lowe's Boswell, covers up the more poignant portions of the final battle by saying, "While anxious to give all the details respecting the last moments of this extraordinary man, I feel that there are some of a medical nature which ought not be made public. A knowledge of the minutiæ of illness is best confined to the nurse and the physician." Why this delicacy? Hitherto no special care had been taken not to offend. Perhaps the closing scenes in their realism might stir up too much sympathy abroad and turn public feeling against the jailer who even now was beginning to suffer from the results of O'Meara's outspoken disclosures and comments.

To the end Lowe organised the pageantry of death — the guard escort of soldiers, salutes of guns, the coffins (there were four — one made from the mahogany dining-table of a St Helena resident), the bands and pall-bearers. It was impressive enough; even more so were the lines of island people watching their legend — no longer a prisoner — depart down the winding road to Geranium Valley for the last time, to lie by the little spring from which for years his servants had drawn water in silver bottles for his use. Twelve

British Grenadiers took the coffin on their shoulders and bore it over the long garden path to where the hearse awaited. The coffin was covered by the Marengo cloak, with Bertrand's sword on top. The corners of the pall were held by Bertrand and his son, Montholon and Marchand. Ali, Napoleon's horse, came behind, led by Archambault, followed by the servants, and last of all a carriage with Madame Bertrand and the two children. Vignali, in his vestments, walked at the head of the procession. Henri Bertrand carried the holy water. After Madame Bertrand's carriage rode the Governor, the Rear-Admiral, the French commissioner and numerous staff. Two thousand garrison troops lined the route. Minute-guns fired a salute. At Hutt's Gate were the Artillery; at the bend of the road the Grenadiers took the coffin. After the religious service Lowe asked Bertrand if he wished to speak but he shook his head; it was all over as far as he was concerned, a page turned and an episode ended. Spectators broke twigs of the willow tree for remembrance. Noticing it, Lowe immediately had a temporary barricade erected around the area of the grave; he wished to prevent any gestures that might give rise to superstition, or undue sentiment.

Of all the women connected with Napoleon, Madame Bertrand, tall, remote, and dignified, was alone to stand behind his coffin. To her it remained to fulfil the obligations of the past with fitting tribute. She represented the elegance, dignity and appearance of the world that had once acclaimed him.

Longwood was in disorder. The two beds used by the Emperor in his last hours were left in their places, but Vignali stripped the altar and took the vestments, drapings and curtains away from the room, also the vessels and relics of the Emperor: his hair, the principal sinew, same of his clothing, the silver cup his dying lips had touched, his handkerchief — all these to be given to his son when he attained the age of sixteen. Certain documents Vignali likewise gathered up, including a copy of the codicil signed by Bertrand, Montholon and Marchand, by which the Emperor bequeathed him 75,000 francs and with it left instructions about the articles he would take away. Vignali wasted no time and removed his belongings before the Governor arrived. Lady Lowe had expressed a wish to see Longwood as it was when Napoleon lived there and the Governor, surveying the disorder, the hurrying servants and the preparation for immediate departure, ordered the house to be restored to its usual form. He went through the Emperor's possessions, his clothing, his personal effects. He found three small boxes heavily sealed, also to be given to his son on attaining his sixteenth year and not to be opened. These Lowe forced, to find they contained small personal gifts and jewellery that the Emperor had worn during his lifetime, with some miniatures and medals added.

On the table lay a snuff-box of gold which he had presented to Doctor Arnott and another of embossed gold, given to him by Pope Pius VII. Lowe opened this, to find a card neatly fitted within and, in Napoleon's writing, "*L'Empéreur Napoléon à 'Lady Holland témoignage de satisfaction et d'estime*" (From the Emperor Napoleon to Lady Holland as a token of appreciation and esteem). Lowe forced the card up with his finger nail and on the back was written, "*Donné par Le Pape Pie, Tolentino, 1797.*"

Bertrand remarked that he had lost a note of Napoleon's that the Emperor wished Wellington to have. It was about Wellington, surprisingly generous and laudatory, but he must have inadvertently destroyed it while disposing of so many rough drafts. He searched widely for it, "*Car c'etait l'éloge du duc*", written in the highest terms of praise of the Duke's military conduct, while Lowe thumbed through the packages of manuscript. Lowe found many works commenced but not completed.

Before the suite vacated Longwood all correspondence and documents were examined by Lowe. He leafed through the bundles of notes on Bertrand's table. There were no incriminating papers — no words that might lead to suspicion of any island people. Bertrand and Montholon, with Marchand, had anticipated this action, and buried, with the personal documents, any they considered would be valuable to posterity. These, somewhere in the Longwood garden, lie undiscovered to this day.

Lady Lowe inspected the house, examined Napoleon's beds and uniforms, appraised the furniture and decided which of the pieces she would take when the place was finally vacated. The clothing she found of small value, being threadbare and much worn.

The *Camel* store-ship in James Roads was made ready to receive the exiles and twelve days after the Emperor's death they embarked, having tidied up most of the loose ends, though for some reason or other — owing to the vigilance of the guards, or fear of servants' disloyalty, or from lack of opportunity — the buried papers were not retrieved. Marchand left a sum of money for a natural son on the island. The other commitments were taken care of.

On 26th May, "A little black group left Longwood, with the children and servants and Sambo, Napoleon's dog." They passed an empty guard-house and at the turn of the road they looked back at the unpretentious home in which they had dwelt with history. Hutt's Gate was also empty; they went by it and down to the tomb in Geranium Valley. Some of the grilles left over from the new Longwood fence now surrounded the grave; "Even in death the hated bars were to be imposed on the captive." They arranged the posies of flowers he had liked the best; yellow immortelles from Marchand's garden, pansies and violets, passion flowers from the arbour that had been made to his direction and copied from the Briars. Vignali again blessed the slabs. The Bertrands knelt, then the Grand Marshal rose, put on his hat, and walked up the path, followed by the others. They turned again for one more glimpse of Longwood, its windows reflecting the sun and its slate roof showing the mottling effect of the weather, looking back across the chasm that lay between. Following the steep little road they saw the "happy terraces of the Briars"; the Pavilion door was open; they noticed the waterfall was swollen by recent rains. Marchand and Ali sighed at the memories that they shared. They had been close to the Emperor in those first months at the Briars, when the valley and the people tempered the bleakness of captivity. Sometimes there had been careless laughter and the sound of singing. Marchand reminded Ali of the wood they gathered for Napoleon's fires during those first weeks, recalled his aversion to coal. The *Camel* took the Longwood household. Montchenu and Gors, for political reasons, preferred to travel on a later vessel. The *Camel* had been used to transport cattle and was dirty beyond words, unsteady and too narrow of beam, but to the exiles it only spelt escape.

A group of people saw them off at the dockside, including Sir Hudson Lowe, his wife and his staff. Montchenu had asked permission to kiss Madame Bertrand. The Reverend Richard Boys was there, pugnacious and kindly, his handclasp Madame Bertrand clung to; Major Hodson ('Hercules') and the elderly Miss Mason had ridden down to see them go.

Others came from the town: Mr Solomon, the diffident Mr Weston, the Commissary-General, Mr Ibbetson and his wife from across the island; the former knew that their departure closed the chapter on the prosperity of St Helena, for now the regiments would leave, and the patrolling fleet sail to further duties; it was a parochial catastrophe.

One journal notes, "The exiles never won any love, but they were carrying away many regrets."

Until darkness interfered, they clung to the rail, watching the cliffs recede, more than cliffs to them — a tomb, of which one of them remarked, "Large enough to be fitting." The black rocks had taken six years out of their lives, yet they felt emotion as Jamestown, the castle and the church were lost to view and only the ramparts remained to guard the Emperor from the ocean, the wheeling gulls and the ever unquiet trade winds.

Madame Bertrand retired to her cabin and remained there during almost all the journey, suffering from seasickness and dysentery.

Nineteen years later the French frigate *Bellepoule*, commanded by a captain-Prince, dropped anchor in James Roads. A quarter of a century had cut a swathe in the continuity of human life, and the description written for the Jamestown paper by an island-born reporter mentions comparatively few of the names that had cropped up with great frequency in past contemporary records. Mr Solomon, now French Consular Agent, was still there. It was from his shop Napoleon once promised a fan for Betsy Balcombe if she burnt off the French commissioner's *queue*. Mr Cole remained postmaster. There was Mr F. Fowler of the Lowe correspondence, a member of the now disbanded firm of Balcombe, Fowler and Cole. Amongst others, Captain Doveton of Sir William's family at Sandy Bay; James Scott, Las Cases's servant, whose coat had once been lined with messages; Mr Janesch, who had elected to stay behind when Sir Hudson Lowe departed; Mr Darling, the carpenter-undertaker who had made for Madame Bertrand the easy-chair coveted by the Emperor; Mr Hodson, the judge advocate, whom Napoleon visited One night when the Balcombe cavalcade rode down to the Admiral's ball at the Castle; Captain Harrison of the 53rd, a brigade-major now, who had been one of the officers present at the autopsy. In them the returning French stirred mixed emotions. In retrospect, the memory of the exile held nothing they could examine with complacency. A small band of English had actively worked for his comfort. O'Meara, Lady Holland, William Balcombe, the Pulteney Malcolms, while Lord Holland, a lone voice in the House of Lords, had upheld his common rights as a prisoner, but the memory had become Unimportant and dim, until the return of the suite.

Now that the frigate awaited his body, to carry it with full honours to France, to lie by the Seine among the people of the nation he loved, Geranium Valley would hold him captive no longer; the island people contemplated his departure with unmixed regret. Apart from pecuniary advantages — for St Helena had become something like the end of a pilgrimage for travellers — he was part of their history and they felt when he departed something of themselves was going also.

The Jamestown reporter gave a meticulous description of the *Bellepoule*'s arrival, which finally occurred after many false alarms. He noted that the subsequent procedure was formal in the extreme. British and French ships lay at anchor, turning to the tide's demands. The frigate *Dolphin*, the East India Company's *Buckinghamshire* and *Repulse* — 1,400 tons; *Cornaline*, *Astrolabe*, *Zelée*, *Junor* — French frigates; *Oreste*, French brig-of-war; *Gloire*, *Bousson*, the *Bellepoule* and *Favourite* — corvettes. He dwelt on "the magnificent French Naval Band" that played during the banquet held at the Castle, and the arrival on shore of the ship's captain, Prince Joinville, son of the reigning Bourbon, who had been commissioned to convey the body home. He went with the visitors to Longwood; to the Briars; to the tomb. He described the men of the suite, nineteen years older, graver, less ebullient, their minds painfully preoccupied by recurrent memories. They visited the well-remembered places and sought out friends, renewed old contacts, felt again the lethargy of an island in the sun and stepped once more into its waking dream. They learned there had been a general exodus after the Emperor's death. The garrison, Plantation House officials, patrolling frigates, had all departed and, after them, the traders and their little ships from Cape Town, no reason for their presence remaining. Emotion coloured the correspondent's description when he saw the visitors' devotion to what he called "a memory", and that France should send a Prince of the reigning house moved him to comment upon it in italics. He also recorded that the people of the island had generally hoped Napoleon's body would repose at St Helena until "the last trump".

He wrote of the young Las Cases, Gourgaud and Bertrand, Marchand and Novarrez, Pierron, Archambault, St Denis, Le Page, young Bertrand, now a man. One wonders why Gourgaud returned, for his sabotage probably did more to hasten Napoleon's end than the ten months' lack of medical attention, yet there he was, among the faithful, walking about the main street, seeing the Castle anew, Mr Solomon's shop, the homes where the commissioners once lived; there with them he had so constantly bewailed ennui and the lack of women. He went into the East India Company's store, formerly crammed with provisions, and to the purveyor William Balcombe's office above; to the post office and to the dives further along the street where the "inferior people subsisted principally by the fleets and mostly kept wine shops for the accommodation of soldiers and sailors." Old wording, a century back, but amply demonstrated today. Young Las Cases likewise remembered the period of detention in the Castle; the town jailer, Mr Weston; the diamond necklace of Queen Hortense around his father's middle and an Englishman saying in a low tone, "I shall walk by you very slowly when I am going out." Bertrand thought of Admiral Cockburn, now dead, of his naval code and bluff demeanour; of Madame Bertrand in her Paris gown at the Admiral's ball; of the lights strung around the courtyard and Ensign Carstairs with his Ensign friends in the archway entrance calling, "Lord W's carriage blocks the way." Those cheerful naval boys were captains today grown like his own sons and bearing the weight of command. He remembered the British Navy's respect for the Emperor; as fighting men and superb seamen they saluted that genius which had brought him to the peak of military greatness. Their recognition stayed in Bertrand's mind as one of the bulwarks of his master's reputation. He remembered that on the *Northumberland* the 'Emperor's gun' had become a legend that still lived, although the ship rotted in a creek. He thought of the two thousand soldiers lining the route from Longwood to Geranium Valley. As he looked at it now, nothing in the Valley had much altered except themselves — grey, elderly men returning to keep faith with a memory. Onlookers, yet participants in the final act of an epoch.

The correspondent marked their interest in the growth of the willow by Napoleon's tomb. They treated their visit to the grave as to a shrine, perhaps doing homage to their own lost youth as well as to the man lying underneath the slab.

They drove to Hutt's Gate above the valley, exclaimed at the size of the trees in Madame Bertrand's garden. They went on foot down to the Briars, where on that first day after arrival Napoleon had ridden, accompanied by Cockburn, and Bertrand, to meet the Balcombe family at the entrance. Las Cases stood once more at the Pavilion door and remembered his inadequate attic above and looked towards Jamestown and the wedge of sea beyond, where the frigates and men-of-war lay at anchor. They had not all been unhappy days. He recalled the Emperor's voice rendering 'Vive Henri Quatre'; the children skylarking in the garden; Betsy and her pranks; coffee after dinner on the lawn, now grown rough with neglect. Plantation House held less happy memories for all of them. With mixed feelings they recognised pieces of Longwood furniture, a sideboard, some china, a few chairs — one that Bertrand was accustomed to draw up to the Emperor's bedside, the green-striped Regency silk still covering the seat — two bookcases, even Napoleon's Empire-style commode.

The Governor was ill and received them informally. A pleasant man, he changed the atmosphere in the house from the chill formality they had once known there. They travelled the steep road to Longwood past the guard-house and saw desolation. The correspondent wrote, "It was difficult to portray their emotion." They saw the little garden, a trodden waste, the building turned into cattle sheds, stables and a granary. The place where they had knelt in homage and watched the Emperor die was a scene of confusion. The gold-starred wallpaper in the drawing-room had been torn from the walls by souvenir-hunters. The green window-shutters hung derelict. Outside, only the trees remained and a vestige of the sunken paths around the fish pond. Greatly distressed they wandered from room to room, recreating fragments of their lives among the litter of farm machinery. Here the Emperor used to sit; here was his bed; the hole in the shutters reminded them of his spyglass and the prowling Nicholls; the black and white tiles were reminiscent of the Montholons' quarters. The Englishmen were embarrassed at the general disrepair of the house; the lack of respect it implied and the obviously disturbed feelings of the visitors made them apologetic and ashamed. They blamed the proprietors of the island, the East India Company. Marchand pointed out to those who had never seen Longwood in the days of the Emperor's residence that, "However dilapidated the house now appeared, yet formerly it had been, though small, a nicely fitted-up residence surrounded by pleasant shrubberies, and handsome gardens once gave it a most picturesque appearance." It eased a moment of awkwardness.

A day later the imperial sarcophagus was landed from the *Bellepoule*. It weighed over one ton, was black, with gold claw feet and bronze laurel wreaths for handles. Napoleon's body rested in a mahogany case, but it was proposed to transfer it in the leaden inner casket to the French catafalque. The single word 'Napoleon' had been inscribed on the lid in "massy gold letters", the reporter's words.

On the twenty-fifth anniversary of the Emperor's arrival on the island, with spades and pickaxes the soldiers commenced to remove the earth from the headstone. Members of the suite stood by the slab that enclosed the grave. The two groups watched in silence as the railings were put aside and the digging was begun. It was found almost impossible to break the cement of the chamber, but by eight o'clock the old sarcophagus was exposed. By nine o'clock the hoist (shears) raised it to the surface and Dr Guillard caused two augur holes to be bored in the top and bottom. Men of the Royal Artillery carried it to a tent nearby. The lids of the old leaden and secondary mahogany coffins were cut through, and the tin coffin, the last covering, was removed at one o'clock. A satin sheet shrouded Napoleon and the doctor raised it gently. The correspondent tells of the suite bending over the body of their master, recognising him, gazing at the familiar features once again, tears on their cheeks, seeing a face miraculously preserved, a young face. Marchand cried out that he had grown more like what he had been as Consul. The satin cover had adhered a little to the side of his cheek. The body was in excellent condition. There was an appearance of mould, but the hands which the doctor touched were perfect and firm, as if he had been mummified, or, at best, recently interred. His eyes were fallen and the bridge of his nose a little sunk, but the lower portion of his face remarkable for its great breadth and fullness. His epaulets and the stars and orders had become tarnished, his black boots mildewed. His cocked hat lay across him and the two silver urns between his calves had become bronze in colour. The body remained exposed for two or three minutes and then the doctor sprinkled some chemical composition over it and the coffin was soldered up.

(The Balcombe family's recollections tell that an eyewitness described the remarkable youthfulness of Napoleon's face; his nails and beard had grown, but after a minute or two, from the action of the air, his face commenced, as they told it, to 'crumple' even as they watched.)

The final scene in the ceremony was the slow departure of the catafalque between lines of soldiers and island folk, minute-guns echoing among the hills, bands playing; the pall held by Marchand, Gourgaud, Las Cases and Bertrand. Nineteen years before, the first pall had been fashioned by two Englishwomen and fulfilled the same purpose in the local church until it finally wore out. France sent a magnificent pall of purple velvet with a wide cross of silver tissue. A deep band of ermine surrounded the velvet and at each corner of it an eagle and the Imperial crown with the letter 'N' were worked in gold. 'Massy bullion tassels' were at each corner for the purpose of being held by the pall-bearers. The remainder of the velvet was studded with golden bees.

CHAPTER 28

Present-day St Helena

After one hundred and forty years of tides and seasons and of changing conditions, Jamestown remains unaltered and the Chinese picture of the eighteenth century still faithfully reproduces its lines.[22]

Monsieur Gilbert Martineau, the French Consul, came along the passageway to our cabin in the *Durban Castle* holding a white camellia. "This," he announced with a bow, "I have picked for you from Napoleon's tree." We were transported into a dimension that took no particular account of time. The living flower linked period with period in ageless sequence, while, across the water, Jamestown showed, in faithful reality to the mezzotints and prints of 1815, its silhouetted Georgian roofs unchanged since Betsy and Jane had seen them from a windjammer and Napoleon and his suite from the deck of the *Northumberland*.

The *Durban Castle* lay where the *Northumberland* had once dropped anchor, a solitary visitant in a morning that held the thin quality of spring — the only movement the slow rollers edging the shore with a white line of broken water. For a century James Roads had been empty of barquentines, frigates, seventy-fours and East Indiamen's store-ships, of white sails blooming on mast and spar, of straw-hatted seamen, of calls and ships' bells sounding across the water to the little town. Our vessel, with her lavender hull and almost insolent impression of power, dominated the picture. Rowing-boats and one official launch attended her and the latter had ferried out the Governor's A.D.C. and the French Consul to us. "Does any of this seem familiar?" asked someone as we sidled along the wall of the landing-stage built by the East India Company for eighteenth-century passengers. A voice called from the steps, "Wait for the wave and jump when you are told." There was nothing familiar; in effect, it was a most unusual landing, fraught with the possibility of a wetting.

The flat area of the dock narrowed into the valley of Jamestown, itself a reproduction of a little Georgian English town with whitewashed houses:

241

square-paned windows; steep narrow steps; and the Castle, the Governor's house, behind a wall on the left of the entrance. In that archway young Carstairs and the middies had wedged the farm cart.

A clean street, stretching up between clean houses, became a scene in an island of yesterday; a play set at a slow tempo, the players polite of gesture, talking a curiously pure English. The road presently divided on either side of what had once been the dives and brothels "patronised by the inferior persons of the Fleet", one side becoming Napoleon Street, where the Emperor had first ridden to visit Longwood, later to descend to the Briars in the valley. We, in our turn, went up Napoleon Street in a diminutive car (only the smaller makes can negotiate the hairpin bends), travelling a step behind history.

Mr Martineau, who was in appearance young, dark, with hair *en brosse*, informed us we were seeing what had met the Emperor's eyes on his first ride to Longwood. I stopped by the crossroads that led to the Briars valley, at the three-way junction, where the tutor Huff's body had been buried — to be passed over, trodden on, the grave forgotten, but for a sentence in Betsy's memoirs.

Further up, Mr Martineau pulled the car to the roadside and pointed down to the Briars estate, dwarfed by the elevation, to the thread of waterfall on the cliff face and the tangled growth of the once-luxuriant garden, its shape, however, recognisable. The drive, a straight avenue of trees with an all-over greenness, was sharp in contrast with the blackness of the mountains rising on three sides. Later on, we were due to go to the Briars, but now Hutt's Gate was the destination. Up still higher, around hairpin bends, more stone walls and by patches of white dwarf arums growing on the hills, Hutt's Gate cottage had become a heap of stones, half covered by creeping nasturtium and periwinkle; the garden and a close ring of trees mark the place where the hospitable Madame Bertrand had made her first home.

It was she who planted the trees against the wind's violence and the camellias at the front door to mark the sharp edge of the bank that descended to the spring in Geranium Valley below, also the now wandering border flowers, sweet alice, ageratum and daisy. A wilderness it seemed, and indeed was, yet blooming in great vigour and a yearly tribute to the lady's courage and resource. Plumbago, briars and lantana tangled under sub-tropical trees that grew beside pines and oaks. Between two camellias, with girths of young pines, could be seen the steep descent where Napoleon clambered down to find the spring and later to choose his burial place. They were blooming, and bore the prim pink flowers of the early species. The pigsty had vanished; only a pile of stones and a step or so lay in the centre of the garden to mark the dwelling. The garden was windless in the early morning, filled with sunlight and the sound of birds, the grass rising from its burden of dew, all a demonstration of the timeless arrogance of nature over human affairs. We followed a road past a new prefabricated cottage and an old church, and presently by aloes in sudden patches, flax and portions of English hedgerows. We came to the guard-house which marked the boundary of Napoleon's domain, nowadays a portion of France, the smallest portion in the world; its transference to the French nation was made possible by Queen Victoria, as was also the valley of the Emperor's grave.

Mr Martineau reminded us of the occasion the Balcombe family and others had spent the night at the guard-house after the Ibbetsons' party, flea-bitten and indignant, having omitted to learn the counter-sign. He drew my attention to the outline of the Barn, the bulk of mountain that Napoleon so disliked, bronze against a blue spring day. What did I see? The Emperor's profile? The massive stone outline resembled a mask in gigantic proportion. Nature has graven him into its very self. But none of the exiles appear to have noticed this phenomenon, which is understandable — to them, as yet, there had been no set profile of death by which to match it.

A responsive French Government recently expended £40,000 on the rehabilitation of Longwood House and grounds. Mr Martineau led us to his quarters (once the Montholons'), where the black and white tiles served as a reminder that this had been the part of the house least infested by rats. The front door and the Emperor's portion of Longwood were familiar enough from contemporary prints. The clean paint created a kind of modern addition. Inside, as much as possible of the furnishings was reassembled. In the two bedrooms the beds were set in the identical position of the original beds — green-and-white curtained, correct in detail, the thin mattress showing how four together were needed to extract any comfort from the iron frames. Mr Martineau had found the actual chair depicted in a picture of the death-bed scene. The mirror over the wooden mantelshelf was back in place, the gilt frame renewed, the original, like most of the wood on the island, having succumbed to white ant. He presented me with a piece from which had hung the miniature of the King of Rome, remarking that Betsy had probably looked in the glass quite often. The bookshelves were being returned, he said. Other finds were on the way back. Mr Martineau's persuasive and sympathetic manner had commenced to reap harvests.

From room to room we went. The nankeen folds on the walls had been renewed, as had the wallpapers — faithful reproductions of the Empire stars and patterns and oddly modern. A little ante-room and its copper built-in bath might have been an adjunct to any early Victorian home, with a hole for soap placed in the woodwork; in all a dingy little bathroom, lit by a small window through which buckets of hot water once were passed by Novarrez from the fire outside. It was through that window the orderly officer had peeped, to be discovered and followed down the veranda by a furious and nude victim.

I queried the colours of the nankeen on the bedroom walls, most of the descriptions having mentioned it as being brown. Indeed, the requisition from the East India Company's stores stated 'brown nankeen'. But the Consul informed me he had matched the new material from an original scrap, a pale primrose. One room, indeed, was white-lined. Flooring boards were new, the rat-holes had gone; the old iron grates were freshly blackened and the hand irons remained in place. Here and there stood an original chair or table, not specially renovated, only the patina brightened by polish. The billiard-table was back from Plantation House, whence Lowe had removed it after Napoleon's death, as were the two large globes from the Castle, that the Emperor's hands had once turned as he traced the movement of past battles. The cloth on the table was faded to a yellowish beige; the cues on the rack seemed short and the Emperor's height was demonstrated by the position of the peep-hole cut in the outside shutter. The ivory billiard-balls had yellowed — balls that he had rolled about in aimless boredom or inexpertly aimed to defeat yet another day, or occasionally used in Betsy's games to bump Napoleon's plump fingers during his attempts to instruct her in snooker.

One added item had come into the room, sent by the Bonaparte family: a bust of the Emperor, formerly Madame Mère's cherished possession, which has been installed where he spent so many hours, and where finally, before a group of surgeons, Antommarchi performed the autopsy on his body. The sculptor had demonstrated the rounded chin and beautifully cut lips. ("He had the sweetest smile in the world," said Betsy.)

Outside the billiard-room windows lay the precise form of Napoleon's garden, as designed by his hand and executed by an unwilling suite in conjunction with Chinese gardeners. From his bedroom he could aim a stone to rouse the sleeping Marchand, above in the attic, and with buckets, spades and hoes the staff would labour in the early morning. There is a picture of Napoleon of that time, in a loose flannel suit, slippers and a floppy hat — the type he insisted others wear against the menace of the midday sun. No romantic figure this, sitting sad and disillusioned. His was a material world of hates and discomforts, of bounded vistas and little incidents. Edging the little formal garden were the earthworks that the Chinese labourers had been called upon to build. There, also, were the banks of trees (of great height now) once moved, half-grown, to their position, for privacy and shelter. Specimens had come from the Cape, others transplanted from island gardens.

The trellised walk nearby, Napoleon's own copy of the Briars grape-arbour, was overgrown with passion-fruit. The garden's sunken paths elucidated a statement in several books that Napoleon had excavated a ditch in which to walk unobserved by sentinels. With some ingenuity, he had contrived to lower the paths of the formal garden about two feet, which brought the level of the hibiscus hedge to the skyline, where, stationed in the surrounding mountains, watchers with spyglasses reported any activity on his part to Plantation House. Beside the earthwork a pond received water from the original source as designed by Le Page, the chef. Here it was that the dying goldfish caused a distressed Napoleon to exclaim that ill-fortune met all who touched him. Beside it flowered a loose-petalled, bearded lily — Napoleon's lily — probably replanted by design, yet possibly a bulb from the original clump.

There is a changelessness about St Helena not possible in other less remote places; nature can reproduce a species undisturbed.

It is generally accepted that somewhere buried in Longwood grounds are manuscripts of Bonaparte's, hidden by Bertrand and Marchand, who hoped to recover them at a later date, their anxiety being to keep their contents from Sir Hudson Lowe. The present Consul will have every chance some day to dig them up. He will have time to consider the mentality of those two men and some day will walk to the spot to find something of priceless value.[23]

Ship's visitors wandered about the house, having paid two shillings admission to a secretary in the sentry-box outside, where the warning flags once blew, telling of Napoleon's movements. In the entrance room have been gathered small Napoleonic relics and a few pictures — one of William Balcombe, with a caption, "Purveyor, and reputed son of George III."

Six gardeners are maintained at Longwood, where Napoleon once pushed a water-cart on wheels and Chinese labourers cut green edges along the paths and the spy David pottered and peered and, in turn, was himself watched. Outside the Montholons' quarters, now Mr Martineau's, and almost level with the stone veranda, is the rose garden, in full spring-blooming, the everlastings, sent from England by Lady Holland, creating a yellow carpet under the formal alignment of the standard trees. Napoleon had picked a rose for Lowe's stepdaughter here once, the curious girl who visited unattended and was discovered wandering around, by Montholon.

We went inside Mr Martineau's sitting-room, over the black and white tiles, nothing else remaining of the Montholon occupancy, a modern book-filled room, pleasant and without memories. Talking of the Montholons and the ghostly sounds in the ceiling that had frightened Madame Bertrand from living at Longwood, the Consul unexpectedly said he had often heard them — rolling noises, but quite certainly dating from pre-Napoleonic times. Sometimes, however, when returning late to Longwood, where he lived alone, he felt as if the house were filled with 'busy people' — a pleasant sensation. I asked to see the kitchen, where some flat stones for the floor had been requisitioned by Le Page from William Balcombe, from the East India Company's stores. They were there, as was the little built-in bread oven and beside it what had every mark of being the original stove. Outside I looked at the yard where rats had "flocked like chickens around the foodbowl". The out-house required by Novarrez for laundry purposes appeared to have gone (it was to cost £12), as had the sod walls, the main harbour for the rodents that had gnawed Napoleon's shirts and coat and the doctor's laundry. We walked down the road to the Bertrands' second house, and the lady's personality once again pervaded the garden as it did at Hutt's Gate. Surrounding a plain little house were great trees to break the south-east trades. Here again were the tangles of familiar flowers and shrubs spilling over a minute terrace, and at the steps stood a mud-scraper, set in concrete.

Napoleon had liked the little house, even though it faced Deadwood Valley, where the 53rd had camped, and the hulking Barn shut off the sea beyond. He had coveted Madame's easy-chair, had watched Deadwood races from a hole in an upper window-shutter with his spyglass, had played with the Bertrand children, met Betsy, watched the erection of the new Longwood House in an adjacent field, glowered at the iron railings so reminiscent of captivity, and, when the mood took him, walked past the trees to where there could be caught a sight of the ocean, where seventy-fours beat up-wind to James Roads and the white sails of store-ships disappeared around the Barn to the Cape. The sea was then not so empty of ships as now.

There are briar roses near the terrace, original stock from which the grafts have gone, also parrot lily, strelitzia (probably a portion of the clumps near Longwood, for it is rare on the island). The little house is still habitable, but empty. New Longwood House was subsequently sold and removed. There remain a few sheds and a garage to mark the British Government's venture to ease a national conscience. On the sloping green graze a few cows. Strangely enough, it was windless, so still that the birds' twitterings could be heard. We were conscious of a void — time did not intrude. Madame Bertrand and her flowers were close beside us, and one could understand the Consul's remark about Longwood House, that he felt it to be filled with 'busy people'.

We registered the nineteenth-century atmosphere as distinct from the present day, when walking up the Plantation House steps, though instead of a Hudson Lowe in regimentals, we were presented to Sir James Harford, a Governor in tweeds, product of a hundred and forty more years of Colonial Office diplomacy, whose interest in the past so balances the St Helena present-day problems as to make a nice value. Plantation House, inside as well as outside, appears to have remained unchanged in architecture as well as in furniture. We lunched at the original round table, had coffee in the Georgian drawing-room and walked into the library where Betsy once stood, in riding habit, and apologised for riding the Emperor's horse. The marble mantelpiece and bookcase bore little, if any, marks of time; the guests at the Balmain wedding would have noticed no difference. "Any ghosts?" I asked, seeing, mentally, dozens about the sunny, windowed house — the officers of the 53rd, Major Fehrzen, the Younghusbands and the Balcombes, Baron Sturmer and his wife, who had wept by the crown at the Pavilion; George Carstairs of the epaulets; Admiral Cockburn; the Lowes and the bull-necked Reade; little Major Gorrequer; Gourgaud, ingratiating himself, the pleasant Governor Wilks and the lovely Laura. "Only a mild poltergeist," said someone. "Pre-Hudson Lowe and it keeps to one room."

Jonathan, the turtle, had been specially guided from the bottom of the garden. Two hundred years old, he is nearly blind and perceives only a white object. This time his objective was an arum lily.

The Lowe Papers hold a brief reference to Jonathan. Two monster turtles were brought to the island by a sea-captain and presented to Sir Hudson Lowe, who sent one to Longwood for food Jonathan being the other. A later note comes from the purveyor at Jamestown to Captain Lutyens on 20th February 1821: "I have sent a man to cut up the turtle and to prepare it by boiling the different parts, first being dressed, which is all that can be done." Evidently the Longwood chef was unable to handle it, for the purveyor later told Lutyens he would send his own cook (the only one on the island, he believed, who understood anything of the matter) "at a very early hour tomorrow morning, to assist the cooks at Longwood in dressing it". A contemporary mezzotint of Plantation House shows Jonathan in the foreground in company with another, smaller, turtle, which has since died. Jonathan stands high enough for a boy to ride.

I kept the last hours for the Briars, half-afraid of an anti-climax of disillusion and loss. However, the drive remained as the old prints depicted. The banyan trees were bigger, the gate intact though weather-beaten, but the house, alas, had become a ruin — only the back quarters and the cellar remaining. The twin pines had kept their characteristics, one thin, one spreading, sentinels of a home that is now nearly a mere memory. With the importation of white ant, many of the wooden dwellings on the island have suffered in the same way. But Napoleon's Pavilion is still in order and the little winding path is traceable; the veranda, the balustrading, the room itself, have defied time, though the view to Jamestown and the sea now has no foreground of lovely garden, only a tangle of growth. There are trees along the steep side of the Pavilion leading to the waterfall — pine and banyan and mohur, where once Betsy had run hand in hand with the Emperor to the valley below. The pond, where Tom Pipes swam among the goldfish and showered Napoleon afterwards, still holds water. The grape arbour has vanished.

Las Cases described his first view of the Pavilion in 1815: "As I ascended the winding path leading to the Pavilion, I saw Napoleon standing at the threshold of the door. His body was slightly bent and his hand behind his back. He wore his usual plain and simple uniform and the well-known hat. The Emperor was alone."

Others have stood at that door looking out across the valley to the gap in the mountain, even as I was now doing: Mrs Younghusband anticipating a Christmas week of fun; Madame Sturmer, emotionally envisaging the exile's thoughts; factual Betsy among the wrapping papers, knowing that her heart had gone with the occupant; the mediating Las Cases, censorious of the children's boisterous manners; Admiral Plampin and his 'wife'; Toby, his crown still well-defined on the grass; Gourgaud, fretting for female companionship; the staff, resigned and busy, listening to their master's unmusical rendering of 'Vive Henri IV'. It was behind this door Napoleon clutched Betsy's ball-gown and turned deaf ears to her entreaties, and behind it that he had dictated his first memoirs, had thought and, so far as it was in his power, composed his pattern of life for the future.

In the distance the *Durban Castle* reminded us of time and the need to go. The Briars avenue led past the unremembered Huff,[24] down Napoleon Street by the 'Castle' arch to the dock steps, to which Napoleon's body had been carried for embarkation.

We put out to sea at dusk and presently the ramparts of St Helena hid the pleasant little valley and Jamestown.

Not often is it given to one of another century to complete a sequence of events that commenced one hundred and forty years ago. In acquiring the Briars house and the Pavilion this has been made possible for me, and the French Nation in accepting the site has placed my hand for a brief moment in that of Betsy's, and has afforded me an opportunity to pay homage to "the greatest man since Alexander".

Residents and Visitors on St Helena

Some of the residents and visitors on St Helena, with whom the Emperor Napoleon had contact.

Abell, Mrs Charles: Betsy Balcombe, 1800-1876.[25]

Amherst, Lord: (William Pitt, 1st Earl) — Plenipotentiary to China. Arrived in Jamestown in the *Corsair*, June 1817.

Antommarchi: Physician to Napoleon from 1819 until his death in 1821.

Archambault, brothers: Coachman and groom to the Emperor.

Arnott, Doctor: Surgeon to the 20th Foot Regiment at Deadwood and was one of Napoleon's medical attendants.

Balcombe, William: East India Company agent and purveyor to the Emperor. Ex-British Naval Officer and owner of the Briars, St Helena. First Colonial Treasurer, New South Wales, 1824; died Sydney, 1829; father of Betsy and Jane; of his four children, Alexander Beatson was born on the island.[26]

Balmain, Count: Russian Commissioner, descended from Scottish family of Ramsay, arrived St Helena 1816.

Bathurst, Earl: Colonial Secretary in Castlereagh Government, was responsible for the safe custody of Napoleon.

Baxter, Doctor: Arrived in the *Phaeton* with Sir Hudson Lowe, 1816.

Bertrand, Général Comte de: Grand Marshal to Napoleon, remaining at Longwood until the Emperor's death in 1821. Returned for the exhumation of his body in 1840.

Bertrand, Countess (Emmy): Wife of the Grand Marshal, half-Irish by birth; of her four children, one, Arthur, was born on the island.

Bingham, Brig.-General: In command of the British troops on St Helena.

Blakeney, Captain: Orderly Officer at Longwood, 1817.

Boys, Reverend Richard: Schoolmaster and incumbent of the Country Church. Buried Cipriani.

Buonoavita Abbé: Came to Longwood in 1819 at the instigation of the Bonaparte family.

Burton, Francis: Surgeon of the 66th Regiment, author of the death-mask of Napoleon.

Cipriani: Maître d'hôtel at Longwood; died there 1818.

Cockburn, Admiral Sir George, KC.B.: Selected by the Prince Regent to convoy Napoleon to St Helena, and was in charge of the prisoner until the arrival of Sir Hudson Lowe, 1816.

Cole, Joseph: Postmaster at Jamestown and member of the firm, Balcombe, Fowler and Company.

Crokat, Captain William: Orderly Officer at Longwood at the time of Napoleon's death, 1821. Sailed on the *Herod* on the 7th May with despatch announcing the death of the Emperor. Crokat died in 1879, and was the last to survive of those who had seen Napoleon on his death-bed.

Darling, Andrew: Upholsterer and undertaker. Made arrangements for burial of the Emperor, and was present at the exhumation nineteen years later.

David: Gardener-spy. Sergeant of the 66th Foot.

Denman, Captain Edmund: Commander of the *Redpole*, friend of the Balcombes and with them spent an evening playing whist with Napoleon.

Doveton, Sir William: Member of Council of St Helena and lived at Sandy Bay. Napoleon visited him for the last time in 1820. He was present at the funeral and at the exhumation.

Fehrzen, Major Oliver: Sometime in command of the 53rd Regiment. The Emperor was always ready to receive the Major, whose fine presence and engaging manner made him a favoured visitor. His military career was marked by bravery and success in many important actions. Though fifteen years her senior, he was one of Betsy's suitors. He died in 1820 in India of cholera.

Forsyth, William: Sir Hudson Lowe's 'Boswell' and compiler of the volumes of letters.

Gorrequer, Major: Aide-de-camp to Sir Hudson Lowe, also acting military secretary, travelling with him on the *Phaeton* to the island in 1816. A master in the art of précis-writing, Gorrequer's diary is still unpublished, largely because it contains facts too vital to expose. Betsy called him a little man and very polite.

Gors, Captain Jean: Secretary to the French Commissioner, arriving with him on the *Newcastle*, 1816. Betsy's diary on occasion mentions him as 'Gors'.

Goulburn, Sir Henry: Under-Secretary to the Colonies until 1826.

Gourgaud, Gaspard: 'Master of the Horse' to the Longwood household. Arrived with the Emperor on the *Northumberland*; departed 1818; returned for the exhumation.

Greentree: Sir William Doveton's son-in-law.

Hodson, Major Charles: Judge Advocate of the island, called 'Hercules' by the Emperor, owing to his size.

Holmes, William: Commission agent, Lyons Inn, Holborn. Employed by Longwood to carry through the negotiation of bills.

Huff: Tutor to the Balcombe boys; obsessed by Napoleon's treatment, he became unbalanced and committed suicide, 1815, and was buried under the crossroads near the Briars. His skeleton was discovered there during recent road-building.

Ibbetson, Denzil: Commissary in St Helena; took charge of purveyorship to Longwood after the departure of William Balcombe in 1818.

Janesch, William: Clerk, came to St Helena in the *Phaeton* with Sir Hudson Lowe. His handwriting is a model of legibility, and figures frequently in the Lowe folios.

Johnston, the Misses: Step-daughters of Sir Hudson Lowe; the elder married Count Balmain in 1820.

Las Cases, Emmanuel, Marquis de la Caussade: He and his young son accompanied the Emperor on the *Northumberland* in 1815. Arrested on the order of Sir Hudson Lowe and deported in 1816; he left with his son on the *Griffon*. His son returned for the exhumation.

Le Page: Cook at Longwood.

Lowe, Sir Hudson, K.C.B.: Lieutenant-General and Governor of St Helena. Napoleon's jailer, 1816-1821. Visited him on occasions in 1816, but after bitter quarrels did not speak to him again.

Lutyens, Captain: Orderly Officer at Longwood.

Lyster, Thomas: Friend of Lowe's; appointed Orderly Officer in 1818 for a brief period, but was removed after challenging General Bertrand to a duel.

Malcolm, Admiral Sir Pulteney: Succeeded Admiral Sir George Cockburn at the St Helena Naval Station, 1816. He and his wife were warmly regarded by Napoleon. Left the island in 1817.

Marchand, Louis: First valet to the Emperor. His mother was nurse to the King of Rome, Napoleon's son.

Mason, Miss Polly: She lived in Prosperous Valley, one of the characters who interested Napoleon by habitually riding an ox.

Mitchell, Doctor Charles: Surgeon on the *Vigo*, flagship of the St Helena station, attended the post-mortem on Napoleon's body and signed the report.

Montchenu, Claude, Marquis de: French Commissioner in St Helena from 1816 to 1821. Not a Bonapartist. Betsy is mentioned several times in his subsequent memoirs as a wild girl.

Montholon, Charles, Marquis de Montholon-Sémonville: Came to St Helena with his wife and children on the *Northumberland*, 1815. Remained with Napoleon until he died. Undertook the management of the Longwood household.

Murray, Captain James: Commanded the *Griffon*. Son of Lord William Murray; brought a python to the island.

Napoleon: 1769-1821. Landed at Jamestown, St Helena on the 15th October 1815. Stayed at the Briars for two and a half months after arrival. Died at Longwood 5th May 1821.

Nicholls, George: Captain of the 66th Regiment, Orderly Officer at Longwood. His diary lists the number of 'sightings' of the Emperor and reiterates the 'long hours spent on his legs' during the process.

Novarrez, Jean: Third valet to the Emperor; was with him at his death and returned for the exhumation nineteen years later.

O'Meara, Doctor Barry: Army surgeon and medical attendant to Napoleon from 1815 to 1818. Dismissed the service after disagreements with Lowe, about whose administration he wrote in *A Voice From St Helena*, in 1822. He accused Lowe of wanting to do away with the prisoner. O'Meara died in 1836, and in his will directed that the following statement be engraved on his tomb. "I take the opportunity of declaring that with the exception of some unintentional and trifling errors in the *Voice from St Helena*, the book is a faithful narrative of the treatment inflicted upon the great man Napoleon by Sir Hudson Lowe and his subordinates and that I have even suppressed some facts which, although true, might have been considered to be exaggerated and not credited".

Pierron: Butler to Longwood, who remained all the time and returned for the exhumation.

Piontkowski, Captain Charles: Arrived on the *Cormorant*, 1815, as one of Napoleon's adherents. A man of Polish extraction and something of a mystery, he saw the Emperor only once.

Plampin, Rear-Admiral Robert: Arrived with his 'wife' in 1817. He was unfriendly to Napoleon and was the instrument of Dr Stokoe's dismissal.

Poppleton, Captain: Orderly Officer from 1815 until 1818.

Porteous: Boarding-house keeper at Jamestown, where Napoleon spent his first night on arrival.

Raffles, Sir Stamford: Visited Napoleon during his journey to England, 1816.

Ricketts, Charles: Kinsman of Lord Liverpool. Returning from India, he had a long interview with the prisoner, who was ill in bed, and carried a biased report to

London.

Robinson, Miss: Known as the 'nymph'. She lived in Prosperous Valley and was admired by Napoleon.

Ross, Captain the Hon. Charles: Post-Captain of the *Northumberland*, friend of William Balcombe, who called Ross Cottage after him. Ross presented the Balcombes with the lock of hair Napoleon had given him. It was subsequently stolen.

Rous, Captain the Hon. Henry: Came to St Helena on the *Conqueror* and remained on the station until 1819, transferring to the *Podargus* and other vessels. He had much to do with instituting the race meetings at Deadwood.

St Denis: Second valet to Napoleon.

Santine, John: Usher at Longwood; was deported m 1816. Later became guardian of the Emperor's tomb at Les Invalides, Paris.

Scott, James: Mulatto servant of Las Cases. The discovery of messages to Lucien Bonaparte in his waistcoat led to the arrest and deportation of Las Cases.

Shortt, Doctor Thomas: Chief Medical Officer, St Helena.

Skelton, John: Lieutenant-Governor of the island and much liked by Napoleon. He left the island in 1816.

Sowerby: Spy-gardener at Longwood.

Stokoe, Doctor John: Surgeon on the *Conqueror*; attended Napoleon several times. Suitor of Jane Balcombe.

Sturmer, Barthelemy, Baron de: Austrian Commissioner on St Helena; arrived 1816 with his wife; recalled before the Emperor's death.

Vignali, the Abbé Ange: A Corsican priest sent to the Longwood household in 1819. He was 'low-born, ignorant and illiterate'.

Wallis, Captain: In command of the *Podargus* after years of captivity by the French. Betsy recounted his bitter remarks to the Emperor.

Warden, William: Surgeon on the *Northumberland* and author of some interesting letters.

Welle: Botanist, travelling with Baron Sturmer; secretly carried a lock of hair from the King of Rome to Napoleon.

Wilks, Colonel Sir Mark: Governor until the arrival of Sir Hudson Lowe. A highly intellectual man with charm, much beloved by the island people, as were his wife and daughter, Laura.

End Notes

1. It was a pleasant scene, about which a Mrs Younghusband (the same Mrs Younghusband who was esteemed a disturber of the peace by contemporary writers, but who from her letter appeared to be a jolly and discerning person), little knowing posterity would pinpoint her description, had written about a week or so later to an aunt in England. She described the paths and scents and the aloes, the arbour and English flowers, and of meeting the Emperor there one day with the Balcombe girls, and of her interest and excitement — all corroboration of Betsy's own description, uncovered after one hundred and thirty years in a desk in England to be published in *Blackwood's Magazine* of August, 1947.
2. It was a fashion in England at that time to wear, in the evening, little bodices of a different colour from the skirt.
3. Lady Loudon was the wife of the Governor-General of India.
4. Editor Note: Mabel Brookes does not make this anecdote absolutely clear. What Betsy says in her book is as follows: *He was very fond of cauliflowers, which were rare vegetables in this island; dining with us one day at the Briars, his aide-de-camp, Captain Gor, had omitted to point out to him that there were some at table; and it was only when about to be removed that the marquess espied the retreating dish. His rage was most amusing; and, with much gesticulation, he exclaimed, "Bête! pourquoi ne m'a tu pas dit qu'il y avait des choux-fleurs?"*
5. The Balmain-Johnston wedding created the social incident of the year 1819. The notables of St Helena, the army and the army wives, the naval officers and the commissioners were invited and crowded into the reception rooms, a duty for the latter but great curiosity prompting the ladies of the first group, who had missed the friendly contact of the Wilkses and who infrequently were invited nowadays. Formality and procedure regimented them now and seniority graded the invitation list. The Anglo-Indian pattern of priority held sway here as in all other colonial dependencies. A viceregal tone spread quasi-lustre on the invitation. The Hodsons ('Hercules') were there and the Dovetons, a family group including the Greentrees, the Brooke family, the Bairds, she of the singing voice; the two clergymen — Mr Boys in evidence; the commissioners, mildly supercilious of the parochial flavour; Carstairs as extra aide-de-camp; General and Lady Bingham — in an official capacity: a list resembling in genteel mediocrity any Anglo-Indian guest list. Many faces were missing, for the wedding took place late in the period of the captivity, and the 53rd had gone — as had the Pulteney Malcolms, Balcombes, Madame Montholon, the Las Cases, their absence again fitting into the Anglo-Indian pattern of constant arrival and departure.

6. Editor Note: What Betsy actually said was: *A lady of high distinction at St Helena, whose husband filled one of the diplomatic offices there,*

7. Editor Note: According to other views on this subject, this interview is open to question and is O'Meara's uncorroborated statement.

8. Editor Note: This statement may be incorrect, and that explosive interview witnessed by Sir Pulteney Malcolm may have been Napoleon's final encounter with Lowe.

9. Editor Note: This is an unusual statement; the slave trade had been abolished in 1807 although slavery itself was not abolished in British territories until 1833.

10. Editor Note: Apparently, the Johnston family denied this.

11. Editor Note: In fact, Lowe brought instructions with him. Although Lowe was undoubtedly a disagreeable and unpopular person, Mabel Brookes occasionally does disservice to him.

12. In reality Montholon had informed Major Gorrequer that if it was insisted that any further considerable retrenchments should be made at Longwood, he was directed by the Emperor to say that he had his authority to dispose of about £25,000 of plate in a private manner, either to Mr Balcombe or any other merchant in the town, as he could spare that quantity (not at present being in use).

13. Editor Note: The *Sydney Morning Herald* of 29 September 1953 reported the following: *Miss T. A. Attwood, one the directors of the firm of auctioneers, said yesterday that it was a beautiful instrument, delicately inlaid with ivory and mother of pearl. It was in a polished cedar case which carried the gentle patina of age, she said. Miss Attwood said that documents with the guitar traced its history from the time it was given to Napoleon by his sister Pauline. She said that Napoleon used to play the guitar on St. Helena for one of his favourites, the little daughter of one of the British officials, Mr. Balcombe. When Napoleon died he left the guitar to the child who subsequently came out to Australia as a music teacher. The guitar passed through several hands until, in 1927, it was presented to the late Dr. John Cappie Shand. Snr., of North Sydney. The guitar is now being offered for auction again by the estate of Dr. Shand, she said. It is at present in a safe deposit at the Bank of New South Wales.* The guitar eventually founds its way to the Napoleonic Museum of The Briars Park. The Briars is now a museum where visitors can see the Dame Mabel Brookes Napoleonic Collection, which includes furniture that Bonaparte shared upon his stay with them and a large number interesting items such as some of his hair, papers, letters, a legion d'honneur medal, artworks and cartoons. Most famous of all is a rare death mask of Napoleon that is unbelievably detailed and shows that rats took their toll on the remains of history's greatest general - chewing off parts of his right ear. The 1842 Briars homestead can be found just south of Mt Martha on Victoria's Mornington Peninsula, about an hour south of Melbourne.

    From this fact we may assume that Betsy took the guitar to Australia with her, but left it there on her subsequent return to England. Dame Mabel quite clearly bought the guitar back for the family at the 1927 auction.

14. Mr Boys superseded Mr Jones as senior chaplain, and, far some reason not evident, the St Helena Council appointed Mr Jones to be inspector of the strayed sheep and goats, at which he stigmatised his appointment as a public insult, and Napoleon remarked he was of the opinion that Mr Jones had been "used most shamefully". Mr Jones wrote to the Council that he had already a very wild herd of goats to look after in his congregation.

15. Editor Note: This is all rather ridiculous, for in reality Betsy was much younger than Dame Mabel Brookes makes her out to be.

16. Editor Note: This is conjectural and there is no firm evidence for Napoleon ever having visited England.

17. No trace of Cipriani's grave can be found. The headstone ordered by Napoleon and the record of burial have disappeared.

18. In contradiction to the general assumption on the Continent that Napoleon's star had set, at the end of 1818 rumours commenced to circulate that he had escaped. Napoleon's long periods of seclusion in his own quarters gave rise to suspicious conjecture by Lowe, and anxiety was reflected in ambiguous passages in his correspondence to Bathurst — passages that are incomprehensible unless holding a key to their real meaning that the prisoner had gone.

There were exchanges in the letters over the presence of an American ship lingering on the horizon, out of reach of examination by reason of her superior speed. Concurrent with the time Madame Bertrand wrote in one of her letters home, "Success is ours! Napoleon has left the island," Gourgaud retracted his statements on the Emperor's condition and was deported from England to 'Hamburgh', and William Balcombe came to be closely interrogated by members of the Cabinet on his association with the exile.

During the heyday of his Empire, Napoleon had four doubles, gathered from all over Europe by his agents. One, François Eugène Robéraud, of Baley-court in the Meuse, was a private in the French Army and attached to Napoleon's headquarters. The whereabouts and fate of these men were known: two dying and one crippled in an accident, Robéraud subsequently returning to farming in Baley-court in the Meuse. In the autumn of 1818 he and his sister deserted their cottage. A search was instituted, and a year or so later the sister was discovered living at Nantes on a pension, but gave no satisfactory reason for the sudden and secret departure, nor of the whereabouts of her brother — "a sailor at sea," she told enquirers, "on a long voyage."

Late in 1818, a French traveller, one Revard, arrived in Verona, and, joined in partnership with an Italian — Petrucci by name, optician by trade and, as well, a dealer in diamonds. By his likeness to the Emperor, the newcomer was jokingly called 'Napoleon' by the townsfolk. He had no knowledge of the business, and showed a disregard for money, of which he had plenty.

In August, 1823, he was suddenly called for, and departed by coach, leaving a sealed letter to be given by Petrucci to the King of France if he did not return, saying he was going on a long journey — that "times were evil".

Twelve nights later, when the King of Rome lay seriously ill of scarlet fever in Schönbrunn Castle, an intruder, dropping from the ivy on the wall, was surprised and shot by a sentry. Officers examined the body and, startled, had it locked in a shed, while they communicated with the French Embassy, who claimed it for burial. However, at the earnest request of Marie-Louise, the body was interred in an unmarked grave at Schönbrunn.

Revard never returned to Verona, but French authorities liquidated the shop, paid 100,000 crowns for the letter and for Petrucci's sworn silence. Thirty years later, he divulged the whole story to the Verona authorities, making a statement to them that he believed his partner to be Napoleon Bonaparte.

In the town records of Baley-court there is inscribed the name of François Eugène Robéraud, "Born in this village, died on St Helena ..." [the date obliterated].

Here, indeed is a mysterious and conflicting collection of facts.

Was there an attempt at rescue and substitution of Robéraud in the Emperor's stead? Did the hovering vessel find the hazards too great — or, more likely, was Napoleon unwilling to expose himself to the uncertainties of freedom?

Probably it was Robéraud who became victim of the sentry's gun, in an effort to convey a message to the sick boy. As against that, the likeness to the Emperor was enough to startle both the Austrians and the French into believing they actually saw Napoleon before them, even though two years had elapsed since his official death had been announced on St Helena. The erased date at Baley-court is part of the puzzle, but that Robéraud was actually substituted for Napoleon on St Helena is hardly likely.

19. Editor Note: Mabel Brookes is incorrect here, for Betsy temporarily left her young husband and was with the family on the voyage to Australia. She returned to England in 1826.

20. There is a legend that a violent storm passed over St Helena, blowing down trees and creating havoc, as Napoleon lay dying. This, in fact, is untrue. The usual trade wind blew and the sun sank in its usual tropical splendour. Two of the island doves preened on one of the window-sills of his room and would not go away.

21. Editor Note: The last few paragraphs betray the 'novelist' in Dame Mabel Brookes trying to come out. This is all conjecture and misplaced in a book of this nature. Nevertheless, I am not going to alter what Mabel Brookes wrote.

22. Editor Note: It should be borne in mind that Dame Mabel Brookes wrote this book in the late 1950s. Her text has been left as it was and the reader should understand that a further sixty years has passed by.

23. There is a comment in the memoirs that glass bottles were procured from the kitchen in which to bury the papers.

24. During recent road-mending the skeleton of Old Huff was discovered at the crossroads.

25. Editor Note: Dame Mabel Brookes was incorrect in assessing her great-aunt's date of birth. She was born in 1802 and had only recently turned 13 when she first met Napoleon.

26. Editor Note: Alexander Beatson Balcombe was Dame Mabel Brookes' grandfather.